The sounds of French

An introduction

The sounds of French

An introduction

Bernard Tranel

Department of French and Italian
and Program in Linguistics
University of California, Irvine

CAMBRIDGE
UNIVERSITY PRESS

Published by the Press Syndicate of the University of Cambridge
The Pitt Building, Trumpington Street, Cambridge CB2 1RP
40 West 20th Street, New York, NY 10011–4211, USA
10 Stamford Road, Oakleigh, Victoria 3166, Australia

First published 1987
Reprinted 1989 1992

Printed in Great Britain by Bath Press, Bath, Avon

British Library cataloguing in publication data
Tranel, Bernard
The sounds of French: an introduction.
1. French language – Phonetics
I. Title
441.1'5   PC2135

Library of Congress cataloguing in publication data
Tranel, Bernard
The sounds of French.
Bibliography.
1. French language – Phonetics. 2. French language –
Phonology, comparative – English. 3. English language –
Phonology, comparative – French. I. Title.
PC2135.T73   1987   441.5   87–9331

ISBN 0 521 30443 1 hardback
ISBN 0 521 31510 7 paperback
ISBN 0 521 35002 6 cassette

Contents

Part two: Vowels and glides

3. Vowel systems

4. Distribution of vowels

5. Nasal vowels

6. *E*

Part four: Suprasegmentals

12. Stress and intonation

Part five: Appendices

Preface

This book is an introduction to French phonetics addressed primarily to English speakers who wish to improve their pronunciation of French systematically. Since a contrastive phonetic study of English and French finds a natural place in such a manual, French speakers learning English will also be able to glean useful elements for a better understanding and a more effective correction of pronunciation errors characteristic of a French accent in English.

This manual can be viewed concurrently as an initiation to general phonetics and as an opening to French phonology. As such, it is also addressed to those who are interested in language in general and French in particular, and who wish to familiarize themselves with the study of the production and function of sounds. My goal here is to establish, for readers without previous linguistic background, a bridge allowing them to approach with greater facility more detailed and more technical works on French phonetics and phonology.

Special note to English-speaking students learning French

For English-speaking students learning French, the goal of this manual is two-fold: first, to provide them with a theoretical perspective on the sound system of French, especially in contrast with the English system; and secondly, to guide them in as practical a manner as possible through the development of a better pronunciation of French. These two aspects, theoretical and practical, are closely linked. A theoretical consideration of the French and English sound systems depicts the way in which the two languages structure, each in its own way, the phonetic substance of which speech is made, and thus explicitly characterizes part of the linguistic knowledge internalized by English and French native speakers. From a practical point of view, such an approach naturally leads, through a comparison of the two languages, not only to a systematic inventory of the problems which can trouble English speakers learning French (and French speakers learning English), but also to a wide range of possible remedies for resolving the difficulties. In sum, a theoretical study ensures, through logical understanding, a precise diagnosis of concrete pronunciation problems and a solid basis for an effective resolution of these problems.

A theoretical approach also offers valuable psychological advantages. First, the abstract knowledge of the system to be mastered satisfies a certain instinctive curiosity, and consequently reduces the aura of mystery and inaccessibility that is often bestowed on the phonetic characteristics of a foreign language. Secondly, the comparison of the two sound systems in presence contributes to the understanding that pronunciation errors are actually part of the normal and expected course of events in the acquisition of a foreign language, because they usually result from the natural superimposition of characteristics of the native language's sound system onto the foreign language. Finally, notions of general phonetics lead to the realization that there is nothing physiological ultimately preventing the reduction and elimination of these errors, since, genetically, we all possess the same speech apparatus and the same 'faculté de langage'. In short, a theoretical approach frees students from a number of negative psychological attitudes which are often obstacles to practical progress.

The identification of pronunciation errors, the interpretation of their causes, and the application of appropriate corrective methods constitute important steps toward the mastery of an improved pronunciation. However, the complete integration of new articulatory habits never occurs overnight. Before corrections become truly operational (i.e. automatic, and not just the fruit of conscious reflection), it is usually necessary to have had experience with the language for an extended period going well beyond the time frames of the rigorous study of a chapter, a set of laboratory lessons, or even an entire manual. One of this book's goals is to offer students means of improving their pronunciation and of accelerating the process by classifying problems, identifying their nature, and suggesting remedies; but it cannot be a substitute for the personal efforts required to achieve a better pronunciation in spontaneous speech. In particular, it can substitute neither for the useful oral work generally undertaken by students in class and in the language laboratory under the direction of their instructors, nor for natural verbal interactions with people who speak French fluently. It is also extremely important to keep in mind that under most circumstances, a non-native pronunciation is not an obstacle to adequate communication and should not constitute a psychological obstacle to using a foreign language; in fact, since the acquisition of a native-like pronunciation depends for most people on a lot of trying, both at the listening and at the speaking ends of communication, feeling shy about using the language because of one's pronunciation would clearly be counterproductive to the intention to improve it.

Organization of the book

This book consists of twelve chapters (divided into four parts) and a series of six appendices (Part Five). Part One contains two general chapters introducing basic notions of general phonetics. Through a discussion of the relationship between French orthography and French pronunciation, Chapter 1 justifies the necessity, for our purposes, of transcribing sounds by means of a phonetic notation (specifically, that of the International Phonetic Association) in which a single symbol corresponds to a single sound. Chapter 2 looks at the operation of the speech organs and provides an inventory of the main articulatory parameters which allow the description and classification of sounds.

Part Two comprises four chapters on vowels and one chapter on glides. Chapter 3 opens with the contrast between stress-timed rhythm in English and syllable-timed rhythm in French, a contrast which plays an essential distinctive role in the pronunciation of vowels in the two languages. This chapter continues with a comparison of the English and French vowel systems. Chapter 4 treats questions internal to French concerning vowel length and the distribution of the mid and open vowels. Correlations between the pronunciation and the spelling of the mid and open vowels are considered at various points in the course of the chapter. Nasal vowels and mute *e* are the respective topics of the next two chapters. Chapter 5 examines the different roles played by vowel nasality in French and in English, and analyzes the specific problems which the existence of nasal vowels in French poses for English speakers. A brief history of the emergence of French nasal vowels accompanies an examination of their notation in the orthography. This chapter ends with a study of the behavior of nasal vowels in liaison. Chapter 6 essentially focuses on mute *e* and the principles determining its presence and absence in the pronunciation. Chapter 7 covers glides. Emphasis is placed on the pronunciation difficulties often caused by the existence of the rounded palatal glide found in words such as *puis* 'then' and *huit* 'eight', on the orthographic representations of glides, on their distributional properties in the word, and on their phonetic and functional relationships with closed vowels.

Part Three is composed of four chapters on consonants. Chapter 8 first offers a comparative overview of the French and English consonantal systems, and then focuses on the main articulatory differences separating phonetically close consonants in the two languages. Chapter 9 is devoted to an examination of the consonants *l* and *r*, which present special difficulties for English speakers learning French (as well as for French speakers learning English). Chapter 10 deals with the question of geminate consonants in French and also with the question of the pronunciation of written word-final consonants (considered outside of the phenomenon of liaison). Liaison itself is the subject of Chapter 11. After a brief historical sketch, conditions for the appearance of linking consonants in contemporary French are classified according to phonetic, morphological, syntactic, and stylistic criteria. This chapter ends with a simple set of practical tips for foreign students embattled in the acquisition of liaison.

Part Four contains a single chapter (Chapter 12), which looks briefly at the suprasegmental features of stress and intonation.

Six appendices (A–F) are located in Part Five. They provide complementary information on a few topics mentioned briefly in the body of the text, or offer in synoptic form basic pieces of data for easy reference. Appendix A contains a brief history of the International Phonetic Association and a summary of the essential principles of its alphabet. Appendix B examines the role of diacritic marks (the cedilla, the accents, and the diaeresis) in French orthography. Appendix C outlines the history of French orthography, with a view to explaining how today's orthography came to represent today's pronunciation. Appendix D recapitulates in the form of various charts the classification of French sounds and the main correspondences between sounds and letters. Appendix E offers a list of fairly common h-aspiré words and summarizes their basic distinguishing properties. Finally, Appendix F is a short list of the most typical pronunciation errors made by English speakers learning French; it can function as a memory aid to assist students in remembering the points where particular vigilance is required.

The book closes with a short Bibliography whose main purpose is to provide direct suggestions for further reading and sources of additional material to study.

The language of reference

As is the case in all languages of the world, there exist in French several types of pronunciation. For example, one talks about a Belgian accent, a Swiss accent, a Canadian accent, a southern accent ('accent du Midi'), a Parisian accent ('accent pointu'). These accents are a matter of geographical distribution and can be referred to as *geographical* varieties (or, technically speaking, geographical 'dialects'). There are also *social* dialects, where pronunciation differences correlate with speakers' socioeconomic levels. Pronunciation variations may also occur in the speech of a given speaker, depending on the social situation in which he/she finds himself/herself (a traffic jam, a family dinner, a meeting with a subordinate or with a superior); such variations pertain to what are usually called *stylistic levels* ('niveaux de langue'). Finally, even with speakers who apparently have the same dialect, small pronunciation differences may actually be found which seem to characterize a single individual rather than a readily identifiable group; one then speaks of *idiolectal* distinctions.

Society typically places value judgments on the different pronunciation varieties of a language; thus, some types of pronunciation will be deemed prestigious, while others will be stigmatized. These judgments have absolutely nothing to do with the intrinsic linguistic characteristics of a given dialect or the personal qualities of the individuals who speak it, for from a purely linguistic point of view, nothing is 'more equal' to a given dialect than another dialect. In fact, it frequently happens that pronunciation characteristics held in low esteem at one time become the social norm at another time, and vice versa. An example of this phenomenon of socio-linguistic relativity is the pronunciation of *r* in French, whose social norm went from a rolled front articulation to a barely fricative back articulation. Another example concerns the graphic sequence *oi* (as in the word *roi* 'king'), whose socially unmarked pronunciation went from [we] to [wa] with the Revolution of 1789.

In a book such as this one, it is all the same necessary to choose a specific type of pronunciation which may serve as a model for students and as a reference in the description. We shall follow here the tradition still in effect today, whereby foreign students are generally taught the French of northern France, and Paris in particular, which is considered to be the language of the social norm. This variety of French has received many labels, including Parisian French, standard French, general French, international French, and common French. We shall take this particular dialect as a point of reference, but we shall have numerous opportunities to mention other varieties of French and, consequently, to consider different types of pronunciation.

An illustrative cassette designed to accompany this book provides a recording of most of the examples used in the book, in particular those organised in tables. The recorded illustrations are identified on the tape by chapter, table and page references.

Acknowledgments

This book is a revised English version of a French manuscript (entitled 'Cours de phonétique française') which I have been using as a text for the French phonetics course (French 11) that I regularly teach at the University of California, Irvine, for students with two years of college French. This manuscript, which actually came in two 'editions' (1982 and 1984), itself evolved from lecture notes gathered since 1975, when I first taught French 11.

I would like to thank the many students who took this course over the years and helped me with their feedback (wittingly or unwittingly). Thanks are also due to Carol Sutton, who bravely accepted the merciless task of undertaking the translation for me, so that I could work on the English version with a fresh eye. Finally, for their comments on the first French manuscript, I am grateful to Yves Morin, Doug Walker, two anonymous referees for Cambridge University Press, and especially Monique Burston, who went through the text with a fine-tooth comb.

Regarding the illustrative cassette, I gratefully acknowledge the help of Alice McMurray and Pierrette Manfredi, who contributed their respective native American English and Quebec French to the recording.

Completion of the work was made possible in part by research grants from the School of Humanities at the University of California, Irvine, and summer grants from the Regents of the University of California.

Part One
Introductory concepts

1
Orthography, pronunciation, and phonetic notation

1.1. Introduction

The phonetic study of a language presupposes that one can refer to its sounds without ambiguity; in other words, a system of representation is required where a given sound is always associated with the same symbol and where a given symbol is always associated with the same sound. Because there is no such systematic correspondence between orthography and pronunciation in French, it is necessary for our purposes to resort to a special notation which fulfills this condition (a single symbol for a single sound). The goals of this chapter are to introduce the system of phonetic transcription used in this book (that of the International Phonetic Association) and to justify its use by sketching out the complex nature of the relation between orthography and pronunciation in French.

1.2. Phonetic notation

Every language uses a fixed and restricted number of sounds which are assembled into syllables which in turn form words. In French, there are 35 sounds (17 consonants, 15 vowels, and 3 glides), which will be represented by the symbols in square brackets given in Tables 1.1–3. Each symbol is accompanied by three key-words where the letters corresponding to the phonetic value of the symbol are italicized. These phonetic symbols are taken from the inventory recommended by the International Phonetic Association (see Appendix A). They are commonly used in linguistics, together with some variants linked to different traditions.

The symbols for the consonants present relatively few learning difficulties. In fact, with just three exceptions ([ɲ, ʃ, ʒ]), they are all letters of the Latin alphabet used for writing, among other languages, English and French. In addition, these letters commonly appear in French orthography with the same phonetic values as those attributed to the phonetic symbols. Keep in mind, however, that the phonetic symbol [k], rather than [c], corresponds to the sound represented by the letter *c* in words such as *car* [kar] 'bus', *cou* [ku] 'neck', and *cube* [kyb] 'cube', and that the phonetic symbol [z], rather than [s], corresponds to the sound represen-

Table 1.1. French consonants

[p]	par, apprendre, cep	(by, to learn, vine stock)
[t]	tard, attendre, cet	(late, to wait, this)
[k]	car, accomplir, cinq	(bus, to accomplish, five)
[b]	barre, abbé, baobab	(bar, abbot, baobab)
[d]	dos, addition, corde	(back, addition, rope)
[g]	gare, aggraver, figue	(train station, to aggravate, fig)
[m]	mare, aimer, pomme	(pond, to love, apple)
[n]	notre, année, âne	(our, year, donkey)
[ɲ]	gnon, agneau, montagne	(blow, lamb, mountain)
[f]	phrase, effet, neuf	(sentence, effect, new)
[s]	seau, assez, mince	(pail, enough, thin)
[ʃ]	chat, cacher, recherche	(cat, to hide, search)
[v]	vase, avant, cave	(vase, before, cellar)
[z]	zèbre, raser, gaz	(zebra, to shave, gas)
[ʒ]	jeu, déjà, âge	(game, already, age)
[l]	la, aller, facile	(the, to go, easy)
[r]	rare, arrondir, quatre	(rare, to round, four)

Table 1.2. French vowels

[i]	lit, midi, hibou	(bed, noon, owl)
[e]	été, métier, et	(summer, job, and)
[ɛ]	était, père, sec	(was, father, dry)
[a]	la, attraper, femme	(the, to catch, woman)
[y]	su, hurluberlu, usure	(known, crazy person, wear)
[ø]	feu, heureux, queue	(fire, happy, tail)
[œ]	le, coeur, heure	(the, heart, hour)
[u]	loup, tout, coup	(wolf, all, blow)
[o]	seau, gros, journaux	(pail, big, newspapers)
[ɔ]	or, fort, Paul	(gold, strong, Paul)
[ɑ]	âme, gaz, gras	(soul, gas, fat)
[ɛ̃]	fin, plein, train	(end, full, train)
[œ̃]	un, aucun, commun	(one, none, common)
[ɑ̃]	enfant, grand, étudiant	(child, big, student)
[õ]	on, long, pont	(one [pronoun], long, bridge)

Table 1.3. French glides

[j]	pierre, mayonnaise, billet	(stone, mayonnaise, ticket)
[ɥ]	lui, huit, puis	(him, eight, then)
[w]	Louis, oui, trois (oi=[wɑ])	(Louis, yes, three)

ted by the letter s in words such as bisou [bizu] 'kiss', poison [pwazõ] 'poison', and ruse [ryz] 'trick'.

For the representation of consonants, then, the symbols whose designs and values may be disconcerting at first are limited to [ɲ, ʃ, ʒ]. The symbol [ɲ] is simply the letter n with a descending tail on the left. It represents a sound perceptually close to the sound sequence written ni in the word *panier* [panje] 'basket'. In French orthography, it is represented by the sequence of letters *gn*, as in *gnon* [ɲõ] 'blow', *agneau* [aɲo] 'lamb', and *montagne* [mõtaɲ] 'mountain'. This sound does not exist in English, but is found in Spanish, where it is written *ñ* (an *n* with a tilde above it), as in *español* 'Spanish' and *año* 'year'. In some systems of phonetic transcription, the symbol [ñ] is used instead of [ɲ]. The phonetic symbol [ɲ] must be carefully distinguished from another, similar, phonetic symbol, [ŋ], which is also formed with an *n* as its base, but by adding a descending tail on the right instead of on the left; [ŋ] represents the English sound written *ng* which is found in words such as 'song'.

The phonetic symbol [ʃ] is a sort of *s* stretched vertically on both sides of the line on which one writes. Its design resembles a seahorse. The sound transcribed by this symbol corresponds in English orthography to the sequence of letters *sh*, as in *sheet* and *ash*. In French, it corresponds to the sequence of letters *ch* in words such as *chat* [ʃa] 'cat', *acheter* [aʃte] 'to buy', and *rechercher* [rœʃɛrʃe] 'to search'. Instead of the symbol [ʃ], it is also common to use the symbol [š] (an *s* with an inverted circumflex or wedge above it).

The phonetic symbol [ʒ] is comparable to the numeral 3, but lowered so that the middle bar is positioned on the line on which one writes. This sound is often written *j* in French orthography (*déjà* [deʒa] 'already', *je* [ʒœ] 'I', *jeudi* [ʒødi] 'Thursday', *journal* [ʒurnal] 'newspaper'). It is found in English words such as *measure* and *pleasure*, where it is written *s*. Just as the symbol [š] is often used instead of [ʃ], the symbol [ž] (a *z* with a wedge above it) is often used instead of [ʒ].

The phonetic symbols used to transcribe vowels are perhaps not as straightforward as those for consonants. To begin with, a fair number of these phonetic symbols do not exist as letters in the French and English alphabets. Secondly, some that *are* found in the alphabets of both French and English have different phonetic values in the orthography of these languages and in the phonetic notation.

Let us first consider the major instances where the symbols of the phonetic alphabet exist in the French and English alphabets, but with different phonetic values. In English, the names used to designate the letters *a*, *e*, and *i* correspond to their pronunciations in the words *fate*, *she*, and *sign*, respectively. In no way, therefore, do they correspond to the sounds which these letters represent when they are used as phonetic symbols. There is even a curious sort of interchange, since the pronunciation of the letter *a* in the English word *fate* is transcribed phonetically with the symbol [e], that of the letter *e* in *she* with the symbol [i], and that of the letter *i* in *sign* with the complex symbol [aɪ]. This systematic mismatch is not the result of a perverse conspiracy on the part of the founding members of the International Phonetic Association. In fact, the correspondence works very well for most languages (French, among others). What sets English apart here is a very important linguistic change, The Great Vowel Shift, which occurred around the sixteenth century and which dramatically transformed the pronunciation of vowels in this language. For our purposes, it is sufficient to keep in mind that the phonetic symbols [i, e, a] have the phonetic values of the corresponding letters in the French words *lit* [li] 'bed', *été* [ete] 'summer', and *la* [la] 'the'. Note finally that in English one refers to the letter *u* with a sequence of two sounds: [ju] (pronounced like the pronoun *you*); the second of these sounds is the value of the phonetic symbol [u].

In relation to French orthography, the main difficulty caused by the phonetic notation of vowels concerns the symbols [y] and [u]. Orthographically, the sound [y] is represented by the letter *u* (*rue* [ry] 'street', *sur* [syr] 'on', *hurluberlu* [yrlybɛrly] 'crazy person') and the sound [u] is represented by the sequence of letters *ou* (*roue* [ru] 'wheel', *sourd* [sur] 'deaf', *roucouler* [rukule] 'to coo'). In many other languages, there is a straightforward correspondence between the phonetic symbol [u] and the letter *u* (Spanish *mucho* 'a lot'; German *Fuss* 'foot'). The discrepancy that occurs in French is due to the fact that in the evolution from Latin to French, the sound [u], written *u*, became the sound [y], but without a change in the spelling (cf. Latin *durare* with [u]; French *durer* 'to last' with [y]). When the sound [u] appeared again in French, it was represented in the spelling by the sequence of letters *ou*, as the letter *u* by itself had become associated with the sound [y]. In some systems of phonetic transcription, the phonetic symbol [ü] (the letter *u* with a diaeresis above it) is used instead of [y]; it corresponds to the German orthography of the sound (*Stück* 'piece', *hübsch* 'pretty').

Let us now consider the instances where the phonetic notation for vowels resorts to symbols which do not exist in the French and English alphabets. The novelties are [ɛ, ø, œ, ɔ], the distinction between [a] and [ɑ], and the tilde which is placed above some vowel symbols.

The phonetic symbol [ɛ] is a Greek letter ('epsilon'). This sound is frequently written *è* in French, as in *père* [pɛr] 'father' and *très* [trɛ] 'very'. It is the vowel which one hears in the English words *bet* and *wreck*, for example.

The phonetic symbol [ø] is simply a slashed *o*. This sound is generally written *eu* in French, as in *feu* [fø] 'fire', *heureux* [ørø] 'happy', and *queue* [kø] 'tail'. It does not exist in English, but one finds it in German, where it is written *ö* (the letter *o* with a diaeresis above it), as in *böse* 'naughty' and *König* 'king'. In fact, some linguists transcribe this sound with the symbol [ö]; this choice of transcription is parallel to the substitution of [ü] for [y].

The symbol 'œ' actually occurs in French orthography: it is the combination (or ligature) spelled out 'o–e dans l'o' in French; it is found in words such as *cœur* 'heart', *œuf* 'egg', and *sœur* 'sister'. In these words, the sequence of letters *œu* corresponds to a single sound transcribed by the phonetic symbol [œ] ([kœr], [œf], [sœr]). The sound [œ] may also be written *eu* (as in *heure* [œr] 'hour', *peur* [pœr] 'fear', and *seul* [sœl] 'alone') and *e* (as in *breton* [brœtõ] 'Breton', *je* [ʒœ] 'I', and *le* [lœ] 'the'). This sound does not exist in English. Parallel to the use of [ü] and [ö] for [y] and [ø], respectively, one sometimes finds [ɔ̈] (the symbol ɔ – see next paragraph – with a diaeresis above it) instead of [œ].

The phonetic symbol [ɔ] is a *c* turned toward the left; this symbol is called 'open *o*' ('o ouvert'), in contrast to [o], which is a 'closed *o*' ('o fermé'). The sound [o] (closed *o*) is found, for example, in *sot* [so] 'stupid' and *idiot* [idjo] 'idiot', whereas the sound [ɔ] (open *o*) is found in the corresponding feminine forms *sotte* [sɔt] and *idiote* [idjɔt].

The phonetic alphabet makes a distinction between two kinds of 'a': [a] and [ɑ]. Orthography does not distinguish between the two symbols *a* and *a*; they are simply variants of the same letter, *a* usually appearing in printed texts and *a* in handwritten texts. But as phonetic symbols, [a] and [ɑ] correspond to different phonetic values. In French, they represent the distinction between the pronunciations of *patte* [pat] 'paw' and *pâte* [pɑt] 'dough', which is similar to the phonetic distinction between the *a*s of the English words *cat* and *father* (the vowel of the word *cat* is usually represented by the phonetic symbol [æ], a ligature formed by an *a* and an *e* joined together).

Four of the symbols used to represent French vowels are written with a tilde above them ([ɛ̃, œ̃, ɑ̃, õ]). The tilde serves to indicate a particular quality of the vowels: their nasality; in other words, in the production of these vowels, air passes through both the nose and the mouth instead of passing only through the mouth. In the orthographic system of French, nasal vowels are always represented by a sequence of letters of the type 'vowel(s) + *n* or *m*', as in *fin* [fɛ̃] 'end', *faim* [fɛ̃] 'hunger'; *un* [œ̃] 'one', *parfum* [parfœ̃] 'perfume'; *enfant* [ɑ̃fɑ̃] 'child', *embrasser* [ɑ̃brase] 'to kiss'; *bon* [bõ] 'good', *compter* [kõte] 'to count'.

Let us complete this introduction to the phonetic alphabet by considering the phonetic symbols for the glides: [j], [ɥ], and [w]. Both *j* and *w* are letters which belong to the French and English alphabets, but whereas the phonetic symbol [w] corresponds to the phonetic value of the letter *w* in English words like *we*, *wish*, and *water*, as well as in a few borrowed words in French (such as *kiwi* [kiwi] 'kiwi' and *watt* [wat] 'watt'), the phonetic symbol [j] never corresponds to the phonetic value of the letter *j* in English or in French; [j] is used to represent the phonetic value associated, for example, with the letter *y* in the English words *yes* and *you*. It is probably because of this sound–letter correspondence in English that American linguists often use the symbol [y] rather than [j]. (They are consequently led to use the symbol [ü] instead of [y] to transcribe the vowel in French words such as *rue* [ry] 'street' and *sur* [syr] 'on'.) Note that in German, the letter *j* regularly corresponds to the sound [j] (*ja* 'yes', *jetzt* 'now', *jung* 'young').

The phonetic symbol [ɥ] may be viewed as an *h* that has been rotated 180 degrees, or as a *u* with a vertical line added to the right side. [ɥ] represents the sound written *u* in words such as *huit* [ɥit] 'eight', *nuit* [nɥi] 'night', and *tuer* [tɥe] 'to kill'. This sound does not exist in English. The symbol [ẅ] is sometimes found instead of [ɥ]. In handwritten phonetic transcriptions, it is important to make a clear distinction in the drawing of [ɥ] and [y], as their forms have a tendency to merge.

In French, a very close relationship exists between the glides [j, ɥ, w] and the vowels [i, y, u]. This relationship is reflected in the orthography, where the letters *i*, *u*, and *ou* are usually pronounced [j, ɥ, w] in front of a pronounced vowel (*défier* [defje] 'to challenge', *tuer* [tɥe] 'to kill', *secouer* [sœkwe] 'to shake') and [i, y, u] elsewhere (*défi* [defi] 'challenge', *tue* [ty] 'kills', and *secoue* [sœku] 'shakes').

This cursory overview of French sounds is but a preliminary approach designed to put in place some of the basic tools necessary to the development of the following chapters. Before continuing, however, let us justify resorting to a phonetic notation such as the one just sketched, by outlining the types of complex correspondences which relate (or perhaps more appropriately, separate) orthography and pronunciation in French.

1.3. Orthography

The French alphabet consists of 26 letters, as does the alphabet of English. Traditionally, these letters are separated into two groups: vowels and consonants. In French, there are 6 vowel-letters (A, E, I, O, U, Y) and 20 consonant-letters (B, C, D, F, G, H, J, K, L, M, N, P, Q, R, S, T, V, W, X, Z). In addition, there are five diacritic marks, i.e. supplementary signs which can be combined with certain letters of the alphabet to form other graphic symbols. These marks are the cedilla ('la cédille'), the acute accent ('l'accent aigu'), the grave accent ('l'accent grave'), the circumflex accent ('l'accent circonflexe'), and the diaeresis ('le tréma'). With these marks, 13 additional symbols are created, as shown in Table 1.4. (On the role of diacritic marks in French orthography, see Appendix B.) Altogether, then, we come to a collection of 39

Table 1.4. Diacritic marks in French orthography

ç	ça, garçon, reçu	(that, boy, receipt)
é	été, hétérogénéité, séparé	(summer, heterogeneity, separate)
è	problème, achèvement, après	(problem, completion, after)
ê	bête, être, forêt	(beast, to be, forest)
ë	ambiguë, Noël	(ambiguous, Christmas)
à	à, déjà, là	(at, already, here)
â	âge, grâce, pâte	(age, grace, dough)
ù	où	(where)
û	août, dû, piqûre	(August, due, sting)
ü	Saül, capharnaüm	(Saul, mess)
ô	côté, hôpital, le nôtre	(side, hospital, ours)
î	boîte, connaître, île	(box, to know, island)
ï	caïman, haïr, héroïque	(alligator, to hate, heroic)

distinct 'letters' (18 vowels and 21 consonants), which, at least by their number, would seem to suffice to represent in a fairly simple and direct fashion the 35 sounds of the phonetic system of French (15 vowels, 3 glides, and 17 consonants). In reality, for historical reasons (see Appendix C), the relationship between letters and sounds is relatively complex in French and falls far short of providing a system of one-to-one correspondences (a single symbol for a single sound). The remainder of this chapter is devoted to examining the nature of the relations between orthography and pronunciation in French. The types of correspondences relating letters to sounds and sounds to letters are introduced by means of a few illustrations selected for their particularly revealing character. (For other examples, consult tables in Appendix D.)

1.3.1. From letters to sounds

To illustrate the relations between orthography and pronunciation in the direction of letters to sounds, let us examine in some detail the case of the letter *c*. In words such as *car* [kar] 'bus', *corps* [kɔr] 'body', *cure* [kyr] 'cure', *cloche* [klɔʃ] 'bell', *croche* [krɔʃ] 'eighth note', 'quaver', *sac* [sak] 'bag', and *tic* [tik] 'twitch', the letter *c* has the phonetic value [k]. In contrast, in words such as *cerise* [sœriz] 'cherry', *cire* [sir] 'wax', and *cygne* [siɲ] 'swan', it has the phonetic value [s]. The distribution of these two phonetic values of *c* is not haphazard, but governed by a general principle: one finds the phonetic value [s] in front of the letters *e*, *i*, and *y*, and the phonetic value [k] elsewhere. Since the distribution of the phonetic value [k] is more general than that of the phonetic value [s], which depends on a specific context, one can say that [k] is the *basic phonetic value* ('valeur phonique de base') of the letter *c* and that [s] is its *positional phonetic value* ('valeur phonique de position').

Table 1.5. Silent c at the end of words

tabac	[taba]	'tobacco'	franc	[frɑ̃]	'franc'
estomac	[ɛstɔma]	'stomach'	jonc	[ʒɔ̃]	'bulrush'
accroc	[akro]	'tear'	aspect	[aspɛ]	'aspect'
escroc	[ɛskro]	'swindler'	respect	[rɛspɛ]	'respect'
blanc	[blɑ̃]	'white'	instinct	[ɛ̃stɛ̃]	'instinct'

Table 1.6. c = [k] at the end of words

bac	[bak]	'ferry'	cognac	[kɔɲak]	'cognac'
lac	[lak]	'lake'	cornac	[kɔrnak]	'mahout'
sac	[sak]	'bag'	hamac	[amak]	'hammock'
bec	[bɛk]	'beak'	avec	[avɛk]	'with'
grec	[grɛk]ʃ	'Greek'	échec	[eʃɛk]	'failure'
sec	[sɛk]	'dry'	laïc	[laik]	'secular'
flic	[flik]	'cop'	loustic	[lustik]	'joker'
pic	[pik]	'peak'	pronostic	[prɔnɔstik]	'prediction'
tic	[tik]	'twitch'	trafic	[trafik]	'traffic'
bloc	[blɔk]	'block'	manioc	[manjɔk]	'manioc'
choc	[ʃɔk]	'shock'	mastoc	[mastɔk]	'heavy'
froc	[frɔk]	'frock'	médoc	[medɔk]	'wine from Médoc'
bouc	[buk]	'he-goat'	aqueduc	[akdyk]	'aqueduct'
duc	[dyk]	'duke'	caduc	[kadyk]	'deciduous'
donc	[dɔ̃k]	'then'	viaduc	[vjadyk]	'viaduct'
fisc	[fisk]	'Internal Revenue Service'	abject	[abʒɛkt]	'abject'
Marc	[mark]	'Mark'	direct	[dirɛkt]	'direct'
parc	[park]	'park'	exact	[ɛgzakt]	'exact'
talc	[talk]	'talcum powder'	contact	[kɔ̃takt]	'contact'

The letter c has a third phonetic value, namely [g], that one finds in zinc [zɛ̃g] 'zinc' and second [sœgɔ̃] 'second' (as well as its derivatives, e.g. secondaire [sœgɔ̃dɛr] 'secondary'). This phonetic value does not seem to be regulated by any general principle. In fact, it occurs only in the few words mentioned here. In such cases, one speaks of an idiosyncratic phonetic value ('valeur phonique idiosyncrasique').

A fourth case exists, where the letter c has no phonetic value; the letter is silent, as in the words of Table 1.5. In these examples, one can say that the letter c has a null (or zero) phonetic value ('valeur phonique nulle ou zéro'). The letter c may have the null value only at the end of a word or when it is followed by a word-final t (itself silent). But this null value is limited to a small number of words; far more examples can be found where, in these contexts, the letter c has its basic phonetic value [k] (see Table 1.6).

The letter c plays a fifth role in French orthography: when combined with the letter h, it may form what is called a digraph ('un digramme'), that is, a combination of two letters representing a single sound. There are other digraphs in French, for example *ou*, which serves to represent the sound [u], and *gn*, which serves to represent the sound [ɲ]. In English, *ng* is a digraph which serves to represent the sound [ŋ]. In French, the digraph *ch* serves to represent the sound [ʃ], as in *acheter* [aʃte] 'to buy', *chat* [ʃa] 'cat', *chien* [ʃjɛ̃] 'dog', and *hache* [aʃ] 'axe'. The sequence *ch* does not necessarily function as a digraph, however, since it does not always have the phonetic value [ʃ], but may in certain cases be pronounced [k] (as in *almanach* [almanak] 'almanac', *varech* [varɛk] 'seaweed', *chlore* [klɔr] 'chlorine', *chrome* [krom] 'chrome', *archaïque* [arkaik] 'archaic', *chaos* [kao] 'chaos', and *écho* [eko] 'echo'), as if the letter *h* of the sequence was not there (that is, had a null value), and the letter *c* had its basic phonetic value [k]. Note that the sequence *ch* always has the phonetic value [k] before a consonant (*l* or *r*) and almost always at the end of a word (exceptions are *almanach*, which may alternatively be pronounced without a final [k], and the proper names *Auch* [oʃ] and *Foch* [fɔʃ], which have a final [ʃ]).

However, when the sequence *ch* represents the sound [k] before the vowels *i* and *e* (for example in *chiromancie* [kirɔmɑ̃si] 'palm-reading' and *archétype* [arketip] 'archetype'), one cannot say that the letter *h* has a null value. For if the letter *h* were not present, one would incorrectly read the letter *c* as [s] instead of [k], because it would immediately precede the letters *i* and *e*. So the letter *h* plays an essential role here in the orthography: it keeps the letter *c* separate from the letters *i* and *e*, thereby preventing it from having its positional value [s]. One can say that the letter *h* has an *auxiliary value* ('valeur auxiliaire'): without contributing directly to the representation of a sound, it allows another letter to have a phonetic value that it could not otherwise have in this position. Auxiliary value, then, is to be distinguished from null value, since a letter which has the null value could just as well be absent from the orthography of the word; it would not change the way in which the word would be read (compare, for example, *chœur* 'choir' and *cœur* 'heart', which are both pronounced in the same way: [kœr]; the *h* in *chœur* has the null value). Not so for a letter with an auxiliary value: it is not itself sounded (like a letter with the null value), but its absence from the spelling of a word would lead to a difference in pronunciation (compare, for instance, the initial syllables in *chiromancie* [kirɔmɑ̃si] 'palm-reading' and *cirrocumulus* [sirokymylys] 'cirro-cumulus').

In front of a vowel, the letter *h* in the sequence *ch* may thus have different values; and the distribution of these values is quite arbitrary, because nothing in the system itself allows one to predict the contrast between words which contain [k], and words which contain [ʃ], as the examples in Table 1.7 illustrate.

Table 1.7. *ch* as [k] vs [ʃ]

ch = [k]			*ch* = [ʃ]		
arch*é*ologie	[arkeɔlɔʒi]	'archeology'	arch*e*vêque	[arʃœvɛk]	'archbishop'
*ch*iromancie	[kirɔmãsi]	'palm-reading'	*ch*irurgie	[ʃiryrʒi]	'surgery'
*ch*aos	[kao]	'chaos'	*ch*ahut	[ʃay]	'rowdiness'
*é*cho	[eko]	'echo'	*é*choppe	[eʃɔp]	'small shop'

Finally, the letter *c* is one of the letters of the alphabet which may be combined with a diacritic mark, in this case the cedilla. The cedilla is used with the letter *c* to give this letter the phonetic value [s] (instead of [k]) in front of the letters *a*, *o*, and *u* (compare the words *ça* [sa] 'that', *façon* [fasõ] 'manner', and *déçu* [desy] 'disappointed', which contain the sound [s], with the words *car* [kar] 'bus', *flacon* [flakõ] 'flask', and *décupler* [dekyple] 'to increase tenfold', which contain the sound [k]). In many cases, this mechanism allows a given root to keep the same spelling (except for the cedilla) throughout its family of related words (for example, *balanc-* in *balancer* 'to swing', *balançait*, *balançons*, and *balançoire*; *franc-* in *France* and *français*; *rec-* in *recevoir* 'to receive', *reçoit*, and *reçu*).

The case of the letter *c* just examined in some detail illustrates the diverse roles that letters may play in the conventional orthographic representation of the sounds of French. In summary, a letter does not necessarily correspond to one single sound; it may represent several sounds, or sometimes none. The distribution of the phonetic values of a letter may be governed by general principles sensitive to context, but the variation may also be idiosyncratic. A letter may enter in combination with other letters, either to form sequences having particular phonetic values, or to allow the other letters to maintain their basic phonetic value.

Table 1.8. Summary table for *c* and *h*

A. *Functions of the letter* c

[k]: basic phonetic value	(*car* [kar] 'bus')
[s]: positional phonetic value	(*cire* [sir] 'wax')
[g]: idiosyncratic phonetic value	(*second* [sœgõ] 'second')
null phonetic value	(*tabac* [taba] 'tobacco')
member of the digraph *ch* = [ʃ]	(*chat* [ʃa] 'cat')
addition of the cedilla: ç = [s]	(*ça* [sa] 'that')

B. *Role of* h *in the sequence* ch

member of the digraph *ch* = [ʃ]	(*chat* [ʃa] 'cat')
null phonetic value	(*chœur* [kœr] 'choir')
auxiliary value	(*archéologie* [arkeɔlɔʒi] 'archaeology')

Finally, some letters may be associated with certain diacritic marks, and thereby retain one of their phonetic values in specific contexts. Table 1.8 provides a summary of the preceding discussion (see also Table D.3 in Appendix D).

1.3.2. From sounds to letters

We have just illustrated the types of relations connecting orthography and pronunciation in French, going from letter to sound. Let us now illustrate the types of correspondences which operate in the reverse direction, that is, starting with the sound and ending with its orthographic representation.

Our first example concerns the sound [k]. There are many ways of representing this sound in French orthography. As we saw in the preceding section, [k] may be represented by the letter *c* (*car* [kar] 'bus'); but it may also be represented by the letter *k* (as in *képi* [kepi] 'kepi', *kilo* [kilo] 'kilo', *klaxon* [klaksɔn] 'horn', *okapi* [ɔkapi] 'okapi', and *mark* [mark] 'German mark') and by the letter *q* (as in *équilatéral* [ekɥilateral] 'equilateral', *quadrupler* [kwadryple] 'to quadruple', *cinq* [sɛ̃k] 'five', and *coq* [kɔk] 'rooster'). A sound may thus be represented by several different letters in the orthography.

Several sequences of letters may also serve to represent a single sound. Thus, for the same sound [k], one finds the following:

(i) the sequence *cc*, after a vowel and before *a*, *o*, *u*, *l*, and *r*, as in *occasion* [ɔkazjɔ̃] 'opportunity', *s'accouder* [sakude] 'to lean on one's elbows', *occuper* [ɔkype] 'to occupy', *occlusion* [ɔklyzjɔ̃] 'obstruction', and *accrocher* [akrɔʃe] 'to hang'. (Before *e* and *i*, the sequence *cc* represents the sounds [ks], as in *accepter* [aksɛpte] 'to accept' and *accident* [aksidɑ̃] 'accident');

(ii) the sequence *ch*, as in *chiromancie* [kirɔmɑ̃si] 'palm-reading', *chlore* [klɔr] 'chlorine', and *varech* [varɛk] 'seaweed' (see above);

(iii) the sequence *ck*, which is found in borrowed words such as *bifteck* [biftɛk] 'steak', *blockhaus* [blɔkos] 'bunker', *cockpit* [kɔkpit] 'cockpit', *dock* [dɔk] 'dock', *jockey* [ʒɔkɛ] 'jockey', *stock* [stɔk] 'stock', and *teck* [tɛk] 'teak';

(iv) the sequence *qu*, which occurs before a vowel-letter, as in *équilibre* [ekilibr] 'equilibrium', *loqueteux* [lɔktø] 'in tatters', *quand* [kɑ̃] 'when', and *quotidien* [kɔtidjɛ̃] 'daily';

(v) other combinations, such as *cch* (*ecchymose* [ekimoz] 'ecchymosis', *saccharine* [sakarin] 'saccharine'), *kh* (*khi* [ki] 'khi', *kolkhoze* [kɔlkoz] 'kolkhoz'), and *cqu* (*acquérir* [akerir] 'to acquire', *grecque* [grɛk] 'Greek', *Jacques* [ʒak] 'James', *socquette* [sɔkɛt] 'sock').

Note finally that the sound [k] is the first element in the double phonetic value [ks] of the letter *x*, as in *axe* [aks] 'axis' and *taxi* [taksi] 'cab'. The letter *x* is the only letter which may represent a sequence of sounds in French. This letter may also have the phonetic values [gz] (as in *exemple* [egzɑ̃pl] 'example'), [s] (as in *six* [sis] 'six'), [z] (as in *deuxième* [døzjɛm] 'second'), and zero (as in *deux* [dø] 'two').

Let us now consider briefly another example, a vowel this time, the nasal vowel [ɛ̃]. As mentioned above, there is no single letter in French which allows the orthographic representation of a nasal vowel. Nasal vowels are represented in the orthography by digraphs (or trigraphs): one (or two) vowel-letters followed by the consonant-letters *m* or *n* (for example, *imposer* [ɛ̃poze] 'to tax' and *vin* [vɛ̃] 'wine' contain the vowel [ɛ̃]; *parfum* [parfœ̃] 'perfume' and *un* [œ̃] 'one', the vowel [œ̃]; *emporter* [ɑ̃pɔrte] 'to take away' and *entourer* [ɑ̃ture] 'to surround', the vowel [ɑ̃]; and *sombre* [sõbr] 'dark' and *bon* [bõ] 'good', the vowel [õ]).

The vowel-letters which may combine with a nasal consonant-letter to represent the sound [ɛ̃] are five in number, and even six in the dialects where [œ̃] (written *um* or *un*) has merged with [ɛ̃]. They are:

(i)   *e*, as in *agenda* [aʒɛ̃da] 'agenda', *chien* [ʃjɛ̃] 'dog', and *examen* [ɛgzamɛ̃] 'examination';
(ii) *i*, as in *cinq* [sɛ̃k] 'five', *fin* [fɛ̃] 'end', and *mince* [mɛ̃s] 'thin';
(iii) *y*, as in *syntaxe* [sɛ̃taks] 'syntax', *synthèse* [sɛ̃tɛz] 'synthesis', and *thym* [tɛ̃] 'thyme';
(iv) *ai*, as in *main* [mɛ̃] 'hand', *pain* [pɛ̃] 'bread', and *faim* [fɛ̃] 'hunger';
(v)   *ei*, as in *frein* [frɛ̃] 'break', *peint* [pɛ̃] 'painted', and *sein* [sɛ̃] 'breast';
(vi) *u*, as in *brun* [brɛ̃] 'brown', *opportun* [ɔpɔrtɛ̃] 'opportune', and *un* [ɛ̃] 'one'.

Table 1.9 gives a summary of the variety of orthographic representations for the sounds [k] and [ɛ̃] (see also Appendix D for further illustrations).

These two cases ([k] and [ɛ̃]) exemplify the redundancy in the orthographic representation of French sounds. In sum, not only may one letter have several phonetic values (as in the instance of the letter *c* examined earlier), but further, a given sound may have several different spellings.

1.3.3. Other complications

The relationship between orthography and pronunciation in French is rendered still more complex by the fact that a letter or group of letters within the same written sequence does not necessarily have a constant phonetic value. In many instances, additional linguistic information helps determine the actual pronunciation of the form, but there are also cases which seem arbitrary. Examples of various kinds follow. In *six* and *dix*, the letter *x* has the phonetic value [s] before a pause (*six* [sis], *dix* [dis]),

Table 1.9. Summary table for [k] and [ɛ̃]

A. Orthographic representations of [k]

c	(*car* [kar])	cc	(*s'accouder* [sakude])	cch	(*saccharine* [sakarin])	(bus, to lean on one's elbows, saccharine)
k	(*képi* [kepi])	ch	(*chrome* [krom])	kh	(*khi* [ki])	(kepi, chrome, khi)
q	(*coq* [kɔk])	ck	(*bifteck* [biftek])	cqu	(*grecque* [grek])	(rooster, steak, Greek)
		qu	(*quand* [kɑ̃])	x	(*taxi* [taksi])	(when, taxi)

B. Orthographic representations of [ɛ̃]

eN	(*chien* [ʃjɛ̃])	(dog)
iN	(*impôt* [ɛ̃po]; *cinq* [sɛ̃k])	(tax, five)
yN	(*thym* [tɛ̃]; *syntaxe* [sɛ̃taks])	(thyme, syntax)
aiN	(*faim* [fɛ̃]; *main* [mɛ̃])	(hunger, hand)
eiN	(*Reims* [rɛ̃s]; *sein* [sɛ̃])	([town name], breast)
uN	(*parfum* [parfɛ̃]; *un* [ɛ̃])	(perfume, one)

(Note: *N* represents *m* or *n*)

the phonetic value [z] before a vowel (*six amis* [sizami] 'six friends', *dix amis* [dizami] 'ten friends'), and the null value before a consonant (*six tables* [sitabl] 'six tables', *dix tables* [ditabl] 'ten tables'). In *grand* 'large', the letter *d* has the phonetic value [t] before a vowel-initial word (*grand avion* [grɑ̃tavjõ] 'large airplane'), the phonetic value [d] before a vowel-initial suffix (*grande* [grɑ̃d] 'large' (feminine), *grandeur* [grɑ̃dœr] 'size'), and the null value before a consonant-initial word (*grand château* [grɑ̃ʃato] 'large castle'). In the written forms *couvent* and *expédient*, the sequence of letters *ent* has the phonetic value [ɑ̃] if it is part of the nouns ([kuvɑ̃] 'convent', [ɛkspedjɑ̃] 'expedient'), but the null value if it is part of the verbs ([kuv] '[they] hatch', [ɛkspedi] '[they] send'). In the pair of verb forms *dévient* [devi] '(they) deviate' – *devient* [dœvjɛ̃] '(he) becomes', the same sequence of letters *ent* has the null value in the first case, but the phonetic value [ɛ̃] in the second case. In the sequence of letters *ti* followed by a vowel, the letter *t* may have the phonetic values [t] or [s]: compare *sortie* [sɔrti] 'exit' (cf. *sortir* [sɔrtir] 'to go out'), *nous portions* [nupɔrtjõ] 'we were carrying' (cf. *porter* [pɔrte] 'to carry'), and *chrétien* [kretjɛ̃] 'Christian', which contain [t], with *inertie* [inɛrsi] 'inertia' (but *inerte* [inɛrt] 'inert'), *portions* [pɔrsjõ] 'shares', and *martien* [marsjɛ̃] 'Martian' (cf. *Mars* [mars] 'Mars'), which contain [s]. Finally, as a last example, observe that the group of letters *qui* may represent the sound sequences [ki] or [kɥi]: compare *qui* [ki] 'who' and *équilibre* [ekilibr] 'equilibrium', which contain [ki], with *ubiquité* [ybikɥite] 'ubiquity' and *équilatéral* [ekɥilateral] 'equilateral', which contain [kɥi].

1.4. Conclusion

The relation between French orthography and French pronunciation is not simple. This does not necessarily mean that French orthography is altogether poorly suited to the representation of the language; for example, the fact that a given word keeps the same spelling, even though its pronunciation may vary according to context, may rightly be considered as an economical, practical, and psychologically motivated means of representing the invariability of its semantic value. Among other things, what I have tried to show in the course of this chapter is simply that French orthography is a far cry from being phonetic and that therefore, for our purposes, it is necessary to introduce another tool of representation for the language, a notation wherein a single symbol corresponds to a single sound.

2
Basic notions of phonetics

2.1. Introduction

Phonetics deals with the study of the sounds used in the languages of the world. Its main goals are to catalog the existing sounds, to examine their acoustic properties, and to determine how they are produced and perceived by human beings. Thus, by its very nature, phonetics relates to a wide variety of disciplines: not only general linguistics, but also physics, biology (physiology and neurology), and psychology.

Our own perspective in this chapter will be relatively narrowly circumscribed. First, we shall confine ourselves to what is traditionally known as *articulatory phonetics* ('la phonétique articulatoire'), that is, the study of sound production at the level of the vocal cords and the cavities above the vocal cords (the supraglottal cavities). We shall not consider, for instance, acoustic phonetics or sound perception. Second, rather than aiming for a comprehensive review of the articulation of all the sounds, or even all the sound types, that have been documented in natural languages, we shall for the most part focus only on the knowledge of articulatory phonetics that is required in order to tackle the sound systems of French and English and their contrastive study. In sum, this chapter is simply devoted to an overview of the operation of the speech organs and to a presentation of the main articulatory parameters which permit the description, classification, and comparison of French and English sounds.

2.2. The production and perception of sounds: general outline

When we speak, our brain sends, through motor nerves ('nerfs moteurs'), a multitude of complex orders to the muscles that control the *speech organs* ('les organes de la parole'). The speech organs then react in various ways upon the air contained in the system and create sound waves ('ondes sonores') which propagate from the speaker's mouth to the listener's ears. The air vibrations are ultimately relayed to the brain by sensory nerves ('nerfs sensoriels'). Verbal communication thus comprises a neurophysiological encoding and decoding of the sounds, separated by a stage of airborne acoustic transmission (see Figure 2.1).

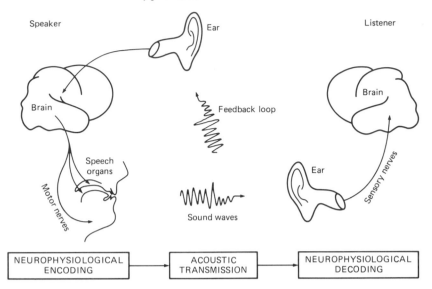

Figure 2.1. The speech chain (adapted from Peter Denes and Elliot Pinson, *The Speech Chain*, 1963, p. 4)

2.3. The production and classification of sounds

2.3.1. Adaptation of the respiratory function

Speech sounds have as their source the various movements communicated by the speech organs to the air located in the respiratory system between the lungs and the lips (see Figure 2.2). Speech sounds are ordinarily produced during the exhalation phase of breathing; they are not produced during the inhalation phase, except in unusual circumstances, for example, when one speaks and sobs at the same time, to disguise one's voice in certain cultures, or to create some stylistic effect with certain words (as with the word *oui* 'yes' in French). When one speaks while inhaling, only brief (and odd-sounding) utterances can actually be produced without interruption, because the inhalation phase cannot be physiologically maintained for very long. In contrast, one can easily control the duration of the exhalation phase. So, while in normal breathing the inhalation and exhalation phases are of approximately equal duration, during speech the exhalation phase can be considerably extended by releasing the air at a slower rate than in normal breathing; this adaptation makes possible the production of relatively long utterances without interruption.

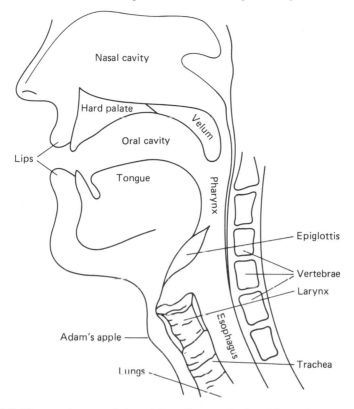

Figure 2.2. The speech organs (adapted from Georges Straka, *Album phonétique*, 1967, p. 2).

2.3.2. The vocal cords

During the exhalation phase of breathing, the air contained in the lungs is compressed and thus pushed outward. The airstream first passes through a cylindrical tube of about ten centimeters in length, the trachea ('la trachée'), and comes to the *larynx* ('le larynx'), a complex structure of cartilages and muscles. There, the air must go through the *glottis* ('la glotte'), a passageway which may be opened and closed by the action of the *vocal cords* ('les cordes vocales'), two muscles in the form of a V pointed toward the Adam's apple. This valve is naturally open during breathing. It closes shut to permit us to fix the rib cage, for example during defecation or when lifting heavy objects. It also closes to prevent undesirable objects, such as food, from entering the trachea. Intruders are catapulted back out by coughing, which is produced by first creating positive air pressure under the closed vocal cords and then abruptly opening the valve.

From a linguistic point of view, the vocal cords function essentially in two ways: either they are apart and leave the glottis open, or else they vibrate very rapidly, opening and closing the glottis 100, 200, 300 times per second. The vibrations of the vocal cords are not caused by extremely rapid contractions of these muscles; rather, it is the airstream coming from the lungs which makes them vibrate. Here is, in slow motion as it were, how these vibrations are produced: the tension and proximity of the vocal cords are regulated in such a way that the air from the lungs may not pass freely through the glottis; consequently, the air pressure under the glottis increases and forces the vocal cords apart; but the passage of the air between the vocal cords automatically reduces the pressure which had created the opening of the glottis in the first place; as a result, the vocal cords come together again and regain their original position; the cycle of one vibration is completed, but all is in place for it to start again. This vibratory phenomenon is known as the Bernoulli Effect (from the name of a Swiss physicist). The very same principle (albeit with different parts of the vocal apparatus) is at work in the lip vibrations performed by many young children and in the production of the rolled *r*s found for example in Spanish (*perro* 'dog') and in some French dialects.

The rate of vibration of the vocal cords (or fundamental frequency) determines *voice pitch* ('la hauteur de la voix'): the more rapid the vibrations, the higher the pitch. The fundamental frequency, and consequently the pitch, depend not only on inherent physiological characteristics of the individual, but also on parameters that each individual is capable of adjusting (in particular, the tension of the vocal cords, the amount of air coming from the lungs, and the velocity of this air). Pitch variations in discourse constitute what is called the *intonation* of sentences. They play a very important linguistic role. For example, the sequence of words *Le petit chat est mort* ('The little cat is dead') denotes an assertion if pronounced with a descending intonation, but a question if pronounced with a rising intonation. It is possible to create all sorts of nuances of meaning through different variations in intonation.

The way in which the air coming from the lungs goes through the glottis, that is, whether the vocal cords vibrate or not, also plays an important linguistic role. Take, for example, the sounds [s] and [z], which are found in the words *poisson* [pwasõ] 'fish' and *poison* [pwazõ] 'poison'. These two sounds are exactly alike in all respects, except that for [s], the air goes through the glottis freely, without making the vocal cords vibrate, whereas in the case of [z], the air causes the vocal cords to vibrate: [s] is *voiceless* ('sourd') and [z] is *voiced* ('sonore' or 'voisé'). For an almost direct tactile feeling of the phenomenon of vocal cord vibration, place your fingers over your Adam's apple and produce [ssss] and

[zzzz] aloud alternately. (Make sure not to whisper, as whispering is precisely speech production without vocal cord vibrations.) For [zzzz], the vibrations of the vocal cords are transmitted to the fingers, but for [ssss], one feels nothing, because the vocal cords do not vibrate. Another way to experience the difference between voiceless and voiced sounds is to plug your ears while producing [ssss] and [zzzz]. For [zzzz], but not for [ssss], you will clearly perceive, through bone conduction, a humming sound which corresponds to the vibrations of the vocal cords.

The vocal cords thus provide an important parameter for differentiating sounds. This parameter is called *voicing* ('sonorité' or 'voisement'). The distinction between [s] (voiceless) and [z] (voiced) is found in other pairs of sounds whose members are otherwise completely identical. Consider, for example, [f]–[v] (*fin* [fɛ̃] 'end' – *vin* [vɛ̃] 'wine') and [ʃ]–[ʒ] (*des chats* [deʃa] 'cats' – *déjà* [deʒa] 'already'), with which the same experiments as with [s] and [z] can be conducted to verify that [f] and [ʃ] are voiceless, whereas [v] and [ʒ] are voiced. The voicing parameter also serves to distinguish [p] (voiceless) from [b] (voiced) (*pain* [pɛ̃] 'bread' – *bain* [bɛ̃] 'bath'), [t] (voiceless) from [d] (voiced) (*thé* [te] 'tea' – *dé* [de] 'thimble'), and [k] (voiceless) from [g] (voiced) (*quai* [kɛ] 'platform' – *gai* [gɛ] 'cheerful').

The consonants [m, n, ɲ, ŋ, l, r] and the glides [j, ɥ, w] are generally voiced, but they can become voiceless next to a voiceless consonant. In a precise phonetic transcription, devoicing ('désonorisation' or 'dévoisement') would be indicated by means of a small subscript circle (*pneu* [pnø̥] 'tire', *snobisme* [snɔbism̥] 'snobbery', *pli* [pl̥i] 'crease', *quatre* [katr̥] 'four', *pied* [pje] 'foot', *puis* [pɥi] 'then', *poids* [pwɑ] 'weight').

Ordinarily, vowels also are voiced, but it is possible for them too (particularly [i, y, u]) to be voiceless when they occur between two voiceless consonants. Again, in a detailed phonetic transcription, this devoicing would be marked with a small subscript circle (*quitter* [kite] 'to leave', *occupation* [ɔkypasjɔ̃] 'occupation', *découper* [dekupe] 'to cut out'). We shall not be further concerned with vowel devoicing in this book.

2.3.3. The supraglottal cavities

Having passed the glottis, the airstream reaches the cavities above the glottis (or supraglottal cavities, 'les cavités supraglottiques'), namely, the *pharynx* ('le pharynx'), the *oral cavity* ('la cavité buccale'), and the *nasal cavity* ('les fosses nasales') (see Figure 2.3).

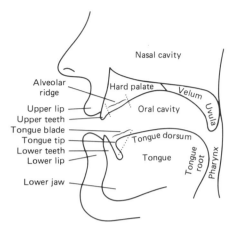
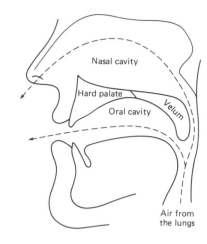

Figure 2.3. The supraglottal cavities
(raised velum) (adapted from Straka,
Album phonétique, p. 15)

Figure 2.4. The supraglottal cavities
(lowered velum) (adapted from Straka,
Album phonétique, p. 29)

The nasal cavity. Whether the air goes through the nasal cavity is
determined by the position of the *soft palate* or *velum* ('le voile du palais'
or 'palais mou' or 'vélum'). If the soft palate is raised, the airstream can
pass only through the oral cavity (see Figure 2.3); if the soft palate is
lowered, the airstream passes through both the nasal cavity and the oral
cavity (see Figure 2.4). The air then necessarily goes into the oral cavity,
but it may or may not pass through the nasal cavity.

This parameter, *nasality* ('nasalité'), plays an important linguistic role.
For instance, the vowels [ɛ] of *mais* [mɛ] 'but' and [ɛ̃] of *main* [mɛ̃] 'hand'
are very similar in all respects, except that for [ɛ], the airstream passes
only through the oral cavity, whereas for [ɛ̃], it goes through both the oral
cavity and the nasal cavity. The same opposition arises in the pairs of
vowels [œ]–[œ̃] (*le* [lœ] 'the' – *l'un* [lœ̃] 'the one'), [ɑ]–[ɑ̃] (*âtre* [ɑtr]
'hearth' – *antre* [ɑ̃tr] 'lair'), and [o]–[õ] (*sot* [so] 'stupid' – *son* [sõ]
'sound'). The vowels [ɛ̃, œ̃, ɑ̃, õ] are said to be *nasal*, because some of the
air passes through the nasal cavity during their production; the other
vowels are said to be *oral*, because the airstream passes through the oral
cavity only.

The parameter of nasality also allows important distinctions to be made
among consonants. Thus, [m, n, ŋ] are in all respects identical to [b, d, g],
except that the air passes the nasal cavity in the first series of
consonants (they are therefore nasal consonants), but not in the second
series (these then are oral consonants). [ɲ] is also a nasal consonant.

The oral cavity. Up until now, two parameters have been isolated which permit the description and classification of sounds: voicing (voiceless/voiced sounds) and nasality (oral/nasal sounds). Sounds are differentiated by many additional criteria, which have to do with the different types of configurations that the oral cavity may adopt through movements of the *lower jaw* ('la mâchoire inférieure'), the *tongue* ('la langue'), and the *lips* ('les lèvres'). If the airstream passes freely through the oral cavity, vowels are produced, such as [i, u, a]; if, on the contrary, an obstruction or a constriction occurs somewhere in the oral cavity, consonants are produced, such as [p, n, v, l].

2.3.4. Consonants

Let us first consider consonants and examine the parameters that allow us to differentiate among them according to their articulation in the oral cavity. Here, it is essentially a matter of determining (i) how the articulation is produced (for example, by a complete blockage of the airstream) and (ii) where in the oral cavity the articulation occurs (for example, at the lips).

Consonants: manner of articulation. When the airstream in the oral cavity is completely stopped (i.e. when there is an oral occlusion), as in the case of [p], the sound thus produced is called a *stop* ('une occlusive'). [p, b, t, d, k, g] are all stops. [m, n, ɲ, ŋ] are also stops; even though the air is allowed to pass freely through the nasal cavity during their production, these nasal consonants are also characterized by an oral stoppage; they are thus referred to as nasal stops ('occlusives nasales'), whereas [p, b, t, d, k, g] are oral stops ('occlusives orales'). Recall that [b, d, g, m, n, ɲ, ŋ] are voiced stops, and [p, t, k] voiceless stops (see Table 2.1).

Table 2.1. Stops

nasal (voiced)		m	n	ɲ	ŋ
oral	voiceless	p	t		k
	voiced	b	d		g

When the airstream in the oral cavity is only partially obstructed, and there is sufficient constriction to create air turbulence and a friction noise, as in the case of [s], the sound thus produced is called a *fricative* ('une fricative' or 'spirante'). [f, v, s, z, ʃ, ʒ] are fricatives. [f, s, ʃ] are voiceless fricatives, [v, z, ʒ] voiced fricatives (see Table 2.2).

Table 2.2. Fricatives

voiceless	f	s	ʃ
voiced	v	z	ʒ

Some consonants are produced by the rapid succession of an occlusion and a constriction. This is the case, for instance, of the English consonants [tʃ] and [dʒ] that are found at the beginning and end of the words *church* and *judge*, and of the German consonants [pf] and [ts] that are found at the beginning of the words *Pferd* 'horse' and *zehn* 'ten'. These consonants are called *affricates* ('affriquées'). [pf, ts, tʃ] are voiceless affricates, [dʒ] is a voiced affricate (see Table 2.3). Instead of the symbols [tʃ] and [dʒ], one commonly finds [č] and [ǰ].

Table 2.3. Affricates

voiceless	pf	ts	tʃ
voiced			dʒ

The *r* of standard French can be fricative, but not necessarily so; in fact, most often, the constriction produced during its articulation is not sufficiently narrow to create air turbulence and friction; we speak then of an *approximant r*. There is usually friction when the *r* is devoiced, as in *quatre* [katʁ̥] 'four'. The phonetic symbol specifically reserved for the *r* observed in standard French, whether it is fricative or not, is [ʁ] (an upper-case *R* rotated 180 degrees on its horizontal axis. In some works one finds [ʁ], an upper-case *R* rotated 180 degrees on its vertical axis.) The phonetic symbol for a voiceless [ʁ] is [χ] (the Greek letter 'khi', which resembles an upper-case *X* slightly prolonged below the line on which one writes), but one finds [ʁ̥] or [ʁ] more often. For reasons of typographical convenience, the symbols [r] and [r̥] are frequently used instead of [ʁ] and [ʁ̥], at least when this does not lead to a confusion with other types of *r*s (such as the one described in the next paragraph).

In other varieties of French, *r* is produced by a few rapid vibrations of the tip of the tongue against the alveolar ridge. This type of *r* is called a *trilled r* ('r roulé'). It is also found in Spanish, Italian, and Russian, for instance. The phonetic symbol specifically reserved for the alveolar trilled *r* is [r].

The consonant *l* brings us to another type of articulation. During the production of this sound, the airstream is blocked in the center of the oral cavity by placing the tongue tip behind the upper front teeth, but the air can flow through on both sides of the tongue (or on just one side, depending on the speaker). For this reason, the consonant is said to be *lateral* ('consonne latérale'), whereas the other consonants are said to be *central* ('consonnes centrales'). As a rule, the airstream in the case of *l* creates no friction, which makes *l* an approximant. But fricative *l*s do occur; for example, in French, the devoicing of *l* after a voiceless consonant is often accompanied by a slight friction noise, as in *peuple* [pœpḷ] 'people'. For functional reasons, the consonants *r* and *l* are often grouped together under the impressionistic label of *liquids* ('liquides').

The distinctions that have just been made between stops, fricatives, affricates, approximants, trills, laterals, and centrals are traditionally subsumed under the heading *manner of articulation* ('mode d'articulation'). As we have seen, this parameter concerns the manner in which the articulators are positioned to create different types of sounds used as consonants in natural languages. But the articulators may, of course, be positioned in various places in the oral cavity, which generates an additional parameter, *place of articulation* ('lieu d'articulation' or 'point d'articulation'). This parameter permits us to make the necessary distinctions among consonants with the same manner of articulation (for instance [p, t, k]), while bringing together into additional natural classes of sounds consonants with the same place of articulation (for instance [t, d, n, s, z, l]).

Consonants: place of articulation. Let us first consider stops, and in particular the nasal stops [m, n, ɲ, ŋ]. What distinguishes these consonants from each other is the place where the occlusion occurs in the oral cavity (cf. the columns in Table 2.1). For [m], the occlusion takes place at the lips; [m] is a *bilabial* nasal stop ('occlusive nasale bilabiale'). [p] and [b] are also bilabial (bilabial oral stops). For [n], the occlusion results from placing the tip ('la pointe') or the blade ('la lame') of the tongue against either the upper front teeth ('les incisives supérieures') or the alveolar ridge ('les alvéoles'); [t] and [d] are formed in the same way; these three consonants are *dental* or *alveolar* stops ('occlusives dentales/alvéolaires') (depending on whether the occlusion is produced with the tongue against the teeth or against the alveolar ridge). For [ɲ], the occlusion is made by placing the front part of the dorsum ('le dos') of the tongue against the hard palate ('le palais dur'); [ɲ] is a *palatal* nasal stop ('occlusive nasale palatale'). For [ŋ], the posterior portion of the dorsum of the tongue is placed against the velum; the same occlusion is produced for [k] and [g]; these consonants are said to be *velar* stops ('occlusives vélaires').

Let us now move on to the fricatives (cf. the columns in Table 2.2). For

[f] and [v], the constriction is produced between the lower lip ('la lèvre inférieure') and the upper front teeth; [f] and [v] are *labio-dental* fricatives ('fricatives labio-dentales'). Consider next two fricatives not mentioned so far, those that are found in English at the beginning of the words *thin*, *thesis*, *thatch*, and *thigh* on the one hand, and *this*, *these*, *that*, and *thy* on the other hand. The first series of words begins with a voiceless fricative transcribed by the phonetic symbol [θ] (the Greek letter 'theta' or, more colloquially, 'the cigar'), whereas the second series begins with a voiced fricative transcribed by the phonetic symbol [ð] (the Anglo-Saxon letter 'eth'). Both fricatives are written *th* in English orthography, and they are indeed exactly alike in all respects, except that the first is voiceless and the second is voiced. Where does the constriction take place? It is produced between the tip or the blade of the tongue and the upper front teeth; these consonants are *dental* fricatives ('fricatives dentales'). These fricatives may also be produced by placing the tip or the blade of the tongue between the upper and lower front teeth; they can then be defined as *inter-dental* fricatives ('fricatives inter-dentales'). For [s] and [z], the constriction occurs between the tip or the blade of the tongue and the alveolar ridge; these are *alveolar* fricatives ('fricatives alvéolaires'). For [ʃ] and [ʒ], the constriction is made with the blade of the tongue slightly further back than for [s] and [z], just behind the alveolar ridge; these are *alveo-palatal* fricatives ('fricatives alvéo-palatales').

The *r* of standard French is generally considered to be the result of a constriction produced between the dorsum of the tongue and the uvula ('la luette'); it is therefore described as a *uvular* consonant ('consonne uvulaire'). The trilled *r* produced by vibrations of the tip of the tongue against the alveolar ridge is an alveolar consonant. Likewise, the consonant *l* mentioned earlier is alveolar.

The sound transcribed [h], which is found, for example, at the beginning of the English words *hat*, *hit*, *house*, and *hut*, is often considered to be a fricative. However, the constriction which characterizes this sound is not located anywhere in the oral cavity, but rather, at the glottis. [h] is therefore described as a *glottal* fricative ('fricative glottale').

In summary, the places of articulation catalogued here for consonants are the following (starting at the lips and ending at the glottis): bilabial, labio-dental, inter-dental, dental, alveolar, alveo-palatal, palatal, velar, uvular, and glottal. Table 2.4 recapitulates the description and the classification of the consonants mentioned up until now. It includes consonants from various linguistic systems (German, English, Spanish, and French).

Table 2.4. Consonants (summary)

Place of articulation / Manner of articulation			bilabial	labio-dental	(inter) dental	dental/alveolar	alveo-palatal	palatal	velar	uvular	glottal
stops	nasal		m			n		ɲ	ŋ		
	oral	voiceless	p			t			k		
		voiced	b			d			g		
fricatives	voiceless			f	θ	s	ʃ			χ	h
	voiced			v	ð	z	ʒ			ʁ	
affricates	voiceless			pf		ts	tʃ				
	voiced						dʒ				
trill						r					
approximants	lateral					l					
	central									ʁ	

2.3.5. *Vowels*

Let us now examine vowels. The production of vowels is different from the production of consonants in that the airstream can pass freely through the oral cavity. We have already seen how the parameter of nasality permits a distinction between oral and nasal vowels. The other distinctions among vowels are produced by means of various configurations of the oral cavity, which are equivalent to different resonating chambers and therefore correspond to different *vowel qualities* ('timbres vocaliques').

Vowels: aperture. Let us begin by comparing the vowels [i] (as in *lit* 'bed') and [a] (as in *la* 'the'). In pronouncing [i], then [a], then [i] again, one notices immediately that the mouth opens, then closes (the lower jaw moves away from and then comes closer to the upper jaw). If one now pronounces [e] (*et* 'and') and [ɛ] (*haie* 'hurdle'), one notices that the lower jaw assumes two intermediate positions between those for [i] and [a]. The progression from [i] to [e] to [ɛ] to [a] is thus accompanied by a progressive opening of the mouth. The word *aperture* ('aperture') is the technical term used to refer to this parameter. [i] is called a *closed vowel* ('voyelle fermée') and [a] is called an *open vowel* ('voyelle ouverte'); [e] and [ɛ] are called *mid vowels* ('voyelles moyennes'), and may be described more precisely as *half-closed* ('mi-fermée') and *half-open* ('mi-ouverte'), respectively.

The degree of aperture correlates with the height of the dorsum of the tongue in relation to the palate. During the production of vowels, the dorsum of the tongue is arched and its highest point in the oral cavity gets progressively further away from the palate as one goes from [i] to [e] to [ɛ] to [a]. It is for this reason that [i] is also described as a high vowel ('voyelle haute') and [a] as a low vowel ('voyelle basse'), and [e] and [ɛ] as high-mid ('mi-haute') and low-mid ('mi-basse') vowels, respectively. In French, the terminology that refers to degrees of aperture is more widely used than that which refers to tongue height ('la hauteur de la langue'), and the reverse is true in English; but we shall follow the prevailing French usage in this book.

When examining the other vowels of French, one notices that [y] and [u] (as in *su* [sy] 'known' and *sous* [su] 'under') have the same aperture as [i] (these are therefore closed vowels), that [ø] and [o] (as in *ceux* [sø] 'those' and *seau* [so] 'bucket') have the same aperture as [e] (these are therefore half-closed vowels), that [œ] and [ɔ] (as in *heure* [œr] 'hour' and *or* [ɔr] 'gold') have the same aperture as [ɛ] (these are therefore half-open vowels), and that [ɑ] (as in *pâte* [pɑt] 'dough') has the same aperture as [a] (both therefore are open vowels).

In sum, the parameter of aperture has allowed us to classify vowels into four groups: closed vowels, half-closed vowels, half-open vowels (these last two can be categorized together as mid vowels), and open vowels.

Vowels: lip position. What distinguishes [i] from [y]? The only distinction is that for [i] the lips are stretched, whereas for [y] they are rounded; apart from *lip rounding* ('arrondissement des lèvres'), these two vowels are pronounced in exactly the same way. This assertion can be easily checked by pronouncing [i] and prolonging it; if during the production of [iiii], you round your lips without changing the position of anything else in the oral cavity (be especially careful not to move your tongue back), you will automatically produce the sound [y].

Lip position is thus an important parameter for distinguishing vowel qualities. The particular distinction just established between [i] (*unrounded* 'non-arrondie') and [y] (*rounded* 'arrondie') occurs in parallel fashion between [e] (unrounded) and [ø] (rounded), and between [ɛ] (unrounded) and [œ] (rounded). It may be further observed that [a] and [ɑ] are unrounded and that [u, o, ɔ] are rounded.

Vowels: place of articulation. The vowels [y] and [u] are both closed rounded vowels. What sets them apart from each other? Going several times from [y] to [u] and again to [y], one notices a movement of the tongue from front to back to front. During the production of [y], the arched portion of the tongue is in a relatively forward position in the mouth, below the hard palate (one can usually feel the tip of the tongue pressing lightly against the lower front teeth); in contrast, during the production of [u], the arched portion of the tongue is in a relatively backward position in the mouth, below the velum (and the tongue is too far back for its tip to be able to press against or even touch the lower front teeth). One says that [y] is a *front* or *palatal* vowel ('voyelle antérieure' or 'd'avant' or 'palatale') and that [u] is a *back* or *velar* vowel ('voyelle postérieure' or 'd'arrière' or 'vélaire').

The vowel [i], which differs from [y] only with respect to lip position, is also a front vowel. Going from [i] to [u] consequently means not only rounding the lips, but also moving the tongue backwards in the oral cavity. The distinction in place of articulation between the closed front vowels [i] and [y] on the one hand, and the closed back vowel [u] on the other hand, is repeated for the other degrees of aperture. Thus, the half-closed vowels [e] and [ø] are front and the half-closed vowel [o] is back; the half-open vowels [ɛ] and [œ] are front, and the half-open vowel [ɔ] is back; finally, the open vowels [a] and [ɑ] are respectively front and back.

The parameters of aperture, lip position, and place of articulation also serve to distinguish among nasal vowels. Even though the articulations of French nasal vowels do not correspond exactly to those of the oral vowels for which the same symbols are used, one can approximately describe [ɛ̃] as a half-open front unrounded nasal vowel, [œ̃] as a half-open front rounded nasal vowel, [ɑ̃] as an open back unrounded nasal vowel, and [õ] as a half-closed back rounded nasal vowel. (In many transcriptions, [ɔ̃] is used instead of [õ], because the denasalization of this vowel results in an open [ɔ] rather than a closed [o]; cf. *bonne* [bɔn] 'good' [feminine] and *bon*, its masculine counterpart, transcribed either [bõ] or [bɔ̃] for the same pronunciation.)

2.3.6. Glides

The glides ('glissantes') remain to be examined. These sounds ([j, ɥ, w]) are akin to consonants (they are also called *semi-consonants* 'semi-consonnes'), because like consonants, they are produced by some degree of constriction in the oral cavity; this constriction is not sufficient, however, to create any friction, as is the case with fricatives (glides are therefore approximants). In addition, glides play the same role in syllables as consonants usually do, in the sense that their existence is linked to the presence of a vowel with which they can be associated.

Table 2.5. Vowel gliding

vowels			*glides*		
défi	[defi]	'challenge'	défier	[defje]	'to challenge'
tue	[ty]	'(he) kills'	tuer	[tɥe]	'to kill'
secoue [sœku]		'(he) shakes'	secouer [sœkwe]		'to shake'

Table 2.6. Vowels and glides (summary)

		front		back	
		unrounded	rounded	unrounded	rounded
glides		j	ɥ		w
oral vowels	closed	i	y		u
	half-closed	e	ø		o
	half-open	ɛ	œ		ɔ
	open	a		ɑ	
nasal vowels		ɛ̃	œ̃	ɑ̃	õ

Glides can be related to vowels as well, particularly closed vowels (they are also called *semi-vowels* 'semi-voyelles'). As indicated briefly in the preceding chapter, in French there is an important functional relationship between [j] and [i], [ɥ] and [y], and [w] and [u]: [i, y, u] generally become [j, ɥ, w], respectively, before a pronounced vowel in the same word, as shown in Table 2.5. There are also important articulatory similarities between the two members of each pair. For [j] as for [i], the lips are stretched, whereas for [ɥ] and [w] as for [y] and [u], the lips are rounded. [j] and [ɥ] are produced by drawing the tongue toward the hard palate; like [i] and [y], [j] and [ɥ] are therefore front (or palatal). But [w] is produced by drawing the tongue toward the velum; like [u], [w] is therefore back (or velar). In sum, [j] is a front unrounded glide, [ɥ] a front rounded glide, and [w] a back rounded glide. The description and classification of these glides are thus quite similar to the description and classification of closed vowels. The essential difference between the two classes of sounds simply has to do with the role that they each play in the syllable: like consonants, glides are the satellites of vowels in the syllable, whereas closed vowels (and vowels in general) form the basic core (or nucleus) of syllables.

Table 2.6 summarizes the description and classification of the vowels and glides mentioned up to now. It corresponds to the system of standard French.

Part Two
Vowels and glides

3
Vowel systems

3.1. Introduction

The object of this chapter is to compare the vowel systems of French and English, to identify the pronunciation problems that a native speaker of English may in principle encounter in the production of French vowels, and to propose a number of remedies to resolve these difficulties. In the next chapter, we shall focus on two specific aspects of French phonetics, vowel length and the distribution of mid and open vowels. Questions relating to nasal vowels and the so-called 'mute *e*' will be treated later, in two separate chapters (Chapters 5 and 6).

3.2. Stress and rhythm

Before we draw up an inventory of French and English vowels and embark on a detailed contrastive study, a few preliminary remarks are necessary concerning stress and rhythm in the two languages, because the fundamental differences separating English and French in this area are the source of a number of traits characterizing an English pronunciation of French and a French pronunciation of English.

By *stress* ('accent') is meant the effect of relative prominence that distinguishes one syllable as salient in relation to others. For example, in the English word *photographer*, the second syllable is stressed, the other three are not: *phoTOgrapher*. In the corresponding French word *photographe*, the last pronounced syllable is stressed, the other two are not: *photoGRAPHe* (the final *e* is not pronounced).

In English, *word stress placement* ('la place de l'accent de mot') varies depending on the word, and a word may receive more than one stress; for instance, *PHOtoGRAPH* is stressed on the first and last syllables, *phoTOgrapher* is stressed on the second syllable, and *PHOtoGRAphic* is stressed on the first and third syllables. The distribution of stress in English words is not random, but the principles that govern it are relatively complicated. In contrast, word stress placement in French is determined by a single simple rule: the stress always falls on the last pronounced syllable: *phoTO*, *photoGRAPHe*, *photograPHIQUe*. It must be added that in French, as in English, word stresses do not all keep the same strength in a phrase or a sentence; phenomena of stress subordination occur which are regulated in particular by the syntactic structure of the phrase or sentence. We shall return to this subject in Chapter 12. What is important to remember for now is that word stress placement is fundamentally different in French and in English, so that one cannot apply the principles of one language to the other without sounding foreign.

Another essential difference between the two languages is the *strength of the stress* ('la force de l'accent'): stress is much stronger in English than in French. Thus, all else being equal, the stressed syllable of the English word *phoTOgrapher* is much more prominent than the stressed syllable of the French word *phoTO*. Looking at things from the reverse perspective, one can say that unstressed syllables in English are much less prominent than unstressed syllables in French. In fact, unstressed syllables in English generally contain a reduced vowel, usually transcribed with the phonetic symbol [ə] (this symbol, called 'schwa', is like the letter *e* rotated 180 degrees). For example, comparing the pronunciation of the sequence *photograph-* in the English words *photograph*, *photographer*, and *photographic*, one notices that the consonantal skeleton remains more or less the same in all three words ([f-t-gr-f]), whereas the vowel melody varies considerably depending on the position of the stress: [-ó-ə-ǽ-], [-ə-á-ə-], [-ò-ə-ǽ-] (in phonetic transcriptions, the symbol ′ over a vowel indicates main or primary stress ['accent principal'] on the syllable containing the vowel and the symbol ` indicates secondary stress ['accent secondaire']); we see here that a full vowel under stress ([o], [ɑ], [æ]) reduces to [ə] when it is no longer stressed. (Observe also that even though we have not indicated it in the phonetic transcriptions, the pronunciation of the *t* actually changes in relation to stress placement.) The phenomenon of *vowel reduction* ('réduction vocalique') in the absence of stress is characteristic of English but radically unlike what occurs in French (or at least standard French). In standard French, unstressed syllables are never reduced; vowels always maintain their full quality ('un timbre plein'); thus, the sequence *photograph-* is always pronounced [fɔtɔgraf-] in the French words *photographe* [fɔtɔgráf] and *photographique* [fɔtɔgrafík]. In a sense, one could say that the relative strength of stress in English imposes a compensatory reduction of unstressed syllables, whereas in French, the relative weakness of stress allows all syllables to preserve the full quality of their vowels. The motto in French, then, is: 'Do not reduce vowels to [ə]'.

The dominant role played by stress in English – as opposed to French – in the pronunciation of vowels within words naturally has repercussions at the level of the sentence for its rhythm. In English, the basic rhythmic element is stress, whereas in French it is the syllable. A brief consideration of traditional poetry and children's rhymes in the two languages vividly illustrates the fundamental distinction between the *stress-timed rhythm* of English ('rythme accentuel') and the *syllable-timed rhythm* of French ('rythme syllabique'). In poetry, the regularity of the lines with respect to a given schema is determined by counting the number of 'feet' in each line. In English poetry, stresses are counted. In French poetry, syllables are counted. In the rhymes that children use in their games in order to determine who will be 'it' ('qui va coller'), the child who recites the formulas must match each of the participants with a specific linguistic unit of text. In English, to each child corresponds a stressed syllable and to each stressed syllable corresponds a child; unstressed syllables are as it were ignored:

> EEni MEEni MIni MO
> CATCH a TIger BY the TOE
> IF he HOLlers LET him GO
> EEni MEEni MIni MO.

In French, to each child corresponds a syllable and to each syllable corresponds a child; word stresses do not come into the picture:

UN PETIT COCHON	[ɛ̃-pœ-ti-kɔ-ʃõ]	A little pig
PENDU AU PLAFOND	[pɑ̃-dy-o-pla-fõ]	Hanging from the ceiling
TIREZ-LUI LA QUEUE	[ti-re-lɥi-la-kø]	Pull his tail
IL PONDRA DES ŒUFS	[il-põ-dra-dɛ-zø]	He will lay eggs
COMBIEN EN VOULEZ-VOUS?	[kõ-bjɛ̃-ɑ̃-vu-le-vu]	How many do you want?

The stress-timed rhythm of English and the syllable-timed rhythm of French are absolutely fundamental characteristics separating the two languages and they have a deep global influence on the pronunciation of vowels. It is very important, then, to avoid imposing the rhythm of one language onto the other. The basic principle in English is to emphasize strongly the stressed syllables and to reduce the vowels of unstressed syllables. By contrast, the basic principle in French is to pronounce each syllable with approximately equal strength and to maintain for each vowel its full quality.

3.3. Vowel inventories

3.3.1. The French vowel system

The vowel system of French has already been presented in the preceding chapter. I simply reproduce it here with examples (see Tables 3.1–2).

Table 3.1. French vowels

		front		back	
		unrounded	rounded	unrounded	rounded
oral vowels	closed	i	y		u
	half-closed	e	ø		o
	half-open	ɛ	œ		ɔ
	open	a		ɑ	
nasal vowels		ɛ̃	œ̃	ɑ̃	õ

Table 3.2. Examples (French vowels)

[i] lit, dit	[y] lu, du		[u] loup, doux	(bed, said; read, of the; wolf, soft)
[e] blé, dé	[ø] leu*ᵃ*, deux		[o] l'eau, dos	(wheat, thimble; two; the water, back)
[ɛ] lait, dais	[œ] le, de		[ɔ] lotte, dot*ᵇ*	(milk, canopy; the, of; monkfish, dowry)
[a] la, ta		[ɑ] las, tas		(the, your; tired, heap)
[ɛ̃] lin, daim	[œ̃] l'un, d'un	[ɑ̃] lent, dans	[õ] long, dont	(flax, suede; the one, of one; slow, in; long, whose)

Notes:
ᵃ leu as in the expression *à la queue-leu-leu* [alakølølø] 'one behind the other'.
ᵇ The two words *lotte* [lɔt] and *dot* [dɔt] are the only examples in this table where the vowel is not in word-final position; that is because the sound [ɔ] never appears in that context in French (see Chapter 4).

3.3.2. The English vowel system

I shall provide here only a very brief sketch of the vowel system of American English generally considered as standard. My goal is not to go into details, but simply to provide a base to facilitate comparison with the vowel system of French. Tables 3.3–4 and the complementary remarks that follow will suffice for this purpose.

3.3.3. Complementary remarks

A large number of the phonetic symbols used to transcribe French vowels are also found in the table for English vowels. This does not necessarily

Table 3.3. English vowels

		front	central	back	
		unrounded	unrounded	unrounded	rounded
closed	tense	i			u
	lax	ɩ			ω
half-closed (tense)		e			o
half-open (lax)		ɛ	ə		ɔ
open		æ		ɑ	

diphthongs	aɩ	aω	ɔɩ

Table 3.4. Examples (English vowels)

[i] beat, keel			[u] boot, coot
[ɩ] bit, kit			[ω] put, good
[e] bait, Kate			[o] boat, coat
[ɛ] bet, get	[ə] but, cut		[ɔ] bought[a], core
[æ] bat, cat		[ɑ] father, car	
[aɩ] bite, kite	[aω] bout, gout	[ɔɩ] boy, coy	

Note:
[a] For many speakers of American English, this word is pronounced with the vowel [ɑ]; more generally, for such speakers, the distinction between [ɔ] and [ɑ] occurs only before [r] (compare *core* and *car*), and *caught* is pronounced like *cot*, i.e. [kɑt].

mean, however, that these sounds are exactly the same in the two languages; in fact, as we shall see in Section 3.4, there are, in most cases, rather important phonetic differences. That the same symbols are used is certainly an indication that the sounds in question are relatively close phonetically; but above all the same symbols are used to mark the parallel between the relative articulatory characteristics of the vowels within each of the two systems. Thus, the same symbol [i] serves to represent both the vowel of the French word *lit* and the vowel of the English word *beat*, because these vowels have an identical function in the two systems, that of being the front unrounded vowel with the smallest degree of aperture; nevertheless, although similar, French [i] and English [i] are not phonetically identical. We shall return shortly to the nature of the differences.

The table for English vowels also contains some phonetic symbols and some terms which have not yet been explained. The phonetic symbols [ɩ] and [ɷ] represent the vowels with an aperture in between those of [i] and [e], and in between those of [u] and [o], respectively. Instead of the symbols [ɩ] and [ɷ], one also finds [I] and [U]. To describe these vowels, an additional parameter, *tension*, is used. Like [i] and [u], [ɩ] and [ɷ] are considered to be closed vowels, but they are distinguished from [i] and [u] by being *lax* ('relâchées'), whereas [i] and [u] are *tense* ('tendues'). The same terminology is commonly applied to mid vowels to distinguish [ɛ] and [ɔ] (lax) from [e] and [o] (tense). (English [ɔ], however, lacks the phonetic and distributional characteristics typical of the lax vowels and is often classified among the tense vowels.) From a phonetic point of view, lax vowels are typically shorter, more open, and more centralized than their tense counterparts. These two types of vowels also have different distributional properties in English. Thus, the lax vowels are never found in stressed open syllables (an open syllable is one that ends with a vowel). For example, the tense front vowels [i] and [e] may appear in stressed open syllables, as in *bee* and *bay*; but no similar English words may exist with the corresponding lax vowels [ɩ] and [ɛ]. Both types of vowels may, however, appear in most stressed closed syllables (a closed syllable is one that ends in at least one consonant); tense vowels and lax vowels therefore contrast in pairs of words such as *beat* [bit] – *bit* [bɩt] and *bait* [bet] – *bet* [bɛt].

The phonetic symbol [æ] represents a front unrounded vowel slightly more open than [ɛ] and slightly more closed than [a]. One finds [æ] in English words such as *ash*, *cat*, *fat*, and *photograph*.

The phonetic symbol [ə] (schwa) is a central mid vowel, that is to say, neither front nor back, neither closed nor open. As already mentioned, [ə] occurs very frequently in unstressed position, as in *arrest* [ərɛ́st], *photographer* [fətɑ́grəfər], and *sofa* [sófə], but it is also found in stressed position, as in *but* [bə́t], *come* [kə́m], and *tug* [tə́g]. When stressed, [ə] may be slightly more open than in unstressed position, and some linguists then prefer to use the phonetic symbol [ʌ] ('the caret', an inverted letter *v*) (compare the two vowels in *above* [əbʌ́v]).

Table 3.3 also contains the three diphthongs [aɩ, aɷ, ɔɩ]. As the complex phonetic symbols used to represent them indicate, diphthongs ('diptongues') are vowels whose quality is not constant: it changes from one vowel sound to another during their production. For the diphthongs just mentioned above, the first symbol represents the main element (or nucleus) of the diphthong. The second symbol is the transitory element or off-glide; it indicates the direction of movement of the articulators once the nucleus has been pronounced. These diphthongs are said to be falling ('décroissantes'). In rising diphthongs ('diptongues croissantes'), the order of the two elements is reversed: the transitory element precedes the nucleus and is then called the on-glide. Some linguists consider that in English words like *cute* [kjut] and *few* [fju], [ju] constitutes a rising diphthong (rather than a 'glide + vowel' sequence). One can also analyze as rising diphthongs the sounds [je] and [we] that are found in Spanish words such as *pienso* [pjɛnso] 'I think' and *cuento* [kwɛnto] 'I count' (cf. the corresponding infinitives *pensar* [pensar] and *contar* [kontar]). There also exist in French certain 'glide + vowel' sequences (for example, [wa] in the word *oiseau* [wazo] 'bird') which may advantageously be thought of as rising diphthongs rather than as two separate units (this view will not be adopted for the purposes of this chapter, but will be considered in Chapter 7).

In English, there are other diphthongs in addition to the ones already mentioned. In particular, as will be seen shortly, the tense vowels of Table 3.3 generally have a tendency to be falling diphthongs rather than monophthongs ('monophtongues'). (Monophthongs are vowels whose quality is constant throughout their production.)

To conclude these preliminary remarks, I note that several systems of phonetic transcription are in common use for diphthongs; the variations in the notation essentially concern the transitory element. For example, for [aɩ] and [aɷ], one may also find [ai, aI, aj, ay] and [au, aU, aw], respectively.

3.4. Contrastive study

Comparing the English and French vowel inventories reveals that the transition from one language to the other presupposes the elimination of certain vowels and the acquisition of new ones (cf. in particular the diphthongs and the lax vowels [ɩ] and [ɷ] of English; the nasal vowels and the front rounded vowels of French). What these inventories do not show is that some vowels which may at first seem transferable from one language to the other in fact require, as already suggested, important modifications in their articulations.

3.4.1. Diphthongization

The vowel system of English includes several falling diphthongs. This type of vowel does not exist in modern standard French, where all of the vowels are monophthongs. In Old French and Middle French, there were diphthongs and even triphthongs, but these complex vowels have been

Table 3.5. Old French dipthongs

	Modern pronunciation	Old French	
eux	[ø]	[eus]	'them'
foi	[fwa]	[foi]	'faith'
pleine	[plɛn]	[plẽĩnə]	'full'
beaux	[bo]	[bəaus]	'beautiful'
aube	[ob]	[aubə]	'dawn'
aime	[ɛm]	[ãĩmə]	'(he) loves'
fous	[fu]	[fɔus]	'mad'

Table 3.6. Quebec French dipthongs

	Quebec French	Standard French	
mère	[mɛɪr]	[mɛr]	'mother'
chaise	[ʃaɪz]	[ʃɛz]	'chair'
curieuse	[kyrjœYz]	[kyrjøz]	'curious'
fleur	[flaⱷr]	[flœr]	'flower'
chose	[ʃɔⱷz]	[ʃoz]	'thing'
fort	[fɔⱷr]	[fɔr]	'strong'
pâle	[pɑⱷl]	[pɑl]	'pale'
mince	[mɛ̃ɪs]	[mɛ̃s]	'thin'
viande	[vjãⱷd]	[vjãd]	'meat'
longue	[lɔ̃ⱷg]	[lõg]	'long'

progressively reduced to simple vowels. The old diphthongal and triph-
thongal pronunciations are still reflected today in the way some vowels
are represented in the orthography, as the examples in Table 3.5
illustrate.

Some contemporary dialects of French do have falling diphthongs, for
example Quebec French. As a rule, the diphthongs of Quebec French
appear in stressed closed syllables. Table 3.6 gives some characteristic
examples taken from Montreal French.

As indicated earlier, in addition to [aɪ, aⱷ, ɔɪ], there are other English
vowels with a diphthongal character. The tense vowels [i, u, e, o], in
particular, do not maintain exactly the same quality during the entire
duration of their pronunciation. Even though the degrees of diphthongization of these vowels can vary from one aperture to another, from
one speaker to another, and from one context to another, the following
transcriptions generally reflect phonetic reality more closely: [iɪ, uⱷ, eɪ,
oⱷ]. In standard French, by contrast, vowels always carry the same
quality during the entire duration of their pronunciation. To keep vowel
quality constant for each vowel is thus absolutely essential for a good
pronunciation of standard French; the vowels [i, u, e, o] should be the

Table 3.7. Closed and half-closed French vowels

[i]			[u]		
si	[si]	'if'	sous	[su]	'under'
lit	[li]	'bed'	loup	[lu]	'wolf'
riz	[ri]	'rice'	roux	[ru]	'red'
qui	[ki]	'who'	cou	[ku]	'neck'
nid	[ni]	'nest	nous	[nu]	'us'
didi	[didi]	'pinky'[a]	Doudou	[dudu]	'Eddy'
[e]			**[o]**		
et	[e]	'and'	eau	[o]	'water'
B	[bɛ]	(the letter *B*)	beau	[bo]	'beautiful'
fée	[fe]	'fairy'	faux	[fo]	'false'
été	[ete]	'summer'	auto	[oto]	'car'
Dédé	[dede]	'Andy'	dodo	[dodo]	'sleep'[b]
g.d.b.	[ʒedebe]	'hangover'[c]	rododo	[rododo]	'fast'[d]

Notes:
[a] *didi*: childish term for 'finger'
[b] *faire dodo*: childish expression for 'to sleep' (*dodo* comes from *dormir* 'to sleep')
[c] *avoir la g.d.b.*: 'to have a hangover' in familiar speech (*g.d.b.* stands for *gueule de bois*, literally 'wooden mouth')
[d] *y aller rododo*: 'to go fast' in familiar speech

object of particular vigilance, since their English counterparts are generally diphthongized.

Not only do French vowels maintain a constant quality, but at least in open syllables, they are also relatively short. For example, the words *si* [si] 'if', *sous* [su] 'under', *C* [se] (the letter *C*), *sot* [so] 'stupid' end quickly and abruptly compared with the English words *sea* [si], *Sue* [su], *say* [se], and *so* [so]. In fact, in English, as we intimated earlier in our brief discussion of lax and tense vowels, it is impossible to have short vowels in this context. The distributional properties of English vowels are such, then, that the native speaker of English has a natural tendency to lengthen and diphthongize the French vowels [i, u, e, o] in an open syllable, when they should be short and monophthongal. The French words in Table 3.7, which contain [i, u, e, o] in open syllables, can be used to practise the short and monophthongal pronunciation of these vowels.

We shall see in Chapter 4 (pp. 49–51) that in French, vowels in some closed syllables are lengthened when stressed, as in the following words (in phonetic transcriptions, a colon after a vowel indicates that this vowel is long):

ivre	[i:vr]	'drunk'	ouvre	[u:vr]	'open'
chèvre	[ʃɛ:vr]	'goat'	pauvre	[po:vr]	'poor'

Given that long vowels are usually diphthongized in English, native speakers of English must often make a particular effort to ensure that lengthened vowels in French also remain monophthongs.

In general, the elimination of diphthongized vowels and the production of monophthongal vowels constitute one of the most important goals for the native speaker of English desiring to acquire a good pronunciation of standard French.

3.4.2. Rounded vowels

As Tables 3.1 and 3.3 show, there are many more rounded vowels in French than in English. The front rounded vowels of French in fact constitute a series of entirely new vowels for native speakers of English. Perhaps the easiest way to learn how to pronounce these vowels is to produce the corresponding front unrounded vowels, and then to round the lips, taking great care not to move the tongue backwards. A backward movement of the tongue, in tandem with the rounding of the lips, is natural for native speakers of English, because in English, rounded vowels are found only among the back vowels. By pronouncing a prolonged [i] and then rounding the lips (without moving the tongue), one automatically produces [y]; one can similarly go from [e] to [ø] and from [ɛ] to [œ]. Practise with pairs of words such as those in Table 3.8.

One may also produce front rounded vowels by starting with the corresponding back rounded vowels. In this case, it is a matter of maintaining the rounding of the lips while moving the tongue forward (until one feels the tip of the tongue against the lower front teeth). One thus automatically goes from [u] to [y], from [o] to [ø], and from [ɔ] to [œ]. Practise with pairs of words such as those in Table 3.9.

When students focus on learning the front rounded vowels, particularly [y], the pronunciation attained is frequently so perfect and apparently so gratifying that the [u] is lost. By a process of hypercorrection, *roue* [ru] 'wheel' becomes *rue* [ry] 'street', *sourd* [sur] 'deaf' becomes *sur* [syr] 'on', and *tout* [tu] 'all' becomes *tu* [ty] 'you' for example. This phenomenon of overgeneralization, far from being a discouraging sign of degradation of the pronunciation acquired up until then, should be appreciated as a positive sign of learning. This sort of apparent regression occurs very commonly in many natural circumstances. Thus, it is well known that children make overgeneralizations when they acquire their native language; for example, children who correctly said *broke* suddenly begin to say *breaked*. The regression is, of course, only apparent; there is in fact acquisition of a general principle concerning the formation of the past in English; the child regains *broke* later. An example perhaps closer

Table 3.8. French front vowels (unrounded vs rounded)

Stretched lips			Rounded lips		
si	[si]	'if'	su	[sy]	'known'
C	[se]	(the letter *C*)	ceux	[sø]	'those'
serre	[sɛr]	'claw'	sœur	[sœr]	'sister'

Table 3.9. French rounded vowels (back vs front)

Tongue toward the back			Tongue toward the front		
sous	[su]	'under'	su	[sy]	'known'
sot	[so]	'stupid'	ceux	[sø]	'those'
sort	[sɔr]	'fate'	sœur	[sœr]	'sister'

to the case which interests us here concerns native speakers of French who are learning English; they often have serious difficulties with the English fricatives [θ] and [ð] (because these sounds do not exist in French) and they usually substitute [s] and [z] for them. But when they strive to learn to pronounce [θ] and [ð] and integrate these new sounds in their speech, many [s]s and [z]s incorrectly become [θ] and [ð] (for example, *something*, which was at the beginning *somesing*, becomes *thomething*). It is only later that the competing fricatives find their correct distribution and that order is restored. The same goes for [y] and [u] in the case of native speakers of English learning French.

Not only are there more rounded vowels in French than in English (because of the existence in French of the front rounded series), but furthermore, the rounding of the lips for the types of rounded vowels that exist in the two languages is more marked in French than in English. In French, the lips are extremely rounded and projected forward, whereas in English they are, comparatively speaking, held back. In addition, both the rounding and the forward projection of the lips occur as early as the preceding consonant and deeply affect its articulation, as in *tout* [tu] 'all', *doux* [du] 'sweet', *cou* [ku] 'neck', *goût* [gu] 'taste', *su* [sy] 'known', *zut* [zyt] 'darn!', *rue* [ry] 'street', and *lu* [ly] 'read', which contrast with words such as *titi* [titi] 'street urchin', *dit* [di] 'said', *qui* [ki] 'who', *gui* [gi] 'mistletoe', *si* [si] 'if', *hésite* [ezit] 'hesitates', *riz* [ri] 'rice', and *lit* [li] 'bed', where the lips remain stretched throughout. In the production of French rounded vowels, native speakers of English should therefore not hesitate to feel that they are exaggerating, both in space and in time, the described required position of the lips. It is useful to practise on words or expressions such as those in Table 3.10 (where the rounded vowels are italicized).

Table 3.10. French rounded vowels

	[u]			[y]	
toujours	[tuʒur]	'always'	*turlututu*	[tyrlytyty]	(exclamation)
roudoudou	[rududu]	'(type of candy)'	*hurluberlu*	[yrlyberly]	'crazy person'
coucou	[kuku]	'cuckoo clock'	*Lustucru*	[lystykry]	(pasta brand name)
tout à coup	[tutaku]	'all of a sudden'	*tu l'as vu*	[tylavy]	'you saw him'
	[o]			**[ø]**	
au dodo	[ododo]	'in bed'	*à la queue-leu-leu*	[alakølølø]	'in a line'
trop tôt	[troto]	'too early'	*peu à peu*	[pøapø]	'little by little'
beau roseau	[borozo]	'beautiful reed'	*deux œufs creux*	[døzøkrø]	'two hollow eggs'
à vau-l'eau	[avolo]	'adrift'	*heureux*	[ørø]	'happy'

Mixed rounded vowels

eux ou nous	[øunu]	'them or us'	*tout heureux*	[tutørø]	'very happy'
rue du Four	[rydyfur]	(street name)	*sous l'eau chaude*	[suloʃod]	'under hot water'

To grasp visually the difference between rounded vowels in English and in French, it is revealing to consider the pronunciation of French syllables containing a rounded vowel such as [u] or [o] when they are used in English in borrowed words or in proper names (for example, *coup* [ku], in *coup d'état* or *coup de grâce*; [so], in *Marcel Marceau or sautéed*). During TV newscasts, for instance, one may often observe how the lips of English-speaking journalists are relatively retracted in comparison with the position required for an authentic French pronunciation. One can also usefully compare French and English films and focus on the lips of the actors when they speak, in particular on close-ups; the difference is often striking, amusing, and extremely instructive.

3.4.3. Closed vowels

The closed lax vowels [ɪ] and [ɷ] of English are not found in standard French. This difference between the two languages creates problems mostly for native speakers of French who are learning English, because for them it is a matter of learning a new vowel distinction (whose absence may result in confusing or embarrassing situations: cf. *beat–bit*, *feat–fit*, *reap–rip*, *sheet–shit*; *fool–full*, *pool–pull*). For the native speaker of English who is learning French, it is more simply a matter of eliminating the distinction.

Note, however, that in some dialects of French, such as Quebec French, the closed lax vowels [ɪ, Y, ɷ] do exist. In Quebec French, they usually appear in stressed closed syllables, where they replace the closed tense vowels [i, y, u] of standard French. Some characteristic examples are given in Table 3.11. Closed vowel laxing may optionally spread leftward to other closed vowels inside the word, even if they are in an open syllable. Such cases exemplify what is called vowel harmony ('l'harmonisation vocalique'), a process by which vowels acquire certain

Table 3.11. Quebec French closed lax vowels

	Quebec French	Standard French	
électrique	[elɛktrɪk]	[elɛktrik]	'electric'
il s'habille	[isabɪj]	[isabij]	'he gets dressed'
pipe	[pɪp]	[pip]	'pipe'
jupe	[ʒYp]	[ʒyp]	'skirt'
luxe	[lYks]	[lyks]	'luxury'
rhume	[rYm]	[rym]	'cold'
grenouille	[grœnɷj]	[grœnuj]	'frog'
ours	[ɷrs]	[urs]	'bear'
toute	[tɷt]	[tut]	'all'

Table 3.12. Quebec French closed lax vowels and vowel harmony

	Quebec French	Standard French	
liquide	[lɪkɪd]	[likid]	'liquid'
musique	[mYzɪk]	[myzik]	'music'
boutique	[bʊtˢɪk]	[butik]	'shop'
tumulte	[tˢYmYlt]	[tymylt]	'uproar'
pilule	[pɪlYl]	[pilyl]	'pill'
toujours	[tʊʒʊr]	[tuʒur]	'always'
coutume	[kʊtˢYm]	[kutym]	'custom'
difficile	[dᶻɪtɪsɪl]	[difisil]	'difficult'
inutile	[ɪnYtˢɪl]	[inytil]	'useless'
ridicule	[rɪdᶻɪkYl]	[ridikyl]	'ridiculous'

characteristics of nearby vowels. Some illustrations are given in Table 3.12. (Notice also that the stops [t] and [d] become the affricates [tˢ] and [dᶻ] before closed front vowels in Quebec French.)

We saw earlier that the vowels [i] and [u] of standard French differ from the corresponding English vowels in that they are monophthongs. They are also characterized by more extreme articulations: thus, French [i] is more closed and more front than English [i], and French [u] is more closed and further back than English [u]. Some of these characteristics are easily verifiable. In particular, concerning the question of the frontness of [i], the tongue being more forward for French [i] than for English [i], the tip of the tongue, which points downward in both cases, presses more against the lower front teeth in French than in English: compare, for example, the French word *mie*, in *la mie de pain* 'the soft part of the bread', with the English word *me*.

3.4.4. Mid vowels

Native speakers of English often have difficulties interpreting the distinction between the half-closed and the half-open mid vowels in French, in particular in the cases of [e]–[ɛ] and [ø]–[œ]. This problem can be easily explained. The distinction between [e] and [ɛ] takes on many forms in English: (i) [e] is more closed than [ɛ]; (ii) [e] is generally a diphthong, whereas [ɛ] is a monophthong; and (iii) [e] is longer than [ɛ]. But in French, there is only one difference: [e] is more closed than [ɛ]; otherwise, the two vowels are both monophthongs and they have the same length in comparable contexts.

From the standpoint of aperture, English [e] and [ɛ] are much closer to each other than French [e] and [ɛ]. While French [ɛ] is only slightly more open than English [ɛ], French [e] is definitely more closed than English [e]. French [e] is, in fact, relatively similar to English [ɪ]; thus, when

Table 3.13. French mid vowels

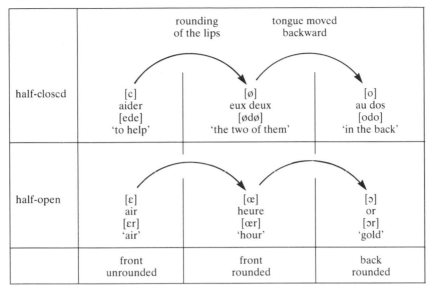

	rounding of the lips	tongue moved backward	
half-closed	[e] aider [ede] 'to help'	[ø] eux deux [ødø] 'the two of them'	[o] au dos [odo] 'in the back'
half-open	[ɛ] air [ɛr] 'air'	[œ] heure [œr] 'hour'	[ɔ] or [ɔr] 'gold'
	front unrounded	front rounded	back rounded

native speakers of French learning English have difficulties in producing [ɪ] in the frequently used sequence *it is*, they are often advised, and with good results, to use French [e], and therefore to produce in this case the French word *été* [ete] 'summer' followed by [z]. To produce French [e], an English speaker can conversely think of his own native [ɪ]. Once the pronunciations of [e] and [ɛ] are learned, those of [ø] and [œ] follow immediately, by rounding of the lips (see Section 3.4.2 above and Table 3.13).

Concerning the back mid vowels, it must be noted that French [o] is more closed and more back than English [o]. As already indicated, it is also more rounded and it is, of course, a monophthong, whereas English [o] is diphthongized. As to French [ɔ], it is less open and much less back than English [ɔ]. In fact, speakers from Paris often produce [œ] instead of [ɔ]; thus, the verb form (*vous*) *donniez* '(you) gave' and the noun *denier* 'penny' can be homophones (pronounced the same) ([dœnje]); other examples of words where [œ] is used in place of [ɔ] are *absolu* [apsœly] 'absolute', *belotte* [bœlœt] (card game), *chausson* [ʃœsõ] 'slipper', *joli* [ʒœli] 'pretty', *personnage* [pɛrsœnaʒ] 'character'. The vowels [o] and [ɔ] can be automatically derived from [ø] and [œ], respectively, by moving the tongue backward in the oral cavity (see Section 3.4.2 above and Table 3.13).

3.4.5. Open vowels

The distinction between the two French open vowels [a] (the front [a])
and [ɑ] (the back [ɑ]) can be a source of some minor difficulties and slight
irritation for the native speaker of English. There are two main reasons
for the problem. One concerns the articulation of these sounds, the other
their distribution. Even though the front [a] (*patte* [pat] 'paw') resembles
English [æ] (*cat* [kæt]) and even though the back [ɑ] (*pâte* [pɑt] 'dough')
resembles English [ɑ] (*father* [fɑðər]), the two French vowels generally
tend to be more central than the English vowels and thus closer to each
other from both an articulatory and a perceptual point of view. It is,
however, interesting to note that in some dialects, particularly in a
(stigmatized) variety of Paris French, these two vowels tend to grow
apart, [a] becoming more front and slightly less open ([æ]) and [ɑ]
becoming rounded ([ɒ]); hence the following pronunciations, for example: *Paris* [pari] becomes [pæri], *pas* [pɑ] 'not' becomes [pɒ]. The
phonetic distinction between the two vowels is thus not necessarily the
same for everybody. In addition, a number of speakers blur the distinction in favor of front [a], particularly in spontaneous speech.

The question becomes further complicated by the fact that speakers
who do make a distinction do not all necessarily distribute the two vowels
in the same way. For example, some have the front [a] in *casse* 'breaks'
and the back [ɑ] in *tasse* 'cup', but for others the reverse is true. There are
also, of course, those who use the same vowel, either [a] or [ɑ], in both
words. We shall return to the problem of the distribution of front [a] and
back [ɑ] in the next chapter (see pp. 62–5). For now, and from a purely
practical point of view, the generalized use of front [a] is to be recommended to foreign students for two reasons: (i) the frequency of [a] in
French words is far greater than that of [ɑ]; and (ii) when the distinction is
not made, [a], rather than [ɑ], is used. It is always possible to determine
later and learn progressively the cases where back [ɑ] is possible or
preferred in standard French.

3.5. Contrastive study: conclusion

In closing this contrastive study of the vowel systems of English and
French, two golden rules should be emphasized concerning the pronunciation of standard French: (i) maintain a full and constant quality for each
vowel (no reduction, no diphthongization), and (ii) make sure to round
and project the lips forward in the production of the rounded vowels (no
rounded vowels with half-hearted lip-rounding).

4
Distribution of vowels

4.1. Introduction

In this chapter, we shall address questions purely internal to French concerning vowel length, the distribution of the mid vowels, and the distribution of the two *a*s. From a pragmatic perspective, we shall also try to establish a number of useful correlations between the pronunciation of the mid and open vowels and their representations in the orthography.

4.2. Vowel length

It is a general phonetic fact across languages that, all else being equal, vowels are longer in front of voiced consonants than in front of voiceless consonants. For example, in English, the nucleus of the diphthong [aɪ] is longer in *ride* and *rise* than in *rite* and *rice*. Likewise, in French, the vowel [a] is longer in *rade* 'anchorage' than in *rate* 'spleen'. This type of distinction does not require any particular effort in the acquisition of English or French pronunciation, because it is a universal phenomenon.

There exist in French, however, specific cases of vowel lengthening which go beyond universal tendencies. As a rule, French vowels can be lengthened in this specific way only if they are both stressed (thus, normally in the final syllable of a word) and in a closed syllable. More precisely, two principles govern the specific lengthening of vowels in French, one affecting any vowel in a word-final syllable closed by a restricted set of consonants, and the other affecting a restricted set of vowels in a word-final syllable closed by any consonant:

    (i) under stress, any vowel in a syllable closed by the consonants [r, z, ʒ, v, vr] is lengthened;

    (ii) under stress, the vowels [ɑ, ø, o] and the nasal vowels are lengthened when they are in a closed syllable (closed by any consonant).

These vowel lengthenings are all the more prominent in syllables with a more prominent stress. Thus, the vowel [ɑ] of the word *pâte* 'noodle' receives a stronger stress and is consequently longer in the sentence *Marie aime les pâtes* ('Mary likes noodles') than in *Marie aime les pâtes au fromage* ('Mary likes noodles with cheese'). Recall that in phonetic transcriptions, the lengthening of a vowel is generally indicated by a colon

Table 4.1 Vowel-length and vowel-quality contrasts

[a] – [ɑ:]	patte – pâte	[pat] – [pɑ:t]	'paw'	– 'noodle'
[œ] – [ø:]	jeune – jeûne	[ʒœn] – [ʒø:n]	'young'	– 'fasting'
[ɔ] – [o:]	sotte – saute	[sɔt] – [so:t]	'stupid'	– 'jumps'
[ɛ] – [ɛ̃:]	messe – mince	[mɛs] – [mɛ̃:s]	'mass'	– 'thin'
[a] – [ɑ̃:]	bac – banque	[bak] – [bɑ̃:k]	'ferry'	– 'bank'
[ɔ] – [õ:]	mode – monde	[mɔd] – [mõ:d]	'fashion'	– 'world'

after the vowel ([pɑ:t]); to represent a less prominent lengthening, only the upper dot is used ([pɑ·t]).

Stress, then, plays an important role in the lengthening of French vowels, but it is also necessary for the syllable to be closed. For example, the vowels [ɑ], [ø], [o], and [ɑ̃] in *pâte* 'noodle', *feutre* 'felt', *saute* 'jumps', and *chante* 'sings' are long ([pɑ:t], [fø:tr], [so:t], [ʃɑ̃:t]), since they occur in closed stressed syllables; but the same vowels are short in *pas* 'step', *feu* 'fire', *saut* 'jump', and *chant* 'song' ([pɑ], [fø], [so], [ʃɑ̃]), since the stressed syllables are open. In *pâté* 'pâté', *feutré* 'soft', *sauter* 'to jump', and *chanter* 'to sing' ([pɑte], [føtre], [sote], [ʃɑ̃te]), these vowels are short for two reasons: they are neither in a closed syllable, nor stressed.

The second rule of vowel lengthening, the one which affects only certain vowels, creates in some contexts vowel-length contrasts on top of the existing vowel-quality contrasts. Examples are given in Table 4.1. But it is the vowel-quality contrasts which really play the determining role in the distinction which speakers make between words. In fact, since vowel length in standard French is predictable given vowel quality and context, this characteristic alone is not as a rule sufficient to mark differences of meaning between words. Length is said to play no distinctive role in standard French (although a very small number of speakers may still make a distinction between [ɛ] and [ɛ:] in a few pairs of words, such as *mettre* [mɛtr] 'to put' – *maître* [mɛ:tr] 'master', *lettre* [lɛtr] 'letter' – *l'être* [lɛ:tr] 'the being', and *belle* [bɛl] 'beautiful' (feminine) – *bêle* [bɛ:l] 'bleats'). There are other dialects, however, where vowel-length contrasts do correspond quite generally to distinctions in meaning, and where length can therefore be said to play a distinctive role. Thus, in Belgium, some speakers have long vowels in syllables which immediately precede a 'mute *e*' in word-final position; for example, the feminine forms *amie* [ami:] 'friend' and *sûre* [sy:r] 'sure' contrast with the masculine forms *ami* [ami] and *sûr* [syr], *roue* [ru:] 'wheel' contrasts with *roux* [ru] 'reddish', and *tousse* [tu:s] 'coughs' contrasts with *tous* [tus] 'all'. Historically, vowel length in these cases correlates with the loss of final *e* in the pronunciation and is known as compensatory lengthening ('allongement compensatoire').

4.3. Distribution of mid vowels

In the preceding chapter (p. 38), we saw that the English lax vowels [ɪ] and [ɷ] could not appear in a stressed open syllable, whereas their tense counterparts [i] and [u] could occur much more freely. This type of situation is common in the languages of the world: for a given language, it frequently happens that some sounds may appear in practically unrestricted fashion in words, whereas others have reduced distributions. The French mid vowels are a case in point: they obey special constraints limiting their possibilities of occurrence. The goal of this section is to examine the restrictions which affect the distribution of these vowels.

French mid vowels function in pairs: [e] and [ɛ], [ø] and [œ], [o] and [ɔ]. Under certain conditions, for a given pair, one member of the pair must occur, to the exclusion of the other. Contrary to what might be hoped, the principles which govern the distribution of the members of each pair are not uniformly valid in all three cases, at least in standard French. For this reason, we shall examine each pair separately. We shall consider first the situation in word-final syllables, where the facts are relatively clear and salient, and then we shall look at what occurs in syllables that are not word-final, where the interaction of a number of factors renders the description of the facts and their interpretation more delicate.

4.3.1. Mid vowels in word-final syllables

4.3.1.1. [e]–[ɛ] in word-final syllables
In an *open* final syllable, the vowels [e] and [ɛ] allow meaning distinctions to occur between words; thus, they play a *distinctive role* ('rôle distinctif'), as shown in the examples of Table 4.2.

Table 4.2. [e] vs [ɛ] in word-final open syllables

allée	[ale]	allait	[alɛ]	'path'	– 'went'
dé	[de]	dais	[dɛ]	'thimble'	– 'canopy'
épée	[epe]	épais	[epɛ]	'sword'	– 'thick'
été	[ete]	était	[etɛ]	'summer'	– 'was'
fée	[fe]	fait	[fɛ]	'fairy'	– 'fact'
foré	[fɔre]	forêt	[fɔrɛ]	'drilled'	– 'forest'
gré	[gre]	grès	[grɛ]	'will'	– 'sandstone'
gué	[ge]	gai	[gɛ]	'ford'	– 'happy'
piquer	[pike]	piquet	[pikɛ]	'to sting'	– 'stake'
vallée	[vale]	valet	[valɛ]	'valley'	– 'valet'

All the same, it must be noted that in the distribution of these two vowels, variations may exist from one speaker to another. In a few words, for example *fait* 'fact', *gai* 'happy', and *quai* 'platform', some speakers have [e] whereas others use [ɛ]. In the grammatical words *les*, *des*, *ces*, *mes*, *tes*, *ses*, *est*, the pronunciation of the vowel commonly varies between [e] and [ɛ], even for a given speaker. In addition, in the first person singular of the simple past and imperfect (*je chantai* 'I sang' – *je chantais* 'I was singing'), as well as in the future and conditional (*je chanterai* 'I shall sing' – *je chanterais* 'I should sing'), some speakers maintain a distinction between [e] (for the ending *ai*) and [ɛ] (for the endings *ais*, *ait*, *aient*), whereas most eliminate it in favor of [ɛ]. The distribution of [e] and [ɛ] in word-final open syllables is thus not absolutely fixed, which shows that there exists between these two vowels a particular affinity that does not exist for example between [i] and [e] or between [ɛ] and [a].

Orthography may serve as a practical guide for foreign students to determine whether [e] or [ɛ] is possible. In general, in a final open syllable, spellings containing *é*, *er*, and *ez* correspond to [e] (e.g. *beauté* [bote] 'beauty', *vallée* [vale] 'valley'; *pâtissier* [pɑtisje] 'pastry-cook', *chanter* [ʃɑ̃te] 'to sing'; *chez* [ʃe] 'at', *chantez* [ʃɑ̃te] 'sing'), whereas spellings containing *è*, *ê*, *et* (with the exception of the conjunction *et* 'and', which is usually pronounced [e]), and *ai* correspond to [ɛ] (e.g. *après* [aprɛ] 'after', *très* [trɛ] 'very'; *forêt* [fɔrɛ] 'forest'; *billet* [bijɛ] 'ticket', *complet* [kɔ̃plɛ] 'complete'; *paix* [pɛ] 'peace', *raie* [rɛ] 'stripe', *trait* [trɛ] 'feature'; all verb forms).

In a *closed* final syllable, there is *neutralization* ('neutralisation') of the potential distinction between [e] and [ɛ] in favor of [ɛ]; in other words, [e] is never found in this context. Only [ɛ] is permitted, as the examples in Table 4.3 show.

The particular distribution of [e] and [ɛ] in closed final syllables explains the alternations that are found between many masculine adjectives or nouns and their feminine forms (see Table 4.4). In the masculine, these words end in [e]; in the feminine, the consonant [r] is added. The final syllable, open in the masculine forms, becomes closed in the feminine forms and thus cannot keep its [e], which it turns into [ɛ]. An identical phenomenon occurs in the course of word-shortening processes placing an interior [e] in a closed final syllable; here also, [e] becomes [ɛ] (see Table 4.5). The same thing may be observed in the conjugation of first group verbs ending in *éCer* (where *C* designates at least one consonant). In the present singular of the indicative, for example, the absence of a pronounced vowel after *C* places the preceding [e] in a closed final syllable, causing it to change to [ɛ] automatically (see Table 4.6).

Table 4.3. [ɛ] in word-final closed syllables

b*e*lle	[bɛl]	'beautiful'
gr*e*c	[grɛk]	'Greek'
m*e*r	[mɛ:r]	'sea'
m*è*re	[mɛ:r]	'mother'
m*ai*re	[mɛ:r]	'mayor'
s*ei*ze	[sɛ:z]	'sixteen'
t*ê*te	[tɛt]	'head'

Table 4.4. [e]~[ɛ] alternations (masculine–feminine)

masculine		feminine		
premier	[prœmje]	première	[prœmjɛ:r]	'first'
entier	[ãtje]	entière	[ãtjɛ:r]	'entire'
boucher	[buʃe]	bouchère	[buʃɛ:r]	'butcher'
poissonnier	[pwasɔnje]	poissonnière	[pwasɔnjɛ:r]	'fishmonger'

Table 4.5. [e]~[ɛ] alternations (word shortening)

agrégation	[agregasjõ]	→	agr*e*g	[agrɛg]	(type of exam)
bén*é*fice	[benefis]	→	bén*e*f	[benɛf]	'benefit'
z*é*phir	[zefir]	→	z*e*f	[zɛf]	(type of wind)

Table 4.6. [e]~[ɛ] alternations (verb conjugation)

céd*er*	[sede]	il cède	[ilsɛd]	'to yield' – 'he yields'
gên*er*	[ʒene]	il gêne	[ilʒɛn]	'to bother' – 'he bothers'

4.3.1.2. [o]–[ɔ] *in word-final syllables*

While [e] and [ɛ] play a distinctive role in word-final open syllables, [o] and [ɔ] are neutralized in this position: only [o] is possible in a final *open* syllable; [ɔ] is impossible in the same position (see Table 4.7). This distribution explains the alternation between [ɔ] and [o] illustrated in

Table 4.7. [o] in word-final open syllables

b*eau*	[bo]	'beautiful'
gr*o*s	[gro]	'fat'
h*au*t	[o]	'high'
t*ô*t	[to]	'early'

Table 4.8. [ɔ]~[o] alternations

A. *Feminine–masculine*[a]

| sotte | [sɔt] | sot | [so] | 'stupid' |
| rigolote | [rigɔlɔt] | rigolo | [rigolo] | 'funny' |

B. *Word shortening*[b]

| métropolitain | [metrɔpɔlitɛ̃] | → | metro | [metro] | 'subway' |
| automobile | [ɔtɔmɔbil] | → | auto | [oto] | 'car' |

C. *Reduplication*[c]

| dormir | [dɔrmir] | (faire) dodo | [dodo] | 'to sleep' |
| communiste | [kɔmynist] | coco | [koko] | 'communist' |

Notes:
[a] The feminine forms on the left end in a consonant which does not occur in the masculine forms on the right.
[b] The words on the right preserve the first two syllables of the words on the left.
[c] The words on the right are formed by taking the initial consonant–vowel sequence of the words on the left and making a copy of it (hence the technical term 'reduplication').

Table 4.8. The words on the left contain an internal *o* pronounced [ɔ]. This *o* is found in final position in the related words on the right and is automatically pronounced [o]. Notice that in four of the examples (*rigolo*, *auto*, *dodo*, and *coco*), the preceding syllable also exhibits a change from [ɔ] to [o], but this time to match the final [o] (vowel harmony).

In *closed* final syllables, two cases need to be distinguished, depending on the nature of the consonants which close the syllable: (i) neutralization of the distinction between [o] and [ɔ] before [z], [r], and [ɲ] and (ii) contrast between [o] and [ɔ] before other consonants.

(i) Neutralization between [ɔ] and [o]:
Only [o] is found before [z], never [ɔ] (see Table 4.9), and only [ɔ] is found before [r] and [ɲ], never [o] (see Table 4.10).
(ii) Contrast between [ɔ] and [o]:
[o] and [ɔ] play a distinctive role before other consonants, as the examples in Table 4.11 indicate.

The vowel-quality difference is often accompanied by a vowel-length difference, because the vowel [o] is one of the vowels which is systematically lengthened in a closed final syllable, whereas the vowel [ɔ] is lengthened only when its syllable is closed by certain word-final consonants (see Section 4.2).

Aside from the cases where the distribution of [o] and [ɔ] is fixed by the phonetic context (namely, in a word-final open syllable and in a word-

Table 4.9. [o] before word-final [z]

cause	[ko:z]	'cause'
chose	[ʃo:z]	'thing'
dose	[do:z]	'dosage'
ose	[o:z]	'dares'
rose	[ro:z]	'rose'

Table 4.10. [ɔ] before [r] and [ɲ] in word-final syllables

corps	[kɔ:r]	'body'	cigogne	[sigɔɲ]	'stork'
dort	[dɔ:r]	'sleeps'	cogne	[kɔɲ]	'hits'
fort	[fɔ:r]	'strong'	grogne	[grɔɲ]	'grumbles'
Laure	[lɔ:r]	'Laura'	rogne	[rɔɲ]	'anger'
or	[ɔ:r]	'gold'			
amorphe	[amɔrf]	'amorphous'			
corde	[kɔrd]	'rope'			
forme	[fɔrm]	'form'			
gorge	[gɔrʒ]	'throat'			
orgue	[ɔrg]	'organ'			
sorte	[sɔrt]	'kind'			

Table 4.11. [o] vs [ɔ] in word-final closed syllables

taupe	[to:p]	tope	[tɔp]	'mole'	– 'agreed!'
haute	[o:t]	hotte	[ɔt]	'high'	– 'basket'
(le) nôtre	[no:tr]	notre	[nɔtr]	'ours'	– 'our'
rauque	[ro:k]	roc	[rɔk]	'hoarse'	– 'rock'
l'aube	[lo:b]	lobe	[lɔb]	'dawn'	– 'lobe'
Maude	[mo:d]	mode	[mɔd]	'Maud'	– 'fashion'
heaume	[o:m]	homme	[ɔm]	'helmet'	– 'man'
cône	[ko:n]	conne	[kɔn]	'cone'	– 'asshole'
gaufre	[go:fr]	coffre	[kɔfr]	'waffle'	– 'coffer'
fauve	[fo:v]	love	[lɔ:v]	'beast'	– 'coils'
pauvre	[po:vr]	Hanovre	[anɔ:vr]	'poor'	– 'Hanover'
Beauce	[bo:s]	bosse	[bɔs]	name of region	– 'lump'
l'ébauche	[lebo:ʃ]	les Boches	[lebɔʃ]	'sketch'	– 'the Jerries'
l'auge	[lo:ʒ]	loge	[lɔ:ʒ]	'trough'	– 'box'
saule	[so:l]	sol	[sɔl]	'willow'	– 'ground'

final syllable closed by [z], [r], or [ɲ]), orthography provides useful information about vowel quality ([ɔ] or [o]) in word-final syllables. Spellings with *ô*, *au*, and *eau* generally correspond to the pronunciation [o]: e.g. *drôle* [dro:l] 'funny', *le nôtre* [lœno:tr] 'ours', *le vôtre* [lœvo:tr] 'yours', *Saône* [so:n] (name of river); *aube* [o:b] 'dawn', *sauf* [sof] 'except', *taupe* [to:p] 'mole'; *Beauce* [bo:s] (name of region). By contrast the spelling *o* tends to correspond to the pronunciation [ɔ]: e.g. *sol* [sɔl] 'ground', *notre* [nɔtr] 'our', *votre* [vɔtr] 'your', *sonne* [sɔn] 'rings', *robe* [rɔb] 'dress', *étoffe* [etɔf] 'material', *hop* [ɔp] (interjection), *bosse* [bɔs] 'lump'. It should, however, be noted that [ɔ] occurs in *Paul* [pɔl] 'Paul' (but with a feminine *Paule* [po:l] 'Paula') and that [o] appears in particular in some words in *-one* (e.g. *amazone* [amazo:n] 'Amazon', *cyclone* [siklo:n] 'cyclone', *zone* [zo:n] 'zone'); in words in *-drome* (e.g. *hippodrome* [ipodro:m] 'race-track', *vélodrome* [velodro:m] 'cycle-track'); in some words ending in *-ome* (e.g. *arome* [aro:m] 'aroma', *atome* [ato:m] 'atom', *idiome* [idjo:m] 'idiom', *chrome* [kro:m] 'chrome'); in a few words in *-osse* (e.g. *fosse* [fo:s] 'pit', *grosse* [gro:s] 'fat'); and in most words ending in *-os* with *s* pronounced (e.g. *albatros* [albatro:s] 'albatross', *calvados* [kalvado:s] (type of brandy), *cosmos* [kosmo:s] 'cosmos', *tétanos* [tetano:s] 'tetanus'; but notice *os* [ɔs] 'bone' and *rhinocéros* [rinɔserɔs] 'rhinoceros'). Note finally that the spelling *-um* generally represents the pronunciation [-ɔm] (e.g. *album* [albɔm] 'album', *capharnaüm* [kafarnaɔm] 'mess', *harmonium* [armɔnjɔm] 'harmonium', *post-scriptum* [pɔstskriptɔm] 'postscript', *référendum* [referɛ̃dɔm] 'referendum', *rhum* [rɔm] 'rum', *sanatorium* [sanatɔrjɔm] 'sanatorium').

4.3.1.3. [ø]–[œ] *in word-final syllables*

The case of the vowels [ø] and [œ] is similar in part to the case of the vowels [o] and [ɔ]. In an *open* final syllable, there is the same neutralization (with one exception): as a rule, only [ø] is found word-finally, never [œ] (see Table 4.12).

This restriction explains why the [œ] in *dégueulasse* [degœlas] 'dirty' becomes [ø] in the abbreviation *dégueu* [degø]. The only cases where [œ] is found in an open final syllable are the nine monosyllabic grammatical words *je*, *me*, *te*, *se*, *le*, *ce*, *de*, *ne*, and *que*; note that these words are written with the letter *e* (and not with the digram *eu*, as in the other cases) and that, as will be seen in Chapter 6, they have the property of being able to lose their vowel entirely under certain conditions.

In a *closed* final syllable, parallel to the case of [o] and [ɔ], there is neutralization of the distinction between [ø] and [œ] before [z] and [r]: only [ø] is found before [z], never [œ], and only [œ] is found before [r], never [ø] (see Table 4.13). But whereas [o] and [ɔ] contrast before many

Table 4.12. [ø] in word-final open syllables

c*eux*	[sø]	'those'
eux	[ø]	'them'
f*eu*	[fø]	'fire'
p*eut*	[pø]	'can'
qu*eue*	[kø]	'tail'
y*eux*	[jø]	'eyes'

Table 4.13. [ø] before final [z] and [œ] before final [r]

[ø] before final [z]			[œ] before final [r]		
creuse	[krø:z]	'digs'	cœur	[kœ:r]	'heart'
chanteuse	[ʃɑ̃tø:z]	'singer' (fem.)	chanteur	[ʃɑ̃tœ:r]	'singer'
heureuse	[ørø:z]	'happy' (fem.)	heure	[œ:r]	'hour'
menteuse	[mɑ̃tø:z]	'liar' (fem.)	menteur	[mɑ̃tœ:r]	'liar'

Table 4.14. [ø] vs [œ] in word-final syllables

veule	[vø:l]	veulent	[vœl]	'spineless'	–	'want'
jeûne	[ʒø:n]	jeune	[ʒœn]	'fasting'	–	'young'
beugle	[bø:gl]	aveugle	[avœgl]	'bellows'	–	'blind'
meugle	[mø:gl]			'moos'		

Table 4.15. [œ] in word-final closed
syllables

peuple	[pœpl]	'people'
club	[klœb]	'club'
meuble	[mœbl]	'furniture'
aveugle	[avœgl]	'blind'
neuf	[nœf]	'nine'
neuve	[nœ:v]	'new'
œuvre	[œ:vr]	'work'
seul	[sœl]	'alone'
seuil	[sœj]	'threshold'

Table 4.16. [ø] in word-final closed syllables

leude	[lø:d]	'vassal'
meute	[mø:t]	'pack'
neutre	[nø:tr]	'neutral'
Pentateuque	[pɛ̃tatø:k]	'Pentateuch'
Polyeucte	[pɔljø:kt]	(name)
neume	[nø:m]	'neume'
Maubeuge	[mobø:ʒ]	(name of town)

other consonants, [ø] and [œ] contrast only before the consonants [l, n, gl], and this in very limited fashion, since there are only four instances (see Table 4.14). In addition, [œ] is used more and more frequently in these four words, *veule, jeûne, beugle*, and *meugle*. This tendency reflects the fact that in word-final closed syllables (excluding those closed by [z] or [r]), [œ] is overall much more prevalent than [ø]. Thus, [œ] appears in about 100 words in front of the word-final consonants [pl, b, bl, gl, f, v, vr, l, j] (see Table 4.15), whereas [ø] appears in only about a dozen words (most of them very rare) in front of the consonants [d, t, tr, k, kt, m, ʒ] (see Table 4.16).

Table 4.17. Mid vowels in word-final syllables (summary)

	open syllable	closed syllable
[e]–[ɛ]	[e] – [ɛ] (*et*) – (*haie*)	[ɛ] (*air*)
[ø]–[œ]	–[ø] generally (*eux*) –[œ] (grammatical words: *je, de, que,* etc.)	–[ø] before [z] (*-euse*) –[œ] before [r] (*heure*) and elsewhere in general
[o]–[ɔ]	[o] (*eau*)	–[o] before [z] (*ose*) –[ɔ] before [r] (*or*) –elsewhere generally: [o] = *au, ô* (*haute, hôte*) [ɔ] = *o* (*hotte*)

4.3.1.4. Summary: mid vowels in word-final syllables

Table 4.17 presents in synoptic form the distribution of mid vowels in word-final syllables in standard French. Certain details mentioned above are omitted so as not to encumber the diagram.

We should not close this examination˙ of mid vowels in word-final syllables without mentioning that the principles which govern their distribution may, of course, vary from dialect to dialect. Southern French, for example, can be characterized as having the half-closed vowels in open syllables (*haie* [e] 'hedge', *de* [dø] 'of') and the half-open vowels in closed syllables (*creuse* [krœz] 'digs', *rose* [rɔz] 'rose'), a much simpler system than the one operating in standard French.

4.3.2. Mid vowels in non-final syllables

4.3.2.1. Introduction

In standard French, the distribution of the mid vowels in non-final syllables is subject to greater variability than in word-final syllables. This is because numerous factors can come into play. To try to clarify matters in the presentation, I shall first describe a general tendency toward neutralization of the potential contrasts, and then examine how other factors may create deviations from this basic neutralization pattern.

In natural languages, there are generally more vowel contrasts possible in stressed syllables than in unstressed syllables; in other words, some potential distinctions are neutralized in unstressed syllables. Thus, in numerous languages, for example English, unstressed vowels are often reduced to schwa (see Chapter 3, p. 34). In Russian, while the five vowels [i, e, a, o, u] are found in stressed syllables, this system is reduced to three possibilities in unstressed syllables: [i, a, u]. In French, the mid-vowel system similarly tends to be reduced in unstressed syllables (i.e. in non-final syllables): an unrounded mid vowel tends to be half-closed, whereas a rounded mid vowel tends to be half-open. In non-final syllables, the basic phonetic tendency is thus to pronounce [e, œ, ɔ] rather than [ɛ, ø, o]. Numerous other factors may, however, reverse this general tendency, or, on the contrary, favor it still more. I shall now turn to these factors.

4.3.2.2. Role of syllable structure
As we have already seen, the distinction between open and closed syllables plays an essential role in the distribution of mid vowels in word-final syllables. This distinction continues to have some importance in non-final syllables. Thus, in non-final closed syllables, [ɛ] may in fact be used as an alternative to [e] (see Table 4.18).

If the non-final syllable is closed by [r], [ɛ] is actually always used, never [e] (see Table 4.19). And a non-final syllable closed by [r] also forces the occurrence of [œ] and [ɔ] (as opposed to [ø] and [o]), as was the case in word-final syllables (see Table 4.20). The closing of a syllable by the consonant [r] thus plays an absolute role in the distribution of the mid vowels: it forces in all cases the appearance of the half-open mid vowels, destroying the potential influence of all the other factors which might tend to make the half-closed mid vowels occur.

The presence of the consonant [z] after a rounded mid vowel strongly favors the occurrence of [ø] and [o] and tends to counterbalance the other

Table 4.18. [e] or [ɛ] in non-final closed syllables

*esp*érer	[espere] ~ [ɛspere]	'to hope'
*esp*acer	[espase] ~ [ɛspase]	'to space'
*él*evé	[elve] ~ [ɛlve]	'high'
*él*evage	[elvaʒ] ~ [ɛlvaʒ]	'stockbreeding'
*v*estige	[vestiʒ] ~ [vɛstiʒ]	'vestige'

Table 4.19. [ɛ] before [r] in non-final closed syllables

*f*ermé	[fɛrme]	'closed'
*m*erci	[mɛrsi]	'thank you'
*p*erdu	[pɛrdy]	'lost'
*v*ertige	[vɛrtiʒ]	'vertigo'

Table 4.20. [œ] and [ɔ] before [r] in non-final closed syllables

*h*eurter	[œrte]	'to hit'	*c*orbeau	[kɔrbo]	'raven'
*m*eurtri	[mœrtri]	'bruised'	*m*orbleu	[mɔrblø]	(interjection)

Table 4.21. [ø] and [o] before non-final [z]

deuxième	[døzjɛm]	'second'	groseille	[grozɛj]	'currant'
creuset	[krøzɛ]	'bowl'	Joseph	[ʒozɛf]	'Joseph'

potential factors which favor the occurrence of [œ] and [ɔ] (see Table 4.21).

4.3.2.3. Role of vowel harmony

The distribution of the mid vowels in non-final syllables also depends (through vowel harmony) on the degree of aperture of the vowel found in the following syllable. If this vowel is closed or half-closed, the occurrence of [e] is naturally reinforced (see Table 4.22). If the following vowel is half-open or open, [ɛ] can be found as well as [e] (see Table 4.23).

The rounded mid vowels generally seem less sensitive to vowel harmony than the unrounded mid vowels. Inside words, [œ] and [ɔ] commonly close to [ø] and [o] only under the influence of the vowels [ø] and [o] themselves in the following syllable (see Table 4.24). Vowel harmony does not seem to occur if other closed or half-closed vowels are in the following syllable (cf. *apeuré* [apœre] 'frightened', *feuillu* [fœjy] 'leafy'; *économie* [ekɔnɔmi] 'economy', *rocheux* [rɔʃø] 'rocky').

Table 4.22. [e] in vowel harmony

étirer	[etire]	'to stretch'	
été	[ete]	'summer'	
bêtise	[betiz]	'stupidity'	(cf. *bête* [bɛt] 'stupid')
aimer	[eme]	'to love'	(cf. *aime* [ɛm] 'loves')

Table 4.23. [ɛ] in vowel harmony

était	[etɛ]	~	[ɛtɛ]	'was'	
théière	[tejɛr]	~	[tɛjɛr]	'teapot'	(cf. *thé* [te] 'tea')
étant	[etɑ̃]	~	[ɛtɑ̃]	'being'	
aimait	[emɛ]	~	[ɛmɛ]	'loved'	(cf. *aime* [ɛm] 'loves')
aidant	[edɑ̃]	~	[ɛdɑ̃]	'helping'	(cf. *aide* [ɛd] 'helps')

Table 4.24. [ø] and [o] in vowel harmony

heureux	[œrø]	~	[ørø]	'happy'	(cf. *bonheur* [bɔnœr] 'happiness')
peureux	[pœrø]	~	[pørø]	'fearful'	(cf. *peur* [pœr] 'fear')
auto	[ɔto]	~	[oto]	'car'	
coteau	[kɔto]	~	[koto]	'hillside'	

Table 4.25. [e], [œ], [ɔ] and derivational morphology

th*é*	[te]	th*é*ière	[tejɛr]	'tea'	–	'teapot'
org*u*eil	[ɔrgœj]	org*u*eilleux	[ɔrgœjø]	'pride'	–	'proud'
b*o*sse	[bɔs]	b*o*ssu	[bɔsy]	'hump'	–	'hunchbacked'

Table 4.26. [ɛ], [ø], [o] and derivational morphology

fra*î*che	[frɛʃ]	rafra*î*chir	[rafrɛʃir]	'fresh'	–	'to refresh'
n*eu*tre	[nø:tr]	n*eu*tralité	[nøtralite]	'neutral'	–	'neutrality'
gr*o*sse	[gro:s]	gr*o*ssesse	[grosɛs]	'fat'	–	'pregnancy'

4.3.2.4. Role of derivational morphology

Derivational morphology ('la morphologie dérivationnelle') may also play a role in the distribution of the mid vowels in non-final syllables. Starting with a base word such as *clair* 'clear', it is possible to derive other words related to it in meaning and in sound by adding affixes (prefixes and suffixes): for example, *clairement* 'clearly', *éclairer* 'to light', *éclaircir* 'to clear up'. This type of process is called 'derivational morphology'. When a base word contains a mid vowel in its final syllable, and this mid vowel then appears in a non-final syllable of a derived word, the vowel quality found in the base word may be preserved in the derived word. This tendency may favor the occurrence of [e, œ, ɔ] in non-final syllables (as shown in Table 4.25), or on the contrary, it may create the possibility of finding [ɛ, ø, o] (as shown in Table 4.26).

4.3.2.5. Other factors and interactions

The operation of all these phenomena affecting the quality of the mid vowels in non-final syllables is closely linked to the speaker's style. Thus, neutralization to [e, œ, ɔ] and vowel harmony occur naturally in spontaneous speech, where a relatively rapid and unmonitored delivery is generally maintained. By contrast, in elicitation situations or in a formal style, where delivery is usually slower and the pronunciation more deliberate, the derivational morphology factor tends to play a more important role. Under such conditions, an additional factor may also come into play: spelling. The following correlations can then be observed: the letter *é* favors the pronunciation [e], whereas the spellings *è*, *ê*, *ai*, *ei*, and *e* before two written consonants may favor the pronunciation [ɛ]; the letter *o* favors the pronunciation [ɔ], whereas the spellings *ô*, *au*, and *eau* may favor the pronunciation [o].

The various factors influencing the quality of the mid vowels in non-final syllables can, depending on the cases, go in the same direction or, on the contrary, conflict. When they all go in the same direction, or when a particular factor plays an absolute role, speakers generally agree on the pronunciation of the relevant words. But when the factors conflict, one naturally encounters variations from speaker to speaker, and even in the realizations of a given word by a given speaker; these variations can be attributed to the relative weights given to each of the factors. The antagonistic roles played by these factors probably also explain why expert phoneticians are capable of detecting the production of vowel qualities intermediate between [e] and [ɛ], [ø] and [œ], and [o] and [ɔ] in non-final syllables.

4.3.2.6. Summary: mid vowels in non-final syllables

Table 4.27 lists in simplified fashion the main factors influencing the pronunciation of the mid vowels in non-final syllables in standard French. As opposed to the absolute factor, the variable factors can be the source of diverse pronunciations not only among different speakers, but also in the speech of a given speaker.

Table 4.27. Mid vowels in non-final syllables (summary)

absolute factor	syllable closed with [r]: [ɛ, œ, ɔ]
variable factors	*spontaneous speech* – absence of word stress: natural preference for [e, œ, ɔ] – vowel harmony: quality of mid vowel dependent on degree of aperture of vowel in following syllable
	careful speech – derivational morphology: quality of vowel in the base word is kept – spelling: *é* = [e]; *è, ê, ai, ei* = [ɛ] *o* = [ɔ]; *ô, au, eau* = [o]

4.4. Distribution of [a] and [ɑ]

As mentioned in the preceding chapter (p. 48), the distinction between front [a] and back [ɑ] is maintained to a certain extent in standard French, but essentially in word-final syllable (i.e. under stress). In non-final syllables (i.e. in unstressed syllables), back [ɑ] has practically disappeared in favor of front [a], especially if the vowel is more than one syllable away from the end of the word. All the same, there are a few common words where back [ɑ] can frequently be encountered in non-final syllables (see Table 4.28 for some examples). It must also be noted that words derived from a base word with back [ɑ] in its final syllable may keep this [ɑ] in a non-final syllable (see Table 4.29).

Table 4.28. [ɑ] in non-final syllables

bâtir	[bɑtir]	'to build'	gazon	[gɑzõ]	'lawn'
bâton	[bɑtõ]	'stick'	haillon	[ɑjõ]	'rag'
château	[ʃɑto]	'castle'	maçon	[mɑsõ]	'bricklayer'
gâteau	[gɑto]	'cake'	marron	[mɑrõ]	'brown'
pâté	[pɑte]	'pâté'	scabreux	[skɑbrø]	'risky'
râteau	[rɑto]	'rake'			

Table 4.29. [ɑ] and derivational morphology

âge	[ɑːʒ]	âgé	[aʒe]	'age'	–	'old'
pâle	[pɑːl]	pâlot	[pɑlo]	'pale'	–	'palish'
pâte	[pɑːt]	pâteux	[pɑtø]	'paste'	–	'pasty'
rase	[rɑːz]	rasoir	[rɑzwar]	'shaves'	–	'razor'

Table 4.30. [a] vs [ɑ] in word-final syllables

rat	[ra]	ras	[rɑ]	'rat'	–	'short'
tache	[taʃ]	tâche	[tɑːʃ]	'stain'	–	'task'
patte	[pat]	pâte	[pɑːt]	'paw'	–	'dough'
arabe	[arab]	crabe	[krɑːb]	'Arab'	–	'crab'
table	[tabl]	sable	[sɑːbl]	'table'	–	'sand'
face	[fas]	espace	[ɛspɑːs]	'face'	–	'space'
obstacle	[ɔpstakl]	miracle	[mirɑːkl]	'obstacle'	–	'miracle'
escadre	[eskadr]	cadre	[kɑːdr]	'squadron'	–	'frame'
bagne	[baɲ]	gagne	[gɑːɲ]	'penitentiary'	–	'wins'
détail	[detaj]	rail	[rɑːj]	'detail'	–	'rail'
drame	[dram]	brame	[brɑːm]	'drama'	–	'bleats'
tape	[tap]	râpe	[rɑːp]	'slap'	–	'rasp'
avare	[avɑːr]	rare	[rɑːr]	'stingy'	–	'rare'
moi	[mwa]	mois	[mwɑ]	'me'	–	'month'
(je) bois	[bwa]	(le) bois	[bwɑ]	'(I) drink'	–	'(the) wood'
(je) vois	[vwa]	(la) voix	[vwɑ]	'(I) see'	–	'(the) voice'

Overall, back [ɑ] is found more frequently in the final syllable of a word than in a non-final syllable, but even in this preferred position, it is relatively rare in comparison with front [a]. Table 4.30 lists examples where a contrast may be found between the two sounds in word-final syllables. As in the case of [ɔ] and [o] noted earlier (Table 4.11), the difference in vowel quality between [a] and [ɑ] is frequently accompanied by a difference in length, in accordance with the laws of vowel lengthening described at the beginning of this chapter.

In spite of the variability of the situation concerning the distribution of [a] and [ɑ], it is possible to isolate a number of conditions which seem to favor the appearance of back [ɑ]. As already indicated, the preferred position of back [ɑ] is under stress. In fact, in a word which contains [ɑ] in its stressed final syllable, this [ɑ] often becomes [a] if the stress is lost or

Table 4.31. [ɑ], [a], and stress

s*a*ble [sá:bl]	s*a*blonneux [sablɔnǿ]		'sand' – 'sandy'
r*a*re [rá:r]	rarissime [rarisím]		'rare' – 'very rare'
J'ai été au b*oi*s [ʒeeteobwá]	J'ai été au b*oi*s de Vincennes	[ʒeeteobwadvɛ̃sɛ́n]	
'I went to the woods'	'I went to the Vincennes woods'		
Il a une belle v*oi*x [ilaynbɛlvwá]	C'est la v*oi*x de son maître	[sɛlavwadsõmɛ́tr]	
'He has a good voice'	'It is his master's voice'		

Table 4.32. [ɑ] after [rw] and before [z]

	[rwɑ]			[ɑ:z]	
dr*oi*t	[drwɑ]	'straight'	b*a*se	[bɑ:z]	'base'
cr*oi*x	[krwɑ]	'cross'	c*a*se	[kɑ:z]	'square'
fr*oi*d	[frwɑ]	'cold'	g*a*z	[gɑ:z]	'gas'
hongr*oi*s	[õgrwɑ]	'Hungarian'	phr*a*se	[frɑ:z]	'sentence'
par*oi*	[parwɑ]	'partition'	v*a*se	[vɑ:z]	'vase'
r*oi*	[rwɑ]	'king'			
tr*oi*s	[trwɑ]	'three'			

Table 4.33. [ɑ] and orthography

			as = [ɑ]		
c*as*	[kɑ]	'case'	matel*as*	[matlɑ]	'mattress'
b*as*	[bɑ]	'low'	p*as*	[pɑ]	'step'
gr*as*	[grɑ]	'fat'	rep*as*	[rœpɑ]	'meal'
l*as*	[lɑ]	'tired'	t*as*	[tɑ]	'heap'

			â = [ɑ]		
*â*me	[ɑ:m]	'soul'	gr*â*ce	[grɑ:s]	'grace'
*â*ne	[ɑ:n]	'donkey'	inf*â*me	[ɛ̃fɑ:m]	'infamous'
app*â*t	[apɑ]	'bait'	l*â*che	[lɑ:ʃ]	'coward'
bleu*â*tre	[blǿɑ:tr]	'bluish'	m*â*le	[mɑ:l]	'male'
c*â*ble	[kɑ:bl]	'cable'	P*â*ques	[pɑ:k]	'Easter'
Cléop*â*tre	[kleɔpɑ:tr]	'Cleopatra'	p*â*te	[pɑ:t]	'dough'
cr*â*ne	[krɑ:n]	'skull'	pl*â*tre	[plɑ:tr]	'plaster'
dég*â*t	[degɑ]	'damage'	t*â*che	[tɑ:ʃ]	'task'

reduced, for example because of the adjunction of a suffix or because of the phenomenon of stress subordination in the sentence (see Chapters 3 and 12). The examples in Table 4.31 illustrate this type of alternation.

Back [ɑ] often enters in preferential combination with certain other sounds: thus, [ɑ] is generally found after the sequence [rw] and before [z] (see Table 4.32).

From a purely practical point of view, note that orthography may also provide useful clues. For example, back [ɑ] is found in most of the words ending in -*as* (but *bras* 'arm' and verb forms ending in -*as* have front [a]), and the presence of the circumflex accent (*â*) also favors the pronunciation with [ɑ] (but verb forms in the imperfect subjunctive, such as *chantât*, and in the simple past, such as *chantâmes*, have front [a]). Table 4.33 provides some examples of these two types of cases.

To sum up, it is important to emphasize once again that the presence of back [ɑ] is the object of considerable variations, that the observations made here are only indicative of possible pronunciations, and that, from a practical point of view, if a single type of open vowel is used, it is wise to resort to front [a] rather than back [ɑ].

5
Nasal vowels

5.1. Introduction

The inventories of the French and English vowel systems given in Chapter 3, pp. 36–7, indicate that there are nasal vowels in French, but not in English. For native speakers of English, the existence in French of this additional vowel series poses a number of difficulties which are discussed in this chapter. This chapter also contains an historical sketch of the emergence of nasal vowels in French, an examination of their spelling, and finally a study of the phenomenon of liaison with nasal vowels.

There are four nasal vowels in French: [ɛ̃, œ̃, ɑ̃, õ] (*un bon vin blanc* [œ̃bõvɛ̃blɑ̃] 'a good white wine'). Many speakers do not distinguish [œ̃] from [ɛ̃] and thus have only three nasal vowels [ɛ̃, ɑ̃, õ] (*un bon vin blanc* [ɛ̃bõvɛ̃blɑ̃]). Table 5.1 gives a few examples of words containing nasal vowels.

There are no special letters for transcribing nasal vowels in French orthography, but they are always spelled by means of specific letter combinations: a single vowel-letter or a vowel digraph followed by the consonant-letters *m* or *n*. For [ɛ̃], the most common vowel-letters are *i* (*fin* [fɛ̃] 'end'), *ei* (*plein* [plɛ̃] 'full'), *ai* (*sain* [sɛ̃] 'healthy') and *e*. The letter *e* usually serves to represent [ɑ̃] (see below), but in some well-defined cases, it is also used to represent [ɛ̃], in particular in the word-final sequences *-ien*, *-yen*, and *-éen* (*chien* [ʃjɛ̃] 'dog', *moyen* [mwajɛ̃] 'average', *européen* [œrɔpeɛ̃] 'European'), as well as in forms of the verbs *venir* 'to come' and *tenir* 'to hold' and their derivatives, e.g. *viens*, *vient* [vjɛ̃] and *tiens*, *tient* [tjɛ̃]. (Other words ending in *-ient*, where the sequence *-ent* is not the silent verb ending of the third person plural, contain [ɑ̃] and not [ɛ̃]: e.g. *client* [klijɑ̃] 'client', *conscient* [kõsjɑ̃] 'conscious', *expédient* [ɛkspedjɑ̃] 'expedient', *inconvénient* [ɛ̃kõvenjɑ̃] 'drawback', *ingrédient* [ɛ̃gredjɑ̃] 'ingredient', *patient* [pasjɑ̃] 'patient', *orient* [ɔrjɑ̃] 'Orient', *récipient* [resipjɑ̃] 'container'.) When the letter *e* is not preceded by *i*, *y*, or *é*, it serves to represent [ɛ̃] only in a very small group of words, for example, *Agen* [aʒɛ̃] (name of town), *agenda* [aʒɛ̃da] 'agenda', *appendice* [apɛ̃dis] 'appendix', *appendicite* [apɛ̃disit] 'appendicitis', *examen* [egzamɛ̃] 'examination', *mémento* [memɛ̃to] 'memento',

Table 5.1. French nasal vowels

[ɛ̃]	*fin, vingt, plein, sain, faim, chien*	[fɛ̃, vɛ̃, plɛ̃, sɛ̃, fɛ̃, ʃjɛ̃]	(end, twenty, full, healthy, hunger, dog)
[œ̃] or [ɛ̃]	*un, aucun, chacun, commun, brun, parfum*	[œ̃, okœ̃, ʃakœ̃, kɔmœ̃, brœ̃, parfœ̃]	(a [article], none, each, common, brown, perfume)
[ɑ̃]	*enfant, banc, en, champ, quand, temps*	[ɑ̃fɑ̃, bɑ̃, ɑ̃, ʃɑ̃, kɑ̃, tɑ̃]	(child, bench, in, field, when, weather)
[õ]	*bɔn, pont, fond, plomb, on, mon*	[bõ, põ, fõ, plõ, õ, mõ]	(good, bridge, bottom, lead, one [pronoun], my)

placenta [plasɛ̃ta] 'placenta', *pentagone* [pɛ̃tagon] 'pentagon', *rhododendron* [rɔdɔdɛ̃drõ] 'rhododendron'. The vowel-letter *y* serves to represent [ɛ̃] in just a few words, such as *larynx* [larɛ̃ks] 'larynx', *pharynx* [farɛ̃ks] 'pharynx', *syntaxe* [sɛ̃taks] 'syntax', *synthèse* [sɛ̃tɛz] 'synthesis', *thym* [tɛ̃] 'thyme', and *tympan* [tɛ̃pɑ̃] 'eardrum'.

For [œ̃], the vowel-letter is always *u*, with a single exception, where *eu* is found (*à jeun* [aʒœ̃] 'fasting'). The words which can contain [œ̃] are relatively few, and as already indicated, they are often pronounced with [ɛ̃] rather than [œ̃] (e.g. *un* 'one', *aucun* 'none', *chacun* 'each').

For [ɑ̃], the vowel-letters are almost always *e* and *a*, as in *enfant* [ɑ̃fɑ̃] 'child' (on the ambiguity of *e*, see above). In a few words, *ae* and *ao* are also found: thus *Caen* [kɑ̃] (name of town), *Saint-Saens* [sɛ̃sɑ̃s] (surname); *faon* [fɑ̃] 'fawn', *paon* [pɑ̃] 'peacock', *taon* [tɑ̃] 'ox-fly'; but note that *pharaon* 'pharaoh' is pronounced [faraõ].

For [õ], the vowel-letter is almost always *o* (*ponton* [põtõ] 'pontoon'). The letter *u* serves to represent [õ] in a few words such as *acupuncture* (also written *acuponcture*) [akypõktyr] 'acupuncture', *jungle* [ʒõgl] 'jungle' (also pronounced [ʒœ̃gl] or [ʒɛ̃gl]), and *punch* [põʃ] 'punch' (the name of the drink; *punch* in the sense of 'hit' is pronounced [pœnʃ]).

We shall return to the question of the spelling of nasal vowels in Section 5.6, where we shall examine the cases when *VN* orthographic sequences (vowel-letter + nasal consonant-letter) represent [VN] phonetic sequences (oral vowel + nasal consonant) rather than [Ṽ] (nasal vowels).

5.2. Articulatory characteristics

Nasal vowels are produced by lowering the velum, thus allowing air to pass through the nasal cavity as well as the oral cavity. For French nasal vowels, the position of the tongue and that of the lips are approximately those required for the oral vowels for which the same phonetic symbols are used ([ɛ, œ, ɑ, o]). Thus, [ɛ̃] and [œ̃] are front, [ɑ̃] and [õ] are back; [ɛ̃] and [ɑ̃] are unrounded, [œ̃] and [õ] are rounded; and [ɛ̃] and [œ̃] are half-open, [ɑ̃] is open, and [õ] is half-closed.

From a practical point of view, learning the distinction between [ɛ̃] and [œ̃] can be considered superfluous, inasmuch as many French speakers themselves have only [ɛ̃]. The distinction, when it is made, simply corresponds to the distinction between [ɛ] and [œ], that is, it is a question of lip position: the lips are rounded for [œ̃], but not for [ɛ̃].

By contrast, it is essential to master the distinction between [ɑ̃] and [õ], which is frequently the source of production, as well as perception, difficulties for English-speaking students. From a perceptual point of view, it is true that these two vowels seem relatively close to each other.

Table 5.2. [õ] vs [ã] in different words

	[õ]		[ã]		
tonton	[tõtõ]	*tentant*	[tãtã]	'uncle'	– 'tempting'
ponton	[põtõ]	*pendant*	[pãdã]	'pontoon'	– 'during'
on f*ond*	[õfõ]	*enfant*	[ãfã]	'we melt'	– 'child'

Table 5.3. [õ] vs [ã] within words

	[õ]–[ã]		[ã]–[õ]		
content	[kõtã]	*canton*	[kãtõ]	'happy'	– 'district'
fondant	[fõdã]	*fendons*	[fãdõ]	'melting'	– '(we) split'
son s*ang*	[sõsã]	*sans* s*on*	[sãsõ]	'his blood'	– 'without sound'

But from an articulatory point of view, they clearly differ along two easy-to-grasp dimensions, degree of aperture and lip position: (i) [ã] is more open than [õ], and (ii) [õ] is very rounded, contrary to [ã]. In order to fix the articulatory differences between the two vowels and their respective qualities, it is useful for students to focus on one vowel, and then on the other, by practising repeating words with [õ] and words with [ã] (see Table 5.2). Students can then contrast one vowel with the other in the same word, by working on the pronunciation of words such as those in Table 5.3.

5.3. The role of nasality in French

In French, vowel nasality allows meaning distinctions between words; the examples in Table 5.4 exhibit contrasting oral and nasal vowels. Nasality, then, plays a distinctive role in French.

Nasal vowels also contrast with sequences of the type 'oral vowel + nasal consonant'. Thus, a large number of adjectives and nouns end in a nasal vowel in the masculine, but in an oral vowel followed by the nasal consonant [n] in the feminine. These alternations between [Ṽ] and [Vn] can be divided into several groups, according to the quality of the oral vowel found in the feminine (see Table 5.5). There are only two cases in this type of alternation where the consonant in the feminine is not [n], but [ɲ]: *bénin* [benɛ̃] – *bénigne* [beniɲ] 'benign' and *malin* [malɛ̃] – *maligne* [maliɲ] 'sly' (but *maline* [malin] is also found).

The nasal and oral vowels which take part in these alternations are not generally in direct phonetic correspondence. In particular, with speakers where [œ̃] has merged with [ɛ̃], three different oral vowels correspond to [ɛ̃]: [i] (*fin–fine*), [ɛ] (*plein–pleine*), and [y] (*un–une*). The other two

Table 5.4. Oral vs nasal vowels

[ɛ]–[ɛ̃]	mais–main, sec–cinq, messe–mince	[mɛ]–[mɛ̃], [sɛk]–[sɛ̃k], [mɛs]–[mɛ̃s]	(but/hand, dry/five, mass/thin)
[a]–[ɑ̃]	las–lent, âtre–antre, passe–pense	[la]–[lɑ̃], [ɑtr]–[ɑ̃tr], [pas]–[pɑ̃s]	(tired/slow, hearth/lair, passes/thinks)
[o]–[õ]	peau–pont, faute–fonte, ose–onze	[po]–[põ], [fot]–[fõt], [oz]–[õz]	(skin/bridge, mistake/cast-iron, dares/eleven)

Table 5.5. [Ṽ]~[Vn] alternations (masculine–feminine)

[ɛ̃]~[in]

divin–divine	[divɛ̃]–[divin]	'divine'
fin–fine	[fɛ̃]–[fin]	'thin'
voisin–voisine	[vwazɛ̃]–[vwazin]	'neighbor'

[ɛ̃]~[ɛn]

certain–certaine	[sɛrtɛ̃]–[sɛrten]	'sure'
chien–chienne	[ʃjɛ̃]–[ʃjɛn]	'dog'
plein–pleine	[plɛ̃]–[plɛn]	'full'

[œ̃]/[ɛ̃]~[yn]

brun–brune	[brœ̃]/[brɛ̃]–[bryn]	'brown'
chacun–chacune	[ʃakœ̃]/[ʃakɛ̃]–[ʃakyn]	'each'
un–une	[œ̃]/[ɛ̃]–[yn]	'a'

[ɑ̃]~[an]

faisan–faisane	[fœzɑ̃]–[fœzan]	'pheasant'
Jean–Jeanne	[ʒɑ̃]–[ʒan]	'John', 'Joan'
paysan–paysane	[peizɑ̃]–[peizan]	'peasant'

[õ]~[ɔn]

baron–baronne	[barõ]–[barɔn]	'baron'
bon–bonne	[bõ]–[bɔn]	'good'
breton–bretonne	[brœtõ]–[brœtɔn]	'Breton'

Table 5.6. [Ṽ]~[VN] alternations (singular–plural present indicative)

(i)	[jɛ̃] ~ [jɛn]	il *vient* – ils *viennent*	[vjɛ̃]–[vjɛn]	(to come)
(ii)	[wɛ̃] ~ [waɲ]	il *joint* – ils *joignent*	[ʒwɛ̃]–[ʒwaɲ]	(to join)
(iii)	[ɛ̃] ~ [ɛɲ]	il *craint* – ils *craignent*	[krɛ̃]–[krɛɲ]	(to fear)
(iv)	[ɑ̃] ~ [ɛn]	il *prend* – ils *prennent*	[prɑ̃]–[prɛn]	(to take)

alternations are one-to-one correspondences, but notice that the front oral vowel [a] corresponds to the back nasal vowel [ɑ̃] and that the half-open oral vowel [ɔ] corresponds to the half-closed nasal vowel [õ].

Other alternations between nasal vowels and sequences of 'oral vowel + nasal consonant' characterize the conjugation of some third conjugation verbs and serve to distinguish between the singular and the plural in the present indicative and between the indicative and the subjunctive in the present singular. There are four classes of correspondences, illustrated in Table 5.6 with the present indicative. The verbs which submit to these alternations are relatively few; the following list provides the most common:

    (i) *tenir* 'to hold', *venir* 'to come', and all their derivatives (e.g. *appartenir* 'to belong', *contenir* 'to contain', *retenir* 'to hold', *soutenir* 'to support'; *devenir* 'to become', *prévenir* 'to warn', *revenir* 'to come back', *se souvenir* 'to remember');

    (ii) *joindre* 'to join' and its derivatives (e.g. *rejoindre* 'to rejoin');

    (iii) *craindre* 'to fear', *éteindre* 'to switch off', *peindre* 'to paint', *plaindre* 'to pity';

    (iv) *prendre* 'to take' and its derivatives (e.g. *apprendre* 'to learn', *comprendre* 'to understand', *surprendre* 'to surprise').

5.4. Contrastive study

It is generally held that English, as opposed to French, does not have nasal vowels. Yet English (certain varieties of American and Australian English in particular) is frequently perceived – and rightly so – as a 'nasal' language (one often speaks of a characteristic 'nasal twang', which may be more or less marked depending on the speaker). So, how can one maintain that there are no nasal vowels in English?

We have seen that in French, vowel nasality plays an important functional role (a distinctive role). Like lip rounding (*lit* [li] 'bed' – *lu* [ly] 'read') or degrees of aperture (*dit* [di] 'said' – *dé* [de] 'thimble'), vowel nasality allows meaning distinctions among words (*mais* [mɛ] 'but' – *main* [mɛ̃] 'hand'). By contrast, in English, vowel nasality does not play a distinctive role. Whether the word *bye* (as in *good-bye*) is pronounced with an oral or a nasal vowel does not matter much; this characterizes in part a given speaker's manner of speech, but in either case the same meaning is conveyed. In French, however, the same semantic message is not conveyed if [sɛk] (*sec* 'dry') is pronounced rather than [sɛ̃k] (*cinq* 'five'), or [atɑ̃dr] (*attendre* 'to wait') rather than [ɑ̃tɑ̃dr] (*entendre* 'to hear'), or [po] (*peau* 'skin') rather than [põ] (*pont* 'bridge'). For this reason, it is essential in French to maintain oral vowels as oral as possible, so as to keep them separate from nasal vowels; in English, the same precautions are not necessary. One could say that in English, the velum is much freer than in French; during the production of vowels, it may be lowered indiscriminately and with semantic impunity to allow air to pass through the nasal cavity; this is indeed what often occurs in American and Australian English, hence the general impression of a strong nasality in these varieties of English. When it is, nevertheless, claimed that English has no nasal vowels, it is important to understand that the perspective then is not purely phonetic, but rather functional: vowel nasality does not serve to create meaning distinctions in English; it does not play a distinctive role.

In all languages, when a vowel precedes a nasal consonant, the velum has a tendency to lower before the articulation of the consonant begins, i.e. during the production of the vowel. This anticipation of the lowering of the velum causes a partial nasalization of the vowel; the nasalization may be more or less perceptible, depending on the timing of the lowering of the velum. In standard French, the nasalization of a vowel in front of a nasal consonant is much less striking than in English; from a practical point of view, one may even consider that, in comparison with English, French oral vowels remain completely oral in front of nasal consonants. The examples in Table 5.7 illustrate the difference between standard French and English. (Note, however, that in other varieties of French, such as Quebec French, vowels are strongly nasalized before nasal consonants.)

With this difference between English and standard French, we come to what is perhaps the most acute problem that vowel nasality poses for the English speaker learning French. In a superficially paradoxical way, the difficulty for the English speaker lies not so much in producing the nasal vowels where they should occur, but rather in avoiding producing them where they should not occur. Thus, in alternations of the [Ṽ]–[VN] type described above, and more generally, in all cases where an oral vowel precedes a nasal consonant in French, special care must be taken to maintain the oral vowel which precedes the nasal consonant as oral as possible (that is, to nasalize it as little as possible). In addition to the types of words given in Tables 5.5–7, adverbs of the type *certainement* [sɛrtɛnmɑ̃] 'certainly' are privileged candidates for improper nasalization

Table 5.7. Vowel nasalization (French vs English)

Standard French			English	
il dîne	[ildin]	'he dines'	dean	[dīn]
certaine	[sɛrtɛn]	'sure'	ten	[tɛ̃n]
panne	[pan]	'breakdown'	pan	[pæ̃n]
boum	[bum]	'boom'	boom	[būm]
bonne	[bɔn]	'good'	bone	[bōn]

by English speakers (who tend to say *[sɛrtɛ̃nmɑ̃] or even *[sɛrtɛ̃mɑ̃]; the asterisks indicate incorrect pronunciations).

Thus the nasality of a vowel in English is often due to the presence of a subsequent nasal consonant. Probably because of this natural association, and perhaps also because French orthography marks the presence of a nasal vowel by means of vowel-letters followed by the nasal consonant-letters *m* or *n*, English speakers frequently tend to have French nasal vowels followed by a nasal consonantal appendage, especially when another consonant follows (saying, for example, *[tõ^{m}be] instead of [tõbe] for *tomber* 'to fall', *[tɑ̃^{n}te] instead of [tɑ̃te] for *tenter* 'to tempt'). To avoid this consonantal excrescence, which does not occur in standard French, it is necessary to synchronize the raising of the velum with the ending of the articulation of the nasal vowel. One can gain an idea of the desired objective by isolating the syllable containing a nasal vowel from the following syllable, thus by pronouncing [tõ–be] and [tɑ̃–te], for example, with a slight pause between the two syllables, before moving on to a normal speech rate.

In southern French, nasal vowels *are* followed by a nasal consonantal appendage which has the same place of articulation as the following consonant (if there is one), or which is [ŋ] if the nasal vowel ends the word. In addition, in this type of speech, nasal vowels are often only partially nasalized and their articulations may differ appreciably from what may be observed in standard French.

5.5. Historical sketch

We have seen that in English in particular, a vowel is naturally nasalized before a nasal consonant (compare, for example, the pronunciations of *can* [kæ̃n], *Ben* [bɛ̃n], and *thin* [θĩn] with those of *cat* [kæt], *bet* [bɛt], and *thick* [θɪk]). When the sequence 'vowel + nasal consonant' is followed by a voiceless stop, the nasal consonant may disappear altogether (*can't* [kæ̃t], *bent* [bɛ̃t], *think* [θĩk]). We then have phonetic contrasts of the type [V]–[Ṽ] (oral vowel – nasal vowel): for example, *cat* [kæt] – *can't* [kæ̃t],

Table 5.8. History of French nasal vowels

	bon	*bonne*	*bonté*	Historical phenomena
Old French	[bõn]	[bõnə]	[bõnte]	nasalization: VN → ṼN
Middle French	[bõ]	[bɔnə]	[bõte]	i. nasal consonant deletion: ṼN → Ṽ in the same syllable ii. denasalization: ṼNV → VNV
Modern French	[bõ]	[bɔn]	[bõte]	deletion of final ə

bet [bɛt] – *bent* [bɛ̃t], *thick* [θɪk] – *think* [θɪ̃k]. This phenomenon is comparable to what is found in French, except that in English, the contexts in which these contrasts obtain are limited, and the pronunciations with a nasal consonant sounded are always possible, for example if the speech rate is slower or the pronunciation more deliberate (*can't* [kænt], *bent* [bɛ̃nt], *think* [θɪ̃ŋk]).

The nasalization of an oral vowel before a nasal consonant and the subsequent deletion of the nasal consonant in some contexts are exactly the phonetic processes which resulted in the emergence of nasal vowels in the history of the French language. In Old French, vowels became strongly nasalized before a nasal consonant ([VN] → [ṼN]). Later, in Middle French, the nasal consonants disappeared when they were in the same syllable as the nasal vowels (i.e. when the sequence [ṼN] was at the end of a word or stood before a consonant), whereas the nasal vowels were denasalized when the nasal consonants belonged to the following syllable (i.e. when the sequence [ṼN] preceded a vowel). To illustrate briefly, Table 5.8 schematically traces the historical evolution of the words *bon* 'good' (masculine), *bonne* 'good' (feminine), and *bonté* 'goodness'.

Over the centuries, the qualities of nasal vowels have changed in a special way and their number has been reduced. In particular, [ĩ] became [ɛ̃] (*fin* [fɛ̃] 'thin'), [ỹ] became [œ̃] and then [ɛ̃] (*un* [œ̃]–[ɛ̃] 'a'), and [ẽ] became [ã] and then [ɑ̃] (*vendre* [vɑ̃dr] 'to sell'). We begin to see now why the nasal vowels [ɛ̃] and [ɑ̃] in particular are transcribed in today's orthography by means of several vowel-letters (cf. Section 5.1): the orthography continues to reflect phonetic distinctions which existed in the past, but have been neutralized since.

With denasalization, the nasal vowels which came from the closed vowels [i] and [y] regained their original closed quality (*fine* [fin] 'thin', *une* [yn] 'a'). By contrast, when the [ã] coming from [e] was denasalized (before the change to [ɑ̃]), it did not retrieve the quality of its original oral vowel; it simply became [a]; this is what explains the pronunciation [a] of the letter *e* in words such as *couenne* [kwan] 'rind', *évidemment* [evidamɑ̃] 'obviously', *femme* [fam] 'woman', and *rouennais* [rwanɛ] 'from Rouen'.

5.6. Nasal vowels and orthography

We have already observed that in French, nasal vowels are always represented in the orthography by a *VN* spelling. The question is to know exactly when this spelling actually represents a nasal vowel ([Ṽ]) and when it represents an oral vowel followed by a nasal consonant ([VN]). As a rule, an orthographic sequence of the *VN* type corresponds to a nasal vowel in the pronunciation in two cases: (i) at the end of a word, and (ii) before a consonant-letter other than *m* or *n*. By contrast, in an orthographic sequence of the *VN(N)V* type (the parentheses around *N* indicate that *N* may or may not be present), the string *VN(N)* generally corresponds to an oral vowel followed by a nasal consonant in the pronunciation. Table 5.9 illustrates these general correspondences between spelling and pronunciation (the symbol # designates the end of a word and *C* represents an oral consonant).

The historical sketch presented in the preceding section helps us understand these correspondences, especially if one keeps in mind the principle that, roughly speaking, modern French orthography represents older pronunciations in a fixed state. First, we can grasp why nasal vowels are transcribed by means of vowel-letters followed by the nasal consonant-letters *m* and *n*, and why in general these sequences of letters denote a nasal vowel only at the end of a word or before a consonant: a vowel could be nasalized only before a nasal consonant and the nasal consonant could disappear only if it belonged to the same syllable as the vowel, that is, only if it was at the end of a word or stood before another consonant. Secondly, we can understand better why a vowel-letter which is found before a simple or double nasal consonant-letter followed by another vowel-letter is generally oral: this context is exactly that of denasalization. (The double nasal consonant was once an orthographic device used in certain cases to indicate that the preceding vowel was

Table 5.9. Nasal vowels and orthography

Orthography	*VN#*	*VNC*	*VN(N)V*	
Pronunciation of *VN(N)*	[Ṽ]		[VN]	
Examples	*fin* *certain* *bon* *en*	*intéressant* *plainte* *bonté* *enfant*	*finesse* *certaine* *amener* *femme*	(thin, interesting, subtlety) (sure, complaint, sure [fem.]) (good, goodness, to bring) (in, child, woman)

Table 5.10. The prefix *en*-[ã]

(a)	*em*porter	[ãpɔrte]	(from *porter* 'to carry')	'to take away'
	*en*rager	[ãraʒe]	(from *rage* 'rage')	'to enrage'
	*en*sabler	[ãsable]	(from *sable* 'sand')	'to silt up'
(b)	*em*merder	[ãmɛrde]	(from *merde* 'shit')	'to annoy'
	*em*murer	[ãmyre]	(from *mur* 'wall')	'to wall up'
	*en*noblir	[ãnɔblir]	(from *noble* 'noble')	'to ennoble'
(c)	*en*herber	[ãnɛrbe]	(from *herbe* 'grass')	'to grow grass'
	s'*en*ivrer	[sãnivre]	(from *ivre* 'drunk')	'to get drunk'
	s'*en*orgueillir	[sãnɔrgœjir]	(from *orgueil* 'pride')	'to boast'
	s'*en*amourer	[sãnamure]	(from *amour* 'love')	'to become enamoured'

nasal; it was not meant to indicate that the nasal consonant was doubled in the pronunciation.)

A few special cases do stray from these general principles of correspondence between spelling and pronunciation, but they have their own internal logic. There are five cases to be considered:

(i) After vacillating for a long time between a pronunciation with [ã] and a pronunciation with [a], the word *ennui* 'boredom' and its derivatives (for example, *ennuyer* 'to bore', *ennuyeux* 'boring') are today pronounced with an initial nasal vowel ([ãnɥi], [ãnɥije], [ãnɥijø]), contrary to the general rule.

(ii) All the words which contain the prefix *en*- (or its variant *em*- before the consonant-letters *p*, *b*, and *m*) are pronounced with an initial nasal vowel: [ã]. This principle applies not only when the rest of the word begins with an oral consonant (conforming to the general rule), but also when it begins with a nasal consonant or a vowel (see Table 5.10).

The last three words in Table 5.10 are sometimes pronounced with the oral vowel [e] instead of the nasal vowel [ã]; the tendency then is to write them with the letter *é* (for example s'*énivrer* [senivre]), which causes them to be read in the same manner as, for instance, s'*énerver* [senɛrve] 'to get nervous' and *énoncer* [enõse] 'to enunciate'.

(iii) It is useful to note here the pronunciation of a few words which contain the orthographic sequences *nm* and *mn* between two vowel-letters. The sequence *nm* is rare; it is found in the adverb *néanmoins* 'nevertheless', the noun *mainmise* 'influence', and the simple past forms *nous tînmes* 'we held', and *nous vînmes* 'we came'. In such cases, the *n* serves to indicate nasality on the preceding vowel and is not itself pronounced, but the following *m* is sounded: [neãmwɛ̃] (like *nez en moins* 'minus the nose'), [mɛ̃miz], [tɛ̃m], [vɛ̃m].

There are many more words with the orthographic sequence *mn*; in these words, the preceding vowel is always oral, but the pronunciation of *mn* varies:

(a) In the words *automne* 'autumn', *damner* 'to damn', and their derivatives (*automnal* 'autumnal', *condamner* 'to condemn'), the *m* is silent: [otɔn], [otɔnal], [dane], [kõdane].

(b) In the word *indemne* 'uninjured', it is the *n* which is silent: [ɛ̃dɛm] (but some speakers pronounce [ɛ̃dɛmn]).

(c) In the rest of the words, *mn* is pronounced [mn], for example: *Agamemnon* [agamɛmnõ], *amnésie* [amnezi] 'amnesia', *calomnie* [kalɔmni] 'slander', *gymnase* [ʒimnaz] 'gymnasium', *indemniser* [ɛ̃demnize] 'to indemnify', *indemnité* [ɛ̃demnite] 'indemnity', *insomnie* [ɛ̃sɔmni] 'insomnia', *omnibus* [ɔmnibys] 'omnibus', *omnipotent* [ɔmnipɔtã] 'omnipotent', *somnoler* [sɔmnɔle] 'to drowse'.

(iv) With one exception (see below), the prefix *in-/im-* follows the general rule. Thus, the following pronunciations occur: an oral vowel in words like *inactif* [inaktif] 'inactive', *inoubliable* [inublijabl] 'unforgettable', *inné* [ine] 'innate', *immortel* [imɔrtɛl] 'immortal', and a nasal vowel in words like *impossible* [ɛ̃pɔsibl] 'impossible', and *insortable* [ɛ̃sɔrtabl] 'uncouth'. Notice that in the cases where these words contain a double *n* or a double *m* (one belonging to the prefix, the other to the base word), it is usually possible to pronounce the two *n*s or the two *m*s: *inné* [ine] ~ [inne], *immortel* [imɔrtɛl] ~[immɔrtɛl].

The prefix *in-/im-* does not follow the general rule and is always pronounced [ɛ̃] when the following conditions are met: (a) the prefix is adjoined to an adjective which begins with [n] or [m]; (b) this adjective ends with the suffix *-able*; (c) the adjective ending in *-able* is productively derived from a verb; and (d) the prefixed adjective has the meaning opposite to that of the unprefixed adjective. When these conditions are met, the orthographic sequences *innV* and *immV* are pronounced with a nasal vowel ([ɛ̃nV], [ɛ̃mV]). Consider the following example: from the verb *nettoyer* 'to clean', the adjective *nettoyable* 'cleanable' can be freely constructed, and from this adjective, its antonym, *innettoyable*, can be formed. *Innettoyable* is pronounced [ɛ̃netwajabl], with the initial nasal vowel [ɛ̃] and not the oral vowel [i]. For all adjectives of this type, the prefix *in-/im-* is pronounced [ɛ̃]. (Sometimes, pronunciations with [i] are given for *immangeable* 'inedible', *immanquable* 'inevitable', and *innavigable* 'unnavigable', but the pronunciations with [ɛ̃] seem far more common.)

Counter-examples are only apparent and may be reduced to three main types illustrated by the following cases:

(a) The adjectives *innombrable* and *innommable* have an initial oral vowel ([i(n)nõbrabl], [i(n)nɔmabl]). The reason for this is that condition (d) above is not met. Thus, *innombrable* [i(n)nõbrabl] has the meaning 'very numerous' and is not directly related semantically to the technical terms *nombrer* 'to number' and *nombrable* 'numerable'. (In a technical sense, to express the opposite of *nombrable*, *non-nombrable* [nõnõbrabl] would be used rather than *innombrable* [ɛ̃nõbrabl], and *innombrable* [i(n)nõbrabl] would be impossible.) Likewise, *innommable* [i(n)nɔmabl] has the meaning of 'horrible' and is not directly related semantically to the verb *nommer* 'to name' or to the adjective *nommable* 'nameable'. (Here, to express the opposite of *nommable*, *non-nommable* [nõnɔmabl] would probably be preferred over *innommable* [ɛ̃nɔmabl], and *innommable* [i(n)nɔmabl] would be impossible.)

(b) An initial oral vowel is also found in the adjective *immuable* [i(m)mɥable] 'unchanging'. The reason for this is that this word is not the result of a productive word-formation process, so that condition (c) above is not met. Today, the suffix *-able* can be freely added to a verb only if the verb is transitive (i.e. if it can take a direct object). The presence of the suffix *-able* allows the direct object of the verb to be qualified by the adjective thus formed, which therefore has a passive meaning. For example, *nettoyable* [nɛtwajabl] and *innettoyable* [ɛ̃netwajable] come from the verb *nettoyer*, a transitive verb (cf. *Jean nettoie ses chemises* 'John cleans his shirts'), and they can refer to an object of the verb and describe it as 'being able/not being able to be cleaned'. The situation is completely different in the case of *immuable* [i(m)mɥable]. This adjective refers to something which does not change, rather than to something which cannot be changed; it allows a reference to the subject of the verb *muer* 'to change' and thus has an active meaning. In this particular function, the suffix *-able* is no longer used productively; it is found only in a few adjectives such as *convenable* 'proper' (= 'qui convient'), *durable* 'durable' (= 'qui dure'), and *valable* 'worth it' (= 'qui vaut quelque chose'). The prefix *in-/im-* combines with these adjectives only in restricted and idiosyncratic fashion; thus *immuable* exists, but not **inconvenable*, **indurable*, or **invalable* (the asterisk serves to indicate that these words do not exist in the language). The very formation of the word *immuable* thus excludes it from the productive class of adjectives ending in *-able* described above, where the prefix *in-/im-* has the pronunciation [ɛ̃].

(c) The adjective *immergeable* [i(m)mɛrʒabl] 'that can be submerged' also contains an initial oral vowel. The reason is that this word is not derived from an adjective **mergeable*, which itself would come from a verb **merger*. Neither the verb **merger*, nor the adjective **mergeable* exists in French. Rather, the adjective *immergeable* is derived from the verb *immerger* 'to submerge', which is pronounced [i(m)mɛrʒe], in accordance with the general rules of correspondence between spelling and pronunciation. If a transitive verb *merger* existed, the adjective *mergeable* and its opposite *immergeable* would be possible words, but the latter would be pronounced [ɛ̃mɛrʒabl] and would have a meaning quite different from that of the existing adjective *immergeable* [i(m)mɛrʒabl]; [ɛ̃mɛrʒabl] would mean 'qui ne peut pas être mergé', whereas [i(m)merʒabl] means 'qui peut être immergé'. The same type of demonstration is possible with other adjectives, such as *immolable* [i(m)mɔlabl] 'that can be sacrificed', which comes from *immoler* [i(m)mɔle] 'to sacrifice' and not from **moler* through **molable*, and *immortalisable* [i(m)mɔrtalizabl] 'that can be immortalized', which comes from *immortel* [i(m)mɔrtɛl] 'immortal' through *immortaliser* [i(m)mɔrtalize] 'to immortalize' and not from *mortel* 'mortal' through *mortaliser*, a conceivable verb meaning 'to make mortal' (so that *immortalisable* pronounced [ɛ̃mɔrtalizabl] could only mean 'that cannot be made mortal').

In summary, the pronunciation [ɛ̃] of the prefix *in-/im-* followed by a nasal consonant occurs only when used with adjectives in *-able* derived productively from verbs and when, semantically, the prefix negates the adjective in *-able*.

(v)   The last special case concerns words whose orthographic structure would seem to predict the pronunciation of a nasal vowel, but where in fact a [VN] phonetic sequence is found. Some examples are given in Table 5.11. These words are typically borrowed words whose phonetic structure does not exhibit any feature uncharacteristic of French and which are thus perfectly well integrated in the language from this point of view. However, they maintain an orthographic structure which, given their pronunciation, does not seem to fit the usual mold. The display in Table 5.12 illustrates these two points by contrasting the pronunciation

Table 5.11. *VN* as [VN] word-finally and before consonants

abdome*n*	[abdɔmɛn]	'abdomen'	géran*ium*	[ʒeranjɔm]	'geranium'
alb*um*	[albɔm]	'album'	hare*m*	[arɛm]	'harem'
bi*n*se	[bins]	'mess'	inté*rim*	[ɛ̃terim]	'interim'
Camer*oun*	[kamrun]	'Cameroon'	macad*am*	[makadam]	'macadam'
cla*m*ser	[klamse]	'to croak'	spri*nt*	[sprint]	'sprint'
clo*wn*	[klun]	'clown'	week-*end*	[wikɛnd]	'week-end'

Table 5.12. *VN* as [VN] (pronunciation vs orthography)

Pronunciation		Orthography			
[abdomɛn]	– [amɛn]	abdome*n*	– am*ène*	'abdomen'	– 'brings'
[albɔm]	– [pɔm]	alb*um*	– *pomme*	'album'	– 'apple'
[klamse]	– [amsõ]	cla*m*ser	– ha*meç*on	'to croak'	– 'hook'
[makadam]	– [madam]	macad*am*	– mad*ame*	'macadam'	– 'Mrs'

Table 5.13. *CVN* as [CVN] word-finally

Spelling	Pronunciation	Examples	Exceptions	
Cam	[Cam]	Abraham, islam, quidam, tam-tam	Adam [adɑ̃]	(Abraham, Islam, somebody, tam-tam; Adam)
Cem	[Cɛm]	idem, sachem, tandem, totem		(the same, sachem, tandem, totem)
Cim	[Cim]	intérim		(interim)
Cum	[Cɔm]	maximum, minimum, décorum	parfum [parfɛ̃]	(maximum, minimum, decorum; perfume)
Cen	[Cɛn]	dolmen, hymen, pollen, spécimen	examen [egzamɛ̃] Agen [aʒɛ̃]	(dolmen, hymen, pollen, specimen; examination, name of town)

Table 5.14. Pronunciation of *VN* sequences (summary)

A. *General rules*
  1. [Ṽ] at the end of words and before *C* (*fin* [fɛ̃], *bon* [bõ], *bonté* [bõte])

  2. [VN] before (*N*)*V* (*fine* [fin], *finesse* [finɛs], *bonne* [bɔn], *bonifier* [bɔnifje])

B. *Special cases*
  1. [VN] at the end of words with some specific spellings (*islam* [islam], *idem* [idɛm], *intérim* [ɛ̃terim], *maximum* [maksimɔm], *abdomen* [abdɔmɛn])

  2. [Ṽ] before (*N*)*V*
     (i) *ennui* [ɑ̃nɥi] and derived words
     (ii) the prefix *en-/em-*: *emmurer* [ɑ̃myre]
                                ennoblir [ɑ̃nɔblir]
                                s'enivrer [sɑ̃nivre]
     (iii) *néanmoins* [neɑ̃mwɛ̃]
     (iv) adjectives with the structure [in[verb + able]] (*innettoyable* [ɛ̃netwajabl])

---

and orthography of such words with the pronunciation and orthography of fully integrated words. All the same, it is worth noting that at least at the end of words, a number of spellings of the type *CVN* correlate quite generally with an oral vowel pronunciation. Table 5.13 lists them with examples and exceptions.

We recapitulate in Table 5.14 the relations which hold between orthography and pronunciation for nasal vowels and [VN] sequences.

5.7. Nasal vowels and liaison

Let us consider for a moment the possessive adjective *son* 'his/her/its'. When this word is cited in isolation, it is pronounced [sõ]. To say *son livre* 'his book', one also pronounces [sõ], and then [livr]: [sõlivr]. But to say *son arbre* 'his tree', one does not simply produce [sõ] and then [arbr]; an [n] is introduced between the two words: [sõnarbr]. Liaison (or linking) is said to have occurred. More generally, liaison is the appearance of a consonant between two given words, under certain conditions. The conditions for the appearance of liaison consonants are roughly the following: the second word must begin with a vowel and the syntactic relation between the two words must be relatively close. The nature of the liaison consonant depends on the first word. Thus, there are liaisons not only with [n] (*son arbre* [sõnarbr]), but also with [t] (*petit arbre* [pœtitarbr] 'small tree'), with [z] (*petits arbres* [pœtizarbr] 'small trees'), with [r] (*dernier arbre* [dɛrnjerarbr] 'last tree'), and more rarely, with [p] (*trop actif* [tropaktif] 'too active') and [g] (*long été* [lõgete] 'long summer'). We shall come back to these questions in more detail in Chapter 11. What specifically concerns us in this chapter are the words governing liaison with [n], because these words end in a nasal vowel which in liaison may, depending on the case, remain nasal or on the contrary be denasalized. Thus, in *son arbre*, the [õ] of *son* remains nasal: [sõnarbr]; but in *bon ami* 'good friend' (masculine), the [õ] of *bon* becomes oral: [bɔnami] (so that [bɔnami] may mean *bon ami* as well as the corresponding feminine *bonne amie*).

Before separating the cases of denasalization from the cases where vowel nasality is preserved, let us review the words governing liaison with [n] and the contexts in which this [n] may appear (we shall assume throughout that the phonetic condition requiring the following word to begin with a vowel is met). Our first category of words will comprise noun modifiers. Here we find qualifying adjectives, the most common of which are *bon* 'good', *ancien* 'old', *certain* 'certain', *plein* 'full', and *prochain* 'next', the possessive adjectives *mon* 'my', *ton* 'your', and *son* 'his/her/ its', and the determiners *un* 'a' and *aucun* 'no'. These words enter into *obligatory liaison* ('liaison obligatoire') with the following modified noun or with the qualifying adjective preceding the noun: *bon-ami* 'good friend', *son-ancien-étudiant* 'his former student', *certain-âge* 'certain age', *plein-emploi* 'full employment', *prochain-ambassadeur* 'next ambassador', *un-arbre* 'a tree', *un-ancien-amiral* 'a former admiral', *aucun-animal* 'no animal' (obligatory liaison is indicated here by means of a hyphen).

The words *bien* 'well' and *rien* 'nothing' can be placed together in a second category. The adverb *bien* enters into *optional liaison* ('liaison facultative') with expressions that it modifies: *bien/ancien* 'really old', *bien/appris* 'well learned', *bien/amèrement* 'very bitterly', *il est bien/à plaindre* 'he really is to be pitied' (optional liaison is indicated here by means of a slashed hyphen). Liaison is not made in cases such as *il se plaît bien/à Paris* 'he likes it well in Paris', *est-ce bien/ou mal?* 'is it good or bad?', since *bien* does not modify what follows (*prohibited liaison* 'liaison interdite' is indicated here by means of a slash).

With the word *rien*, the situation seems more complex, but one can very approximately say that *rien* enters into optional liaison with the following word in constructions of the type *rien/à manger* 'nothing to eat', *je n'ai rien/entendu* 'I heard nothing', *ne rien/y voir* 'to see nothing', *sans rien/en dire* 'without saying anything about it', where *rien* in a way plays the role of the (preposed) object of the following verb (*manger*, *entendu*, *voir*, *dire*). Otherwise, *rien* does not link with a following word: *un rien/ effraie ce petit chat* 'the slightest thing scares this little cat', *il n'apprend rien/à l'école* 'he learns nothing at school', *il ne voit rien/et n'entend rien* 'he sees nothing and hears nothing', *rien/ou presque* 'nothing, almost'.

In the cases where liaison with *bien* and *rien* is optional, its presence or absence correlates with the style chosen by the speaker: the absence of liaison gives the impression of a relatively colloquial style, whereas its presence gives the impression of a relatively careful style.

The preposition *en* and the pronouns *on* and *en* can be placed in a third (and final) category. As a rule, these words enter into obligatory liaison with the following word if they belong in a construction with it. More precisely, in a prepositional phrase, the preposition *en* obligatorily links with the noun that it governs (*en-argent* 'made of silver', *en-Irlande* 'in Ireland') or with the determiner preceding the noun (*en-aucun cas* 'in no case', *en-un mois* 'in a month').

The pronoun *on* obligatorily links with a following verb of which it is the subject (*on-arrive* 'we are coming') or with the object pronouns which may intervene (*on-y va* 'we are going there', *on-en vient* 'we come from there'). By contrast, liaison is prohibited in cases such as *va-t-on/arriver?* 'are we going to get there?', *va-t-on/y venir?* 'are we going to come to it?', *va-t-on/à Paris?* 'are we going to Paris?', where *on* is in a construction with the preceding verb – it is the (inverted) subject of *va*, hence the linking *t* – but not with what follows (*arriver*, *y venir*, *à Paris*).

The pronoun *en* obligatorily links with a following verb to which it is 'grammatically attached' (*il en-a* 'he has some', *il en-achètera plusieurs* 'he will buy several', *va en-acheter* 'go buy some'). To understand what I mean by 'grammatically attached', consider the imperative sentence *fais-en/acheter* 'have (somebody) buy some', where liaison does not occur between *en* and *acheter*, and contrast it with the other imperative sentence *va en-acheter* 'go buy some', where liaison must occur between *en* and *acheter*. These two different types of liaison behavior suggest two different types of 'grammatical attachment' between the pronoun *en* and the verb *acheter*. While word order in these imperative sentences is not helpful in determining whether or not *en* 'grammatically attaches' to *acheter*, the corresponding declarative sentences are revealing: one says *J'en fais acheter* 'I have (somebody) buy some', not **Je fais en acheter*, but one says *Je vais en acheter* 'I am going to buy some', not **J'en vais acheter*. These sentences show clearly that in constructions with '*faire* + infinitive', *en* is grammatically attached to *faire*, not to the infinitive, whereas in constructions with '*aller* + infinitive', *en* is grammatically attached to the infinitive, not to *aller*. The facts of liaison in *fais-en/acheter* and *va en-acheter* follow from this distinction. Similarly, in sentences such as *achètes-en/un* 'buy one', liaison is prohibited between *en* and *un* because *en* is grammatically attached to *acheter*, not to *un* (cf. *J'en-achète un* 'I buy one').

Let us now separate denasalization cases from cases where vowel nasality is preserved in liaison. Here there are many dialectal variations. In standard French (Dialect I in Table 5.15), denasalization occurs with

Table 5.15. Nasal vowels in liaison (summary)

	[ṼnV]	[VnV]	Tendencies
Dialect v	all	none	stable
Dialect iv	*ancien, certain,* etc *mon, ton, son* *un, aucun* *bien, rien* *on, en*	*bon*	iv→v
Dialect i	*mon, ton, son* *un, aucun* *bien, rien* *on, en*	*bon, ancien,* etc.	i→iv
Dialect ii	*un, aucun* *bien, rien* *on, en*	*bon, ancien,* etc. *mon, ton, son*	ii→i
Dialect iii	none	all	stable

the qualifying adjectives cited above (*bon, ancien, certain, plein, prochain*), but the other words keep their nasal vowel in liaison. Among these words must be included the adjective *commun* in the expressions *d'un commun accord* [dɛ̃kɔmɛ̃nakɔr] 'in joint agreement' and *par/dans un commun effort* [par/dɑ̃zɛ̃kɔmɛ̃nefɔr] 'in a joint effort', which constitute the only cases where *commun* may naturally appear before a noun.

In some dialects, speakers denasalize in more cases than in standard French. Thus, a second type of pronunciation (Dialect ii in Table 5.15) can be distinguished from standard French in that, in addition to the qualifying adjectives *bon, ancien, certain, plein,* and *prochain,* the possessive adjectives *mon, ton,* and *son* are also denasalized. This type of pronunciation can be heard in the region of Lyons. In a third type of dialect (Dialect iii in Table 5.15), denasalization is found throughout. This pronunciation is characteristic of southern French.

Other dialects also exist which denasalize less than standard French. Thus, there are speakers who keep nasal vowels throughout, except with the adjective *bon* (Dialect iv in Table 5.15). This type of pronunciation can be observed in Paris and in Quebec. Finally, there are speakers who keep nasal vowels throughout, even in the adjective *bon* (Dialect v in Table 5.15). This type of pronunciation is often found in the French spoken in North Africa.

With the exception of the dialect of southern France (Dialect iii), it seems that the dominant tendency is toward keeping nasal vowels in liaison. Thus, the geographic distribution of Dialect ii today seems to have reduced in comparison with what it was, for example, at the beginning of the eighteenth century or even in the first half of the twentieth century. In addition, the pronunciations characteristic of Dialects ɪv and v clearly appear as innovative tendencies in the very domain where standard French is spoken (a summary of these tendencies is diagrammed in the right-hand column of Table 5.15).

Table 5.15 recapitulates across dialects and word categories the different types of distribution of the oral and nasal pronunciations of nasal vowels in liaison.

6

E

6.1. Introduction

We said in Chapter 3 (p. 34) that contrary to vowels in English, vowels in standard French are not reduced and always preserve their full quality. As we shall see in this chapter, there actually exists an important case of vowel reduction in French, but it affects only one particular vowel under certain well-defined conditions. In addition, when this vowel is reduced, it is reduced to nothing: it completely disappears from the pronunciation. Otherwise, it appears as a full-fledged vowel, namely [œ]. The word *petit* 'small' may thus be pronounced [pœti] or [pti], depending on the context. This exceptional vowel is known under many names, among others: mute *e* ('*e* muet'), feminine *e* ('*e* féminin'), unstable *e* ('*e* instable'), fleeting *e* ('*e* caduc'), and schwa. Here we shall simply speak of *e*, since the vowel whose behavior we wish to study is generally written this way in French orthography.

Since orthography, rather than sounds, constitutes our strategic point of departure in this chapter, and since *e* is used in French orthography with many different values, it is necessary to define precisely the specific category of *e* which concerns us here. Briefly, it consists of the *e*s which occur between two consonants or at the end of a word, and which correspond to the sound [œ] when they are pronounced. The words in Table 6.1 contain examples of relevant *e*s.

E has many other values in French orthography; in particular, the following types of *e* can also be found:

(i) *e*s which are part of vowel digraphs or trigraphs such as *ei* (*pleine* [plɛn] 'full', *teint* [tɛ̃] 'complexion'), *eu* (*ceux* [sø] 'these', *peur* [pœr] 'fear'), *œu* (*bœuf* [bœf] 'ox', *sœur* [sœr] 'sister'), *eau* (*beau* [bo] 'beautiful', *peau* [po] 'skin');

(ii) *e*s with an auxiliary value allowing the letters *c* and *g* to have the positional phonetic values [s] and [ʒ], instead of the basic phonetic values [k] and [g] (*douceâtre* [dusɑtr] 'soft', *mangeons* [mɑ̃ʒɔ̃] 'let's eat');

(iii) *e*s which, together with the letters *m* or *n*, serve to represent the nasal vowels [ɑ̃] and [ɛ̃] (*encore* [ɑ̃kɔr] 'again', *temps* [tɑ̃] 'weather'; *chien* [ʃjɛ̃] 'dog', *examen* [egzamɛ̃] 'examination');

(iv) *e*s which are found in front of a double consonant-letter, two pronounced consonants, or one word-final consonant-letter, and which

Table 6.1. Words with *e*

brusqu*e*ment	'abruptly'	l*e*	'the'
ch*e*mis*e*s	'shirts'	parl*e*nt	'(they) speak'
certain*e*ment	'certainly'	p*e*tit	'small'
cord*e*	'rope'	sam*e*di	'Saturday'
fenêtr*e*	'window'	tabl*e*	'table'
gross*e*	'fat' (fem.)	v*e*ndr*e*di	'Friday'

represent the sounds [e] or [ɛ] (*effet* [efɛ] 'effect', *espoir* [ɛspwar] 'hope', *exact* [ɛgzakt] 'exact', *est* [ɛst] 'east', *ciel* [sjɛl] 'sky', *chez* [ʃe] 'at');

(v) *e*s with an acute, grave, or circumflex accent, and which also represent the sounds [e] or [ɛ] (*étang* [etã] 'pond', *succès* [syksɛ] 'success', *forêt* [fɔrɛ] 'forest');

(vi) *e*s which are found after vowel-letters and which are never pronounced (*joue* [ʒu] 'cheek', *balbutiement* [balbysimã] 'stammering', *il crie* [ilkri] 'he shouts').

These six varieties of *e* are not our concern in this chapter, and from now on, we shall not be referring to them when we talk about *e*s. The *e*s which interest us, then, are those which have the sound [œ] when they are pronounced. From a phonetic (rather than orthographic) perspective, this means that the sound [œ] may disappear from the pronunciation under certain conditions. But even if these conditions are met, it is not the case that just any [œ] sound may disappear. For example, the two phrases *dans le rétablissement* 'in the re-establishment' and *dans leur établissement* 'in their shop' can be pronounced in exactly the same way ([dãlœretablismã]), but only the first one may be pronounced without the *e* in the second syllable ([dãlretablismã]), because *le* [lœ], but not *leur* [lœr], may lose its [œ]. It is thus necessary to distinguish between two types of [œ]: stable [œ], which never disappears, and unstable [œ], which may disappear. To separate in a convenient way these two categories of [œ], the following device is often used in the literature: unstable [œ] is transcribed with the phonetic symbol [ə] (schwa) and the phonetic symbol [œ] is reserved for stable [œ]; I shall not use this device in this book, as it sometimes leads to the false impression that the sound labeled [ə] sounds different from [œ] when pronounced. Generally, in the orthography, the [œ]s which may disappear are written *e* (*le* [lœ] 'the', *serait* [sœrɛ] '(it) would be') and those which may not are written *eu* or *œu* (*leur* [lœr] 'their', *sœurette* [sœrɛt] 'little sister').

One of the goals of this chapter is to present a description of the main facts concerning the presence and absence of *e* in the pronunciation of standard French. Another goal is to offer foreign students, by way of this description, a series of relatively simple principles facilitating the progressive acquisition of a coherent and natural pronunciation in spontaneous speech. A third goal is to throw some light on a few interesting properties of the sequential organization of sounds in French which the behavior of *e* helps isolate.

6.2. *E*-deletion: general principles

With respect to the conditions of their deletion in the pronunciation, *es* do not all behave in the same way. This is why it is useful to divide them into three categories:

(i) *Final es* ('les *e* finaux'): these are the *es* found at the end of polysyllables (for example: chemis*es* 'shirts', cord*e* 'rope', fenêtr*e* 'window', parl*ent* '(they) speak', tabl*e* 'table').

(ii) *Initial es* ('les *e* initiaux'): these are the *es* found in the first syllable of words (for example: ch*e*mises 'shirts', f*e*nêtre 'window', p*e*tit 'small'). This category also includes the *es* of the nine monosyllables *je*, *me*, *te*, *se*, *le*, *ce*, *de*, *ne*, and *que*.

(iii) *Internal es* ('les *e* internes'): these are the remaining *es*, those found inside words (for example: brusqu*e*ment 'abruptly', sam*e*di 'Saturday', vendr*e*di 'Friday').

We consider in this section the general principles governing the omission of *e* in the pronunciation. In the majority of cases, two simple rules determine where an *e* may or may not be pronounced. The first rule affects final *es*, the second initial and internal *es*.

Rule 1: Final *es* are not pronounced (see Table 6.2 for examples). There are certain circumstances where final *es* may in fact be pronounced. These particular conditions are examined in Section 6.3.2.

Table 6.2. Silent final *es*

brusqu*e*	[brysk]	'abrupt'	fix*e*	[fiks]	'fixed'
certain*e*	[sɛrtɛn]	'certain' (fem.)	gross*e*	[gros]	'fat' (fem.)
chemis*es*	[ʃœmiz]	'shirts'	parl*ent*	[parl]	'(they) speak'
cord*e*	[kɔrd]	'rope'	phonétiqu*e*	[fɔnetik]	'phonetic'
fenêtr*e*	[fœnɛtr]	'window'	tabl*e*	[tabl]	'table'

Rule 2: Internal and initial *es* may be omitted from the pronunciation only if they follow a single pronounced consonant. In other words, *es* preceded by more than one pronounced consonant are sounded. The deletion of *e* after a single pronounced consonant is obligatory for internal *es*, optional for initial *es*. (See Tables 6.3–4 for examples; note that in all following examples, parentheses around the symbol [œ] indicate that the presence of [œ] is optional.)

Table 6.3. Internal *es*

e-deletion			no-deletion		
grand*e*ment	[grãdmã]	'greatly'	brusqu*e*ment	[bryskœmã]	'abruptly'
phonétiqu*e*ment	[fɔnetikmã]	'phonetically'	fix*e*ment	[fiksœmã]	'fixedly'
sam*e*di	[samdi]	'Saturday'	vendr*e*di	[vãdrœdi]	'Friday'

Table 6.4. Initial *es*

e-deletion possible			no deletion		
trois ch*e*mises	[trwaʃ(œ)miz]	'three shirts'	une belle ch*e*mise	[ynbɛlʃœmiz]	'a nice shirt'
la f*e*nêtre	[laf(œ)nɛtr]	'the window'	une f*e*nêtre	[ynfœnɛtr]	'a window'
Henri l*e* voit	[ãril(œ)vwa]	'Henri sees it'	Luc l*e* voit	[lyklœvwa]	'Luke sees it'
pas d*e* scrupules	[pad(œ)skrypyl]	'no scruples'	un squ*e*lette	[ɛ̃skœlɛt]	'a skeleton'
des p*e*tits chats	[dɛp(œ)tiʃa]	'small cats'	sept p*e*tits chats	[sɛtpœtiʃa]	'seven small cats'

Table 6.5. *E-deletion and syllabification*

grand*e*ment	[grãd-mã]	'greatly'
phonétiqu*e*ment	[fɔnɛtik-mã]	'phonetically'
sam*e*di	[sam-di]	'Saturday'
chez l*e* docteur	[ʃel-dɔktœr]	'at the doctor's'
tout l*e* monde	[tul-mõd]	'everybody'
beaucoup d*e* gens	[bokud-ʒã]	'many people'
ça s*e* fait	[sas-fɛ]	'that is done'

An examination of the possible pronunciations for a sentence such as *il me dit* 'he tells me' illustrates the way Rule 2 works. This sentence may be pronounced [ilmœdi]: in conformity with Rule 2, the *e* of *me* is kept in the pronunciation since two pronounced consonants precede it (the [m] of *me* and the [l] of *il*). But, in front of a consonant-initial word, the pronoun *il* may very well lose its [l] (thus, *il vient* 'he is coming' is pronounced [ilvjɛ̃] or [ivjɛ̃]). If this [l] is omitted before *me* in *il me dit*, the *e* of *me* is preceded by only one pronounced consonant, and it may consequently be omitted from the pronunciation, hence [imdi], a very common way of saying *il me dit* in spontaneous speech.

English speakers sometimes have trouble pronouncing the consonant clusters resulting from *e*-deletion by Rule 2. In such cases, the task can be greatly simplified if it is mentally considered that the consonant in front of the (omitted) *e* is pronounced together with the preceding vowel, rather than with the following consonant. Contiguous consonants are thus distributed in two different syllables, which facilitates pronunciation (see Table 6.5 for examples to practise with).

Table 6.6. *E*-deletion and regressive voicing assimilation

ça *se* voit	[sasœvwa]	→	[sazvwa]	'it is obvious'
plus *de* sucre	[plydœsykr]	→	[plytsykr]	'no more sugar'
mais *je* travaille	[mɛʒœtravaj]	→	[mɛʃtravaj]	'but I work'

When two consonants coming into contact because of *e*-deletion are oral stops or fricatives, they tend to be pronounced both voiced or both voiceless, the first consonant borrowing the voicing of the second by *anticipatory* or *regressive assimilation* ('assimilation régressive'); this tendency is particularly clear and commonplace with the subject pronoun *je* (see Table 6.6.).

6.3. *E*-deletion: refinements

As just presented, Rules 1 and 2 provide a global overview of the pronunciation of *es* in standard French. We shall now examine in more detail how these rules function, focusing first on initial and internal *es* (Rule 2) and then on final *es* (Rule 1).

6.3.1. *Initial* es *and internal* es

6.3.1.1. E *in the initial syllable of a group*
We saw that after the application of Rule 2, the consonant found before the unsounded *e* may be thought of as belonging to the same syllable as the preceding vowel. But what happens when a *Ce* sequence (*C* = a single pronounced consonant) begins a sentence or an intonation group within a sentence? According to Rule 2, the *e* should be able to delete, since it is preceded by a single consonant; but if *e*-deletion occurs, this consonant obviously cannot be pronounced together with what stands to its left, since by hypothesis, nothing precedes it; it can therefore only be attached to the following syllable. Under such conditions, the *e* may indeed be dropped in the pronunciation, but its deletion depends on the pronounce-ability of the resulting consonant cluster. The main restriction here affects initial *es* whose deletion would lead to two oral stops or two identical consonants next to each other in syllable-initial position; thus, in Table 6.7, the examples on the left show no deletion and contrast with the examples on the right, where deletion is possible.

By contrast, *e*-deletion in the initial syllable of a group may occur if the resulting consonant cluster contains consonants of a different enough nature, for instance a fricative and a stop (see Table 6.8).

From a practical point of view, it is useful to note that one can always

Table 6.7. No e-deletion in the initial syllable of a group

no e-deletion		e-deletion possible		
de qui parlez-vous?	[dœkiparlevu]	vous parlez de qui?	[vuparled(œ̯)ki]	'about whom are you talking?' / 'you are talking about whom?'
te casse pas la tête	[tœkɑspɑlatɛt]	ne te casse pas la tête	[nœt(œ̯)kɑspɑlatɛt]	'don't worry' / 'don't worry'
debout	[dœbu]	il est debout	[iled(œ̯)bu]	'standing' / 'he is standing'
depuis quatre ans	[dœpɥikatrɑ̃]	c'est depuis quatre ans	[sɛd(œ̯)pɥikatrɑ̃]	'for four years' / 'it has been four years'
dedans	[dœdɑ̃]	là-dedans	[lad(œ̯)dɑ̃]	'inside' / 'inside there'
je joue	[ʒœʒu]	mais je joue	[mɛʒ(œ̯)ʒu]	'I play' / 'but I play'
le lait	[lœlɛ]	dans le lait	[dɑ̃l(œ̯)lɛ]	'the milk' / 'in the milk'
ce salon	[sœsalɔ̃]	dans ce salon	[dɑ̃s(œ̯)salɔ̃]	'this sitting room' / 'in this sitting room'

Table 6.8. *E*-deletion in the initial syllable of a group

*se*coue pas la tête	[s(œ) kupɑlatɛt]	'don't shake your head'
je pense pas	[ʃpɑ̃spɑ] ~ [ʒœpɑ̃spɑ]	'I don't think so'
ce bon à rien	[zbõarjɛ̃] ~ [sœbõarjɛ̃]	'this good-for-nothing'

pronounce initial *e*s occurring at the beginning of intonation groups and still maintain a perfectly natural delivery.

6.3.1.2. E *in contiguous syllables*

An interesting problem arises when initial *e*s occur in contiguous syllables, for instance, to take an extreme case, in *mais de ce que je ne te le redemandais plus,* (*tu en as déduit que je n'en voulais plus*) 'from the fact that I had no longer asked you for it again, (you inferred that I no longer wanted it'). Since each of the nine successive *e*s in this expression is preceded by a single consonant, Rule 2 should theoretically be able to delete all of them, which would yield the unpronounceable *[mɛdskʒntlrdmɑ̃dɛply] (the asterisk indicates an impossible sequence). This example shows that Rule 2 cannot be applied indiscriminately to *e*s occurring in contiguous syllables and that some additional restriction has to be worked in. One way of obtaining the proper outcome is to assume that Rule 2 applies from left to right in the sentence, and that for each application of the rule, the result obtained by the previous application is taken into account.

A simple example will suffice for the purpose of our demonstration: *mais je le veux* 'but I want it'. If Rule 2 is first applied to the *e* of *je*, [mɛʒlœvø] is obtained. If Rule 2 is now tried on the *e* of *le*, it is immediately apparent that the rule will fail to apply, since this *e* is preceded by two consonants (the [ʒ] of *je* and the [l] of *le*). And, indeed, one may say [mɛʒlœvø], but not *[mɛʒlvø]. Since Rule 2 is optional for initial *e*s, let us suppose next that it is not applied to the *e* of *je*; working on [mɛʒœlœvø], Rule 2 may now operate on the *e* of *le*, because it is preceded by a single consonant; the result is [mɛʒœlvø], another possible pronunciation for our example. Again, since Rule 2 is optional for initial *e*s, it might, alternatively, not be applied to the *e* of *le*; a third possible pronunciation of the expression is then obtained: [mɛʒœlœvø]. It must, however, be noted that the more initial *e*s there are in a row, the less one can afford not to apply Rule 2 without falling into a somewhat unnatural style. As a rule of thumb, it can be considered that two consecutive *e*s deletable by Rule 2 may be kept in the pronunciation; beyond that, the pronunciation usually takes on an artificial character, at least in spontaneous conversation in standard French.

Some sequences of monosyllables containing *e*, probably because they occur frequently in speech, tend to have a fixed pronunciation with the same *e* always mute and the same *e* always sounded. Thus, in *ce que*, only the *e* of *ce* may be deleted by Rule 2, never the *e* of *que* (*ce que la mer est belle!* [skœlamɛrɛbɛl] 'how beautiful the ocean is!'). For the sequence *je te*, it seems more natural to have Rule 2 delete the *e* of *je* than the *e* of *te* (*mais je te dois combien?* [mɛʃtœdwakõbjẽ] 'but how much do I owe you?'). It should be noted that the *e*s of *que* and *te* are obligatorily eliminated before a vowel-initial word (*ce qu'elle dit* 'what she says', *je t'attends* 'I am waiting for you'), but what occurs here is *elision* ('l'éli-sion'), a process distinct from Rule 2. The applications of these two rules are not mutually exclusive ([skɛldi], [ʃtatã]). We shall return briefly to the question of elision at the end of this chapter.

The negative particle *ne* exhibits an interesting property with respect to Rule 2: its *e* usually has priority of deletion over immediately surrounding *e*s, which consequently do not undergo Rule 2 themselves (*mais je ne veux pas* [mɛʒœnvøpɑ] 'but I don't want to', *ça ne me dit rien* [sanmœdirjẽ] 'I don't feel like it'). However, when *ne* begins an intonation group, it is preferable to keep its *e* and delete the initial *e* of the following word (*ne me dis rien* [nœmdirjẽ] 'don't tell me anything', *ne le fais pas* [nœlfɛpɑ] 'don't do it'); consonant clusters not favored in syllable-initial position are thus avoided. In spontaneous speech, the word *ne* is very often completely omitted, without semantic loss, as the negative or restrictive meanings belong entirely to the associated particles *pas, plus, que, rien*, etc. in contemporary French (*mais je veux pas* [mɛʒvøpɑ], *ça me dit rien* [samdirjẽ], *me dis rien* [m(œ)dirjẽ], *le fais pas* [l(œ)fɛpɑ]).

6.3.1.3. *Some special cases*
In constraining *e*-deletion, Rule 2 mentions only what precedes *e*, and nothing of what follows. But what follows *e* may actually play a determining role and prevent *e* from being deleted, even if it is preceded by a single consonant. We shall consider next four such cases, and then a fifth case where in a sense the reverse situation occurs, since, as we shall see, an *e* may delete in violation of Rule 2, that is, even though it is preceded by more than one consonant.

H-aspiré words. Initial *e*s in monosyllabic words cannot be deleted before a special class of words traditionally called 'h-aspiré' words. H-aspiré words can be defined as words which, even though they begin with a vowel phonetically, prevent the realization of phenomena such as liaison and elision. As the examples in Table 6.9 show, French words which phonetically begin with a vowel normally allow liaison and elision, but this is not the case with h-aspiré words.

Table 6.9. Liaison and elision

			Regular vowel-initial words		
liaison			*elision*		
le*s* arbres	[lezarbr]	'the trees'	l'arbre	[larbr]	(cf. *le* bel arbre 'the beautiful tree')
le*s* étoiles	[lezetwal]	'the stars'	l'étoile	[letwal]	(cf. *la* belle étoile 'the beautiful star')
			H-aspiré words		
	no liaison			*no elision*	
	le*s* hiboux	[leibu]	'the owls'	*le* hibou	[lœibu]	'the owl'
	le*s* hauteurs	[leotœr]	'the heights'	*la* hauteur	[laotœr]	'the height'

Table 6.10. *E*- deletion and h-aspiré words

beaucoup *de* hiboux	[bokudœibu]	'a lot of owls'
dans *le* haut	[dãlœo]	'at the top'

In the orthography, h-aspiré words often begin with the letter *h*, hence their traditional name. But, in actuality, the *h* is not pronounced and the presence of an initial *h* in the spelling of a word guarantees nothing as to the properties of this word with respect to liaison and elision. Thus, there are many words beginning with *h* which allow liaison and elision (traditionally these words are said to begin with a 'mute *h*'), for instance *homme* 'man' and *hirondelle* 'swallow': *les hommes* [lezɔm], *les hirondelles* [lezirõdɛl]; *l'homme* [lɔm], *l'hirondelle* [lirõdɛl]. And there are words beginning with a vowel-letter which do not allow liaison or elision (these words can be grouped together with h-aspiré words, even though they do not contain an *h* in their spelling), for instance *onze* 'eleven': *les onze joueurs* [leõzʒwœr] 'the eleven players', *le onze août* [lœõzut] 'August 11'.

That a word belongs to the special class of h-aspiré words is an idiosyncratic property of that word: it cannot be deduced from anything about the phonetic or orthographic shape of the word. These words must therefore be learned one by one, which is presumably how native speakers do it. (See Appendix E for a list of the most common h-aspiré words, together with a summary of their main properties.)

Now that we have defined a special class of vowel-initial words (special with respect to their behavior in liaison and elision), the interesting fact here is that Rule 2 does not operate before these words, as shown in Table 6.10.

Why are h-aspiré words exceptions to Rule 2? One could attribute this phenomenon to an additional requirement on the operation of Rule 2 itself: the *e* must not just be preceded by a single consonant, it must also be followed by a consonant; since h-aspiré words begin with a vowel, Rule 2 cannot apply in front of them. An alternative explanation would be to hypothesize that the failure of Rule 2 to apply before h-aspiré words is due to a special property of h-aspiré words (rather than to a more complex formulation of Rule 2). One could in particular try to relate the behavior of h-aspiré words with respect to Rule 2 to their behavior with respect to liaison and elision. Under this type of approach, it seems that what distinguishes this small group of exceptional words from other vowel-initial words is their refusal to accept the application of a rule leading to a syllable restructuration where an external consonant would become agglutinated to their initial vowel within the same syllable. Thus, since a liaison consonant or a consonant before an elided vowel normally enters into the same syllable with the following vowel, we see why neither liaison nor elision can occur before h-aspiré words, since their initial vowels reject such consonantal contact. Similarly, if Rule 2 applied in front of h-aspiré words, we would expect the consonant preceding the (deleted) *e* to want to attach itself to the following vowel, again a process which the initial vowels of h-aspiré words do not allow. The next question, of course, is why the consonant does not attach itself to the preceding vowel. For instance, for the phrase *dans le haut* [dɑ̃lœo] 'at the top', if we cannot get *[dɑ̃.lo], why not [dɑ̃l.o] (the periods in the phonetic transcriptions indicate the demarcation between syllables)? The impossibility of *[dɑ̃l.o] in standard French seems related to the following two general observations: (a) phonetically, in a sequence [VCV], the syllabification normally goes [V.CV], not *[VC.V]; (b) grammatically, the [l] belongs to the following noun *haut* [o] (it is its determiner), not to the preceding preposition *dans* [dɑ̃]. These two reasons then combine to prevent the attachment of [l] to the preceding vowel [ɑ̃]. Since [l] cannot be attached to the following vowel [o] either (*haut* is an h-aspiré word and as such rejects such attachment), in the end we can have neither *[dɑ̃l.o], nor *[dɑ̃.lo]; in addition, the [l] cannot just stand on its own in a syllable (*[dɑ̃.l.o]). The only way out is for Rule 2 not to apply, hence [dɑ̃.lœ.o].

Note in passing that glides which act like consonants, in that they allow neither liaison nor elision, naturally allow the application of Rule 2 (see Table 6.11).

[CLjV] *sequences.* A second case where what follows *e* blocks the application of Rule 2 concerns words containing sequences where the *e* is followed by a liquid ([l] or [r]), a jod ([j]), and a vowel, as in the examples of Table 6.12. If the *e* were deleted in this type of word, phonetic sequences of the form [CLjV] ('consonant + liquid + jod + vowel')

Table 6.11. *E*-deletion and glide-initial words

no liaison			*no elision*		
ces whiskys	[sewiski]	'these whiskeys'	le whisky	[lœwiski]	'the whiskey'
des yaourts	[dejaurts]	'yogurts'	le yaourt	[lœjaurt]	'the yogurt'
les yétis	[lejeti]	'the yetis'	le yéti	[lœjeti]	'the yeti'

Application of Rule 2		
apportez ce whisky	[apɔrtes(œ)wiski]	'bring this whiskey'
donne-lui le yaourt	[dɔnlɥil(œ)jaurt]	'give him the yogurt'
pas de yétis ici	[pad(œ)jetiisi]	'no yetis here'

Table 6.12. *E*-deletion and [CLjV] sequences

atelier	[atœlje]	'workshop'
Richelieu	[riʃœljø]	(surname)
nous chanterions	[nuʃɑ̃tœrjɔ̃]	'we would sing'
vous aideriez	[vuzedœrje]	'you would help'

Table 6.13. The suffix [je] and [CLjV] sequences

sable	[sɑbl]	'sand'	sablier	[sɑblije]	'hourglass'
sucre	[sykr]	'sugar'	sucrier	[sykrije]	'sugar bowl'

Table 6.14. Verb endings and [CLjV] sequences

souffler:	nous soufflions	[nusuflijɔ̃]	'we were blowing'
souffrir:	vous souffriez	[vusufrije]	'you were suffering'

would be produced. It turns out that such sequences are not generally tolerated in French, as can be seen independently by examining other cases where they could in theory arise.

When the suffix *-ier* [-je], which is found, for instance, in the word *banquier* [bɑ̃kje] 'banker' (derived from *banque* [bɑ̃k] 'bank'), is attached to a noun ending in a 'consonant + liquid' cluster, it is not the sequence [CLje] which is finally produced, but rather [CLije] (see Table 6.13). Similarly, words like *peuplier* 'poplar' and *ouvrier* 'worker' contain not [CLje], but [CLije] ([pœplije], [uvrije]).

The same phenomenon can be observed in the speech of many speakers when the endings *-ions* [-jɔ̃] and *-iez* [-je] are added to verb roots ending in a 'consonant + liquid' cluster (see Table 6.14).

The same type of pronunciation regularly occurs when vowel-initial

Table 6.15. Stems ending in [CLi] and [CLjV] sequences

oubli:	oublier	[ublije]	'to forget'
pli:	pliage	[plijaʒ]	'folding'
cri:	nous crions	[nukrijõ]	'we shout'
tri:	vous triez	[vutrije]	'you sort'

endings such as *-er* [-e], *-age* [-aʒ], *-ons* [-õ], and *-ez* [-e] are added to words ending in a [CLi] sequence (see Table 6.15).

In the conditional first and second person plural of first conjugation verbs whose stems end in a consonant (e.g. *demand-: nous demanderions* 'we would ask'; *aim-: vous aimeriez* 'you would like'), some speakers do not always pronounce the *e* which follows the stem. But, significantly, they use the same strategy as that mentioned above to avoid [CLjV] sequences, hence the pronunciations [nudœmãdrijõ], [vuzemrije] (instead of [nudœmãdœrjõ], [vuzemœrje]).

The existence of forms such as *nous parlions* [nuparljõ] 'we were talking' and *vous parliez* [vuparlje] 'you were talking', where [CLjV] sequences are actually found, requires a refinement of our stated constraint on the occurrence of these sequences. In all the cases where a sequence [CLjV] can be found without any restriction, [C] turns out to be a liquid. One could therefore say that sequences of the form [CLjV] are prohibited in French, unless C is a liquid. But a better explanation is available, if one takes into consideration the way in which sounds are allowed to be grouped into syllables. In French words, a syllable break normally occurs between two contiguous liquids (unless they occur word-finally, as in *parle* [parl] 'speak'). Thus, *parler* 'to speak' is syllabified [par.le], and similarly for *parlions* and *parliez*, we have [par.ljõ] and [par.lje]. By contrast, when a stop or a fricative precedes a liquid in a word, the two consonants obligatorily belong to the same syllable; for example, *enfler* 'to swell', *appeler* 'to call', *apprendrons* '(we) will learn', and *demanderons* '(we) will ask' are syllabified [ã.fle], [a.ple], [a.prã.drõ], [dœ.mã.drõ]. The absence of the [œ] after the stem in the verb form *demanderions* [dœmãdœrjõ] would therefore automatically place the [d] in the same syllable as the [r], hence a final syllable [drjõ]. As it is precisely this type of configuration which is not tolerated, the following constraint may be proposed: a syllable may not begin with a consonantal sequence of the form [CLj]. (We shall refine and generalize this constraint in the next chapter.) No violation of the constraint arises when the *e* between [d] and [r] in *demanderions* [dœ.mã.dœ.rjõ]) is pronounced. For speakers who do not pronounce the *e*, the potential problem is circumvented by pronouncing [CLijV] ([dœ.mã.dri.jõ]). For *parlions* [parljõ] and *parliez* [parlje], there is no violation of the constraint, because the syllabic break is located between the two liquids ([par.ljõ], [par.lje]).

In sum, the set of facts examined in this section on [CLjV] sequences naturally follows from regularities about syllable structure in French. In particular it explains the absence of *e*-deletion illustrated earlier in Table 6.12.

The pronoun le. A third case where Rule 2 must not be applied concerns certain usages of the pronoun *le*. In the imperative, when *le* is found after the verb of which it is the object, its *e* has to be preserved in the pronunciation (compare, for example, *donnez-le-moi* [dɔnelœmwa] 'give it to me', where the *e* of *le* must be pronounced, and *René le moissonne* [rœnel(œ)mwasɔn] 'René harvests it', where the *e* of *le* may be deleted). This difference in behavior between postverbal *le* and preverbal *le* can be related to the fact that for first and second person singular object pronouns, different forms are found before and after the verb (*me, te* vs *moi, toi*: *ne me regarde pas*/*regarde-moi* 'don't look at me'/'look at me'). It is as if postverbal *le* were a separate word from preverbal *le*, containing a stable [œ] rather than an unstable one, just as *moi–toi* are different words from *me–te*, containing [wa] rather than unstable [œ]. The fact that postverbal *le* is commonly pronounced [lø] reinforces this view, since stable [œ] is usually pronounced [ø] word-finally (see Chapter 4, Section 4.3.1.3).

As we have just seen, Rule 2 may cause the *e* of *le* to be deleted when *le* precedes the verb. But the *e* of preverbal *le* cannot be deleted when *le* combines with the object pronouns *lui* and *leur* (*tu le lui donneras* [tylœlɥidɔnra] 'you will give it to him', *tu le leur diras* [tylœlœrdira] 'you will tell them about it'). One may, however, omit the pronoun *le* altogether (*tu lui donneras, tu leur diras*) and preserve the meaning of the sentences with *le* (i.e. the presence of a direct object is implied). It is worth noting that the restriction on the application of Rule 2 to *le* in front of *lui* and *leur* is strictly limited to these particular pronoun sequences. The following examples show that Rule 2 can operate in identical phonetic sequences made up of other word combinations: *c'est le luisant* (*qui vous plaît dans cette étoffe*) [sɛl(œ)lɥizã] 'it's the sheen (that you like in this material)'; *c'est le leur* [sɛl(œ)lœr] 'it's theirs'; *tu le leurres toujours* [tyl(œ)lœrtuʒur] 'you always deceive him'.

Other cases. There also exist a few polysyllabic words with initial or internal *e*s that are immune to Rule 2, even though a single consonant precedes, and even though the sequences resulting from a deletion would

Table 6.16. Stable *es*

la belotte	[labœlɔt]	(card game)	(cf. *la blonde*	[lablõd]	'the blonde')
la belette	[labœlɛt]	'the weasel'	(cf. *l'ablette*	[lablɛt]	'the ablet')
champenois	[ʃãpœnwa]	'from Champagne'	(cf. *l'apnée*	[lapne]	'the apnea')
soupeser	[supœze]	'to weigh'	(cf. *l'absent*	[lapsã]	'the absent')
la querelle	[lakœrɛl]	'the quarrel'	(cf. *la crème*	[lakrɛm]	'the cream')
un rebelle	[ɛ̃rœbɛl]	'the rebel'	(cf. *un rebond*	[ɛ̃r(œ)bõ]	'a bounce')
il est velu	[ilɛvœly]	'he is hairy'	(cf. *du velours*	[dyv(œ)lur]	'velvet')

Table 6.17. Contiguous *es* within a word

il est chevelu	[ilɛʃœvly]	'he has a lot of hair'
sa chevelure	[saʃœvlyr]	'his hair'
échevelé	[eʃœvle]	'with unkempt hair'
ensevelir	[ãsœvlir]	'to bury'
il est genevois	[ilɛʒœnvwa]	'he is from Geneva'

Table 6.18. Contiguous *es* with the prefixes *de-* and *re-*

il est devenu	[ilɛdvœny]	~	[ilɛdœvny]	'he has become'
il en redemande	[ilãrdœmãd]	~	[ilãrœdmãd]	'he wants more'
nous recevons	[nursœvõ]	~	[nurœsvõ]	'we receive'

not violate any constraint on sound sequences or syllable structure. In such cases, it looks as if speakers have come to view these *es* as stable, rather than unstable, [œ]s. Not unexpectedly, a certain amount of variation can be observed across speakers as to which words must retain their *es*. The list in Table 6.16 contains a few words which fairly regularly belong to this category (they are contrasted with phrases showing that the application of Rule 2 would not result in impossible sound sequences).

The case where two *es* are found in contiguous syllables *within a word* should also be mentioned here. In keeping with what was said earlier about *e* in contiguous syllables (see Section 6.3.1.2), assuming that both are eligible for Rule 2, only one may actually delete. But at least in standard French, it is the second one which must delete, and the first must remain in the pronunciation (see Table 6.17). This restriction does not operate if one of the *es* belongs to a prefix (*de-*, *re-*); either *e* may then delete, although, at least with *re-*, the deletion of the *e* in the prefix sounds more natural (see Table 6.18). In the word *ressemeler* 'to resole', which contains the prefix *re-* followed by two consecutive *e*-syllables, the third *e* must delete, the second must stay, and the first may delete (*à ressemeler* [arsœmle] ~ [arœsœmle] 'to be resoled').

Table 6.19. *E*-deletion in the future and conditional

	deletion possible	
tu gard*e*rais	[tygard(œ)rɛ]	'you would keep'
nous brusqu*e*rons (les choses)	[nubrysk(œ)rõ]	'we will precipitate (things)'
vous vous offusqu*e*rez	[vuvuzɔfysk(œ)re]	'you will be offended'
	no deletion	
nous gard*e*rions	[nugardœrjõ]	'we would keep'
vous brusqu*e*riez (les choses)	[vubryskœrje]	'you would precipitate (things)'
vous vous offusqu*e*riez	[vuvuzɔfyskœrje]	'you would be offended'
il souffl*e*ra	[ilsuflœra]	'he will blow'
ils sucr*e*ront	[ilsykrœrõ]	'they will sugar'

The future and the conditional. We have just examined several cases where Rule 2 does not apply, even though the *e* is preceded by a single consonant. The reverse also occurs, where the *e* may be omitted from the pronunciation in apparent violation of Rule 2. In the future and conditional of first conjugation verbs, the *e* following the verb stem may delete, even if it is preceded by more than one consonant (see the upper portion of Table 6.19).

The *e* cannot, of course, be dropped in the conditional first and second person plural, because the sequences which would result would violate the constraint prohibiting the occurrence of [CLjV] in the same syllable; nor can it be dropped when it comes after a stem ending in a stop or fricative followed by a liquid (see the lower portion of Table 6.19). This last restriction is of a general scope in French, where inside a word a sequence of the type [OLC] is impossible ([O] stands here for a stop or a fricative). Consequently, in any sequence of the form [OLœC], the [œ] absolutely must be pronounced.

6.3.2. *Final* es

Rule 1 says very generally that final *e*s are not pronounced. This statement needs to be qualified. A final *e* may actually be pronounced if it is preceded by at least two consonants and if the following word begins with at least one consonant (see Table 6.20; recall that parentheses around [œ] indicate that the presence of the sound is optional). An [œ] may even be pronounced in this context when there is no *e* in the orthography (see Table 6.21). An [œ] also frequently occurs between two words when the first ends in a single consonant and the second begins with a consonant cluster such as [ps] or [sp] (e.g. *un problème psychique*

Table 6.20. Pronounced final *es*

un tex*te* magnifique	[ɛ̃tɛkst(œ)maɲifik]	'a magnificent text'
une ves*te* rapiécée	[ynvɛst(œ)rapjese]	'a patched-up jacket'
une énorm*e* pancarte	[ynenɔrm(œ)pɑ̃kart]	'a huge banner'
une cord*e* spéciale	[ynkɔrd(œ)spesjal]	'a special rope'
ils parl*ent* souvent	[ilparl(œ)suvɑ̃]	'they speak often'

Table 6.21. [œ] word-finally

un contact pénible	[ɛ̃kõtakt(œ)penibl]	'a painful contact'
un film fabuleux	[ɛ̃film(œ)fabylø]	'a fabulous film'
un match prodigieux	[ɛ̃matʃ(œ)prɔdiʒjø]	'an extraordinary match'
un ours mal léché	[ɛ̃nurs(œ)malleʃe]	'a rude person'
en mars dernier	[ɑ̃mars(œ)dɛrnje]	'last March'

[ɛ̃prɔblɛm(œ)psiʃik] 'a psychological problem', *un tarif spécial* [ɛ̃tarif(œ)spesjal] 'a special price').

Several factors influence the probability of occurrence of an [œ] under these conditions. In the three series of examples which follow (Tables 6.22–4), all else being equal, the pronunciation of [œ] is more probable in the expressions of the left-hand column than in those of the right-hand column.

(i) The tightness of the syntactic connection between the words favors the presence of the [œ] (see Table 6.22). In the first pair of contrasting examples, a relatively tight syntactic group (adjective + noun) contrasts with a less cohesive one (subject noun + verb). In the second pair of examples, *le risque d'avancer* constitutes a syntactic unit in the sentence on the left (as the object of *prennent*), but not in the sentence on the right (where *le risque* is the object of *aiment* and *d'avancer* is the complement of *empêche*).

(ii) The nature of the consonant clusters located at the edge of the words also plays an important role. For example, the final sequences [lk] and [sk] favor the occurrence of the [œ] more than final sequences of the form [rC] (see Table 6.23). It is important to note (given their high frequency of use) that in fact the words *quelques* 'a few' and *presque* 'almost' followed by a pronounced consonant practically always keep their final *e* in the pronunciation, in particular when they modify the following word (i.e. when they have a close syntactic relationship with it): *quelques paquets* [kɛlkœpakɛ] 'a few packages', *quelques avions* 'a few airplanes' [kɛlkœzavjõ], *presque toujours* [prɛskœtuʒur] 'almost always'.

(iii) If the second word is monosyllabic and stressed, the occurrence of the [œ] is also favored (see Table 6.24). A parallel phenomenon can be

Table 6.22. Pronounced final *es* and syntactic cohesion

l'énorme chagrin	les normes chagrinent	'the enormous sorrow'	/ 'norms cause sorrow'
il aime ceux qui prennent le risque d'avancer	il empêche ceux qui aiment le risque d'avancer	'he loves those who take the risk of moving'	/ 'he prevents those who like risks from moving'

Table 6.23. Pronounced final *e*s and consonant clusters

quelqu*e*s paquets	d'énorm*e*s paquets	'a few packages' / 'huge packages'
quelqu*e*s avions	de superb*e*s avions	'a few planes' / 'beautiful planes'
presqu*e* fissuré	de larg*e*s fissures	'almost split' / 'wide splits'
presqu*e* toujours	quatorz*e* touristes	'almost always' / 'fourteen tourists'
un calqu*e* réussi	une cart*e* réussie	'a well-done tracing' / 'a well-done map'
un risqu*e* démesuré	une firm*e* démesurée	'an excessive risk' / 'too big a firm'

Table 6.24. Pronounced final *e*s and stress

la cart*e* verte	la cart*e* vermeille	'the green card' / 'the red card'
un text*e* plat	un text*e* plausible	'a flat text' / 'a plausible text'
il parl*e* trop	il parl*e* trop peu	'he talks too much' / 'he talks too little'

Table 6.25. Pronounced final *e*s and compounds

port*e*-clé	[pɔrtœkle]	port*e*-drapeau	[pɔrtdrapo]	'key-ring' / 'standard-bearer'
port*e*-voix	[pɔrtœvwa]	port*e*-parole	[pɔrtparɔl]	'megaphone' / 'spokesman'
port*e*-poisse	[pɔrtœpwas]	port*e*-document	[pɔrtdɔkymɑ̃]	'jinx' / 'briefcase'
gard*e*-fou	[gardœfu]	gard*e*-malade	[gardmalad]	'railing' / 'nurse'

observed in compounds ('mots composés'). When the first term of a compound has at least two consonants before its final *e*, this *e* must be pronounced if the second term is monosyllabic and begins with at least one consonant (see Table 6.25).

Words ending in a *CLe* spelling sequence deserve special mention at this point. In these cases, the final *e* may, of course, be pronounced if the following word begins in a consonant; but if the *e* is not pronounced, then the liquid itself disappears from the pronunciation (see Table 6.26). The liquid may also disappear before a pause (see Table 6.27), and in colloquial speech it may even disappear before a vowel-initial word (see Table 6.28). In compounds, the liquid and the *e* must be pronounced if the second (consonant-initial) term is monosyllabic, but they may both be omitted otherwise (see Table 6.29).

It is not the case that all words ending in *CLe* can lose their liquid in the pronunciation. The list of words allowing this deletion may vary from speaker to speaker, but as a rule the high frequency of use of a word favors the possibility of omitting the liquid. At any rate, from a practical point of view, it is useful to remember that one never has to omit the liquid: a final *CLe* sequence can always be pronounced [CL] before a vowel or at the pause and [CLœ] before a consonant.

The presence of a final [œ] under the conditions stated above creates

Table 6.26. Final *CLe* sequences before consonant-initial words

quat*re* garçons	[katrœgarsõ]	~	[katgarsõ]	'four boys'
un pauv*re* type	[ɛ̃povrœtip]	~	[ɛ̃povtip]	'a poor guy'
un aut*re* chat	[ɛ̃notrœʃa]	~	[ɛ̃notʃa]	'another cat'
une tab*le* bien garnie	[yntablœbjɛ̃garni]	~	[yntabbjɛ̃garni]	'a well-provided table'
souff*le* tes bougies	[suflœtɛbuʒi]	~	[suftɛbuʒi]	'blow out your candles'

Table 6.27. Final *CLe* sequences at the pause

ils sont quat*re*	[ilsõkat(r)]	'there are four of them'
il est pauv*re*	[ilɛpov(r)]	'he is poor'
prends-en un aut*re*	[prɑ̃zɑ̃ɛ̃not(r)]	'take another one'
à tab*le*	[atab(l)]	'at the table'
à bout de souff*le*	[abutsuf(l)]	'breathless'

Table 6.28. Final *CLe* sequences before vowel-initial words

quat*re* enfants	[kat(r)ɑ̃fɑ̃]	'four children'
pauv*re* andouille	[pov(r)ɑ̃duj]	'poor schmuck'
une aut*re* histoire	[ynot(r)istwar]	'another story'
une tab*le* en bois	[yntab(l)ɑ̃bwa]	'a wooden table'
souff*le* une bougie	[suf(l)ynbuʒi]	'blow out a candle'

Table 6.29. Final *CLe* sequences in compounds

ouv*re*-boîte	[uvrœbwat]	ouv*re*-bouteille	[uv(rœ)butɛj]	'can-opener' / 'bottle-opener'
coff*re*-fort	[kɔfrœfɔr]	souff*re*-douleur	[suf(rœ)dulœr]	'safe' / 'whipping-boy'

the possibility for Rule 2 to apply when the following word begins with a syllable containing an (initial) *e*. Even though pronunciations here are subject to much variation, as a rule one can say that the more the presence of the final [œ] is favored, the more Rule 2 will be able to apply; conversely, the less the presence of the final [œ] is favored, the less Rule 2 will tend to apply. As a consequence, when *quelques* 'a few' and *presque* 'almost' are followed by a word containing *e* in its initial syllable, Rule 2 will often apply to this initial *e*, leaning as it were on the final *e* of *quelques* and *presque* (see the upper portion of Table 6.30). By contrast, in most other cases, pronounced final *e*s do not generally allow Rule 2 to lean on them for its application. Thus, in the examples of the lower portion of Table 6.30, the initial *e*s are usually sounded, even if they are preceded by a single consonant when the final *e*s of the preceding words are pronounced.

Note as we close this section that final *e*s are often pronounced before h-aspiré words (see Table 6.31). Here again, we can see that h-aspiré

Table 6.30. Final *es* and initial *e* deletion

	deletion of initial e possible	
quelques s*e*condes	[kɛlkœzgõd]~[kɛlkœsœgõd]	'a few seconds'
presque d*e*viné	[prɛskœd(œ)vine]	'almost guessed'
	no deletion of initial e	
une carte d*e* Paris	[ynkart(œ)dœpari]	'a map of Paris'
une veste d*e* luxe	[ynvɛst(œ)dœlyks]	'a luxurious jacket'
un concierge r*e*traité	[ɛ̃kõsjɛrʒ(œ)rœtrete]	'a retired concierge'
quatorze d*e*mandes	[katɔrz(œ)dœmɑ̃d]	'fourteen requests'

Table 6.31. Final *es* and h-aspiré words

un*e* hache	[ynœaʃ]	'an axe'
un énorm*e* hibou	[ɛ̃enɔrmœibu]	'an enormous owl'
quatr*e* héros	[katrœero]	'four heroes'
une petit*e* hausse	[ynpœtitœos]	'a small raise'

words seek in yet another way to protect themselves from possible direct contact with a preceding consonant (cf. p. 95).

The rules of pronunciation for *e* discussed in this chapter characterize standard French. Things are quite different phonetically in southern French, where the general tendency is to pronounce all the *e*s of the orthography that are found in an interconsonantal position. Traditional French poetry also requires these *e*s to be pronounced (except at the end of lines), in order that each line contain the required number of syllables.

6.4. Other cases of vowel deletion

In a few common words, vowels not spelled *e* may drop in the pronunciation. A list of such words, accompanied by brief comments on the usage of the reduced forms, is provided in Table 6.32.

Finally, we turn briefly to a case of vowel deletion alluded to earlier in this chapter (pp. 93–5), namely *elision*. A few monosyllabic grammatical words of the form [CV] elide (i.e. lose) their vowel before a vowel-initial word. Elision applies obligatorily to all monosyllables with *e* (*je, me, te, se, le, ce, de, ne, que*), as well as to the article and pronoun *la*. The orthography captures these cases of elision by means of the apostrophe (e.g. *j'aime* [ʒɛm] 'I like', *l'arbre* [larbr] 'the tree', *l'étoile* [letwal] 'the star'). Elision applies optionally to the conjunction *si* 'if' before *il(s)* 'he/ they' (*s'il vient* [silvjɛ̃] ~ *si il vient* [siilvjɛ̃] 'if he comes'), but not elsewhere (*si elle vient* [siɛlvjɛ̃] 'if she comes'; *si Yves vient* [siivvjɛ̃] 'if

Table 6.32. Other cases of vowel deletion

peut-être	[pøtetr]~[pœtetr]~[ptet]	'maybe'	(very frequent in conversation)
monsieur	[møsjø]~[mœsjø]~[msjø]	'sir'	(used mainly by children)
déjeuner	[deʒœne]~[deʒne]	'lunch'	(in some idiolects)
à tout à l'heure	[atutalœr]~[attalœr]	'see you later'	(very frequent)
maman	[mamɑ̃]~[mɑ̃mɑ̃]~[mmɑ̃]	'Mom'	(frequent in the speech of children when
papa	[papa]~[ppa]	'Dad'	addressing their parents)
déjà	[deʒa]~[dʒa]	'already'	(frequent in conversation)
cet	[sɛt]~[st]	'this' (masc.)	cet homme-là [stɔmla] (colloquial)
cette	[sɛt]~[st] before a vowel	'this' (fem.)	cette omelette [stɔmlɛt] (colloquial)
	[sɛt]~[stœ] before a consonant		cette femme-là [stœfamla] (very colloquial)
voilà	[vwala]~[vla]	'here is'	(frequent in conversation)

Yves comes'). In addition, in colloquial speech, the pronoun *tu* 'you' and the subject relative pronoun *qui* 'who' may also lose their vowel in the pronunciation (*tu attendras* [t(y)atɑ̃dra] 'you'll wait'; *celui qui a fait ça* [sœlɥik(i)afɛsa] 'the one who did that'). Note that elision occurs only before words with which the monosyllables in question are in a close syntactic relationship. Thus, the pronouns *le* and *la* elide obligatorily in *nous l'attendons* [nulatɑ̃dɔ̃] 'we wait for him/her' (*l'* = *le* or *la*), but there is no elision in constructions such as *donne-le à Pierre* [dɔnlœapjɛr] 'give it to Peter' and *fais-la entrer* [fɛlaɑ̃tre] 'have her come in'. This is quite analogous to the conditions described in the preceding chapter (pp. 81–3) for cases of obligatory liaison (see also Chapter 11).

7
Glides

7.1. Introduction

This chapter is devoted to the three French glides, [j, ɥ, w] (*miette* [mjɛt] 'crumb', *muette* [mɥɛt] 'mute', *mouette* [mwɛt] 'seagull'). In particular, we shall focus on how the glides are represented in the orthography, on their distributional properties and their functional relation with the closed vowels [i, y, u], and on remedies for the pronunciation difficulties that the existence of [ɥ] often creates for English-speaking students.

7.2. The front rounded glide [ɥ]

There are two glides in English, [j] (*yes* [jɛs]) and [w] (*we* [wi]). When learning French, then, the English speaker must learn to produce a third: [ɥ]. The goal of this section is to facilitate the acquisition of this sound.

As already mentioned in Chapter 2, p. 30, [j] is the front unrounded glide that corresponds to the closed front unrounded vowel [i], [ɥ] is the front rounded glide that corresponds to the closed front rounded vowel [y], and [w] is the back rounded glide that corresponds to the closed back rounded vowel [u] (see Table 7.1). Given these correspondences, it is not surprising to find, in connection with the existence of the glide [ɥ], pronunciation problems similar to those due to the existence of the vowel [y] (see Chapter 3, p. 42), i.e. an inadequate pronunciation of [ɥ] and in particular some confusion between [ɥ] and [w].

Before working, if need be, on the production of [ɥ] and on the distinction between [ɥ] and [w], it is first desirable to make sure that [y] has been solidly acquired and that there is no confusion between [y] and [u] (see the advice and exercises suggested in Chapter 3, Section 3.4.2). Using the closed vowels as a point of departure, it is then relatively easy to produce the corresponding glides. For example, keeping in mind the fact that what separates [i] from [y] on the one hand, and [j] from [ɥ] on the other hand, is solely lip position, one may begin by repeating several times the following front sequence: [i]–[y] (lips stretched for [i], rounded for [y]). Then, simple words containing these vowels may be produced, such as the verb forms [si]–[sy] (*scie–sue* 'saws'–'sweats'). In a third phase, add a final vowel to these forms, for instance the [e] of the

Table 7.1. French closed vowels and glides

	closed vowels		*glides*		
front unrounded	[i] (défi	[defi])	[j] (défier	[defje])	'challenge' / 'to challenge'
front rounded	[y] (tue	[ty])	[ɥ] (tuer	[tɥe])	'kills' / 'to kill'
back rounded	[u] (secoue [sœku])		[w] (secouer [sœkwe])		'shakes' / 'to shake'

Table 7.2. Simple words with French glides

[j]			[ɥ]			[w]		
bien	[bjɛ̃]	'well'	huit	[ɥit]	'eight'	boîte	[bwat]	'box'
pièce	[pjɛs]	'coin'	lui	[lɥi]	'him'	moi	[mwa]	'me'
pied	[pje]	'foot'	nuit	[nɥi]	'night'	oui	[wi]	'yes'
rien	[rjɛ̃]	'nothing'	puis	[pɥi]	'then'	voir	[vwar]	'to see'

infinitive, but produce (somewhat artificially for the moment) bisyllabic words: [si-e]–[sy-e]. Finally, these words can be pronounced more rapidly and more naturally, in a single syllable, with the appropriate glides: [sje]–[sɥe] (*scier–suer* 'to saw'–'to sweat'). The same type of exercise may be done with [u]–[y] and [w]–[ɥ], keeping in mind the fact that this time, it is only the position of the tongue on the horizontal axis that should change (the lips remain rounded). One may thus proceed from the rounded vowel sequence [u]–[y] (back position of the tongue for [u], front for [y]), to the words [su]–[sy] (*sous–sue* 'under'–'sweats'), then to bisyllabic forms like [su-ɛ]–[sy-ɛ], and finally to the monosyllables [swɛ]–[sɥɛ] (*souhait–suait* 'wish'–'sweated').

Another useful exercise consists in proceeding directly from the glides [j] and [w] (which as a rule do not create pronunciation problems for English speakers) to the glide [ɥ], in the same way that one had arrived at the vowel [y] from the vowels [i] and [u] (see Chapter 3, pp. 42–3). For instance, one may go from [je], as in *yé-yé* (term used in the sixties to refer to 'in' things and people), to [ɥe], as in *huée* 'boo', focusing on the rounding of the lips and on the stability of the front position of the tongue when going from [j] to [ɥ]. Or one may go from [wi], as in *oui* 'yes', to [ɥi], as in *huis* 'door', focusing on the forward movement of the tongue and on the stability of lip rounding when going from [w] to [ɥ].

It is also useful to practise pronouncing simple common words containing [j], [ɥ], and [w], such as those in Table 7.2.

Finally, students may play the 'minimal pair' game, i.e. try to recognize and pronounce correctly words that are distinguished only by the glide they contain (see Table 7.3).

The glide [ɥ] is not necessarily an easy sound to learn to produce and

Table 7.3. French glides in (near) minimal pairs

	[j]			[ɥ]			[w]	
miette	[mjɛt]	'crumb'	muette	[mɥɛt]	'mute'	mouette	[mwɛt]	'seagull'
nier	[nje]	'to deny'	nuée	[nɥe]	'cloud'	nouer	[nwe]	'to knot'
Gien	[ʒjɛ̃]	(town)	juin	[ʒɥɛ̃]	'June'	joint	[ʒwɛ̃]	'joint'
sciait	[sjɛ]	'sawed'	suait	[sɥɛ]	'sweated'	souhait	[swɛ]	'wish'
(pied	[pje]	'foot')	buée	[bɥe]	'fog'	bouée	[bwe]	'buoy'
			lui	[lɥi]	'him'	Louis	[lwi]	'Lewis'
			s'enfuir	[sɑ̃fɥir]	'to flee'	s'enfouir	[sɑ̃fwir]	'to burrow'

Table 7.4. Glides and their basic orthographic representations

	[j] = i/y			[ɥ] = u			[w] = ou	
pierre	[pjɛr]	'stone'	lui	[lɥi]	'him'	fouet	[fwɛ]	'whip'
biniou	[binju]	'bagpipes'	Suède	[sɥɛd]	'Sweden'	jouer	[ʒwe]	'to play'
biologie	[bjɔlɔʒi]	'biology'	persuader	[persɥade]	'to persuade'	Louis	[lwi]	'Lewis'
bien	[bjɛ̃]	'well'	juin	[ʒɥɛ̃]	'June'	ouate	[wat]	'cotton'
yacht	[jɔt]	'yacht'						
yéti	[jeti]	'yeti'						
Lyon	[ljõ]	(town)						

above all to integrate into spontaneous speech. In fact, it is not a particularly common sound in the languages of the world; most languages which use glides limit their inventory to [j] and [w], as is the case for English. And some French dialects actually do not have [ɥ]; thus, in Belgium, [ɥ] is generally replaced by [w] (for example, *puis* 'then' is pronounced [pwi], rather than [pɥi]).

7.3. The representation of glides in the orthography

There are no special letters reserved for the transcription of the glides in French orthography. The letters *i/y*, *u*, and *ou* in front of a pronounced vowel generally serve to represent [j], [ɥ], and [w] respectively (see Table 7.4).

7.3.1. The representation of [ɥ]

The letter *u* in front of a pronounced vowel is actually the only way in which the glide [ɥ] is represented in French orthography. It must be noted, however, that after the consonants *g* and *q*, the letter *u* before a pronounced vowel is usually silent (*gué* [ge] 'ford', *gui* [gi] 'mistletoe'; *liquide* [likid] 'liquid', *quand* [kɑ̃] 'when'). After *g*, it ordinarily serves to indicate the basic phonetic value [g] of the consonant when the vowels *e* or *i* follow: compare, for example, *mangue* [mɑ̃g] 'mango' and *mange* [mɑ̃ʒ] 'eat', *guide* [gid] 'guide' and *Gide* [ʒid] (proper name). As to *q*, it is always followed by *u* (*quai* [kɛ] 'platform', *que* [kœ] 'that', *qui* [ki] 'who', *quotidien* [kɔtidjɛ̃] 'daily', *piqûre* [pikyr] 'sting'), except at the end of a word (*cinq* [sɛ̃k] 'five', *coq* [kɔk] 'rooster'). After *g* and *q*, the letter *u* is pronounced [ɥ] only in a few words where [i] follows (e.g. *aiguille* [egɥij] 'needle', *linguiste* [lɛ̃gɥist] 'linguist', *équidistant* [ekɥidistɑ̃] 'equidistant', to be contrasted with *anguille* [ɑ̃gij] 'eel', *languir* [lɑ̃gir] 'to languish', *équitable* [ekitable] 'equitable').

7.3.2. The representation of [w]

For the glide [w], one finds, besides *ou* in front of a pronounced vowel, the letter combinations *oi* and *oin*, which represent the sound sequences [wa]/[wɑ] and [wɛ̃] respectively (see Table 7.5).

In rather rare cases, the spellings *oe/oê* are found for [wa] or [wɑ] (*moelle* [mwal] 'marrow', *moelleux* [mwalø] 'soft', *poêle* [pwal] 'skillet'). In a number of borrowed words, the letter *w* is also found for [w] (*kiwi* [kiwi] 'kiwi', *sandwich* [sɑ̃dwitʃ] 'sandwich', *tramway* [tramwɛ] 'streetcar', *water* [watɛr] 'toilet', *watt* [wat] 'watt'; but note that *wagon*

Table 7.5. [w] in *oi* and *oin*

cr*oi*re	[krwɑr]	'to believe'	gr*oin*	[grwɛ̃]	'snout'
l*oi*	[lwɑ]	'law'	l*oin*	[lwɛ̃]	'far'
*oi*seau	[wazo]	'bird'	m*oin*s	[mwɛ̃]	'less'
p*oi*gnet	[pwaɲɛ]	'wrist'	p*oin*t	[pwɛ̃]	'period'
tr*oi*s	[trwɑ]	'three'	s*oin*	[swɛ̃]	'care'

'(railway) car' is pronounced [vagõ]). Finally, observe that in a few words, the spellings *qua* and *gua* represent [kwa] and [gwa], rather than [ka] and [ga] (*adéquat* [adekwa] 'adequate', *aquarelle* [akwarɛl] 'watercolor', *aquarium* [akwarjɔm] 'aquarium', *aquatique* [akwatik] 'aquatic', *équateur* [ekwatœr] 'equator', *équation* [ekwasjõ] 'equation', *quadragénaire* [kwadraʒenɛr] 'quadragenarian', *quadrupède* [kwadrypɛd] 'quadruped', *quartz* [kwarts] 'quartz', *square* [skwar] 'park'; *iguane* [igwan] 'iguana', *jaguar* [ʒagwar] 'jaguar').

7.3.3. The representation of [j]

For the glide [j], besides the letters *i* and *y* in front of a pronounced vowel, two other spellings are common: *ill* and *il*. After a glide, *ill* represents [ij] (*aiguille* [egɥij] 'needle', *cuillère* [kɥijɛr] 'spoon', *juillet* [ʒɥijɛ] 'July'). After a vowel sound, *ill* simply represents [j] (*conseiller* [kõseje] 'adviser', *feuille* [fœj] 'leaf', *fouiller* [fuje] 'to search', *paille* [pɑj] 'straw'). After a consonant, *ill* represents [ij] or, more rarely, [il] (see Table 7.6). (Note that *ill* is always pronounced [il] or [ill] at the beginning of a word: *illuminer* [i(l)lymine] 'to illuminate', *illustration* [i(l)lystrasjõ] 'illustration'.)

The spelling *il* can represent [j] only at the end of a word (elsewhere it always stands for [il]: *îlot* [ilo] 'island', *bilan* [bilɑ̃] 'balance sheet'). If a vowel precedes immediately, then *il* is always [j]; if a consonant precedes immediately, the spelling *il* usually indicates the pronunciation [il] or, more rarely, the pronunciation [i] (see Table 7.7).

Table 7.6. Pronunciations of *ill* after a consonant

ill = [ij]			*ill* = [il]		
briller	[brije]	'to shine'	billevesée	[bilvœze]	'rubbish'
cédille	[sedij]	'cedilla'	mille	[mil]	'thousand'
famille	[famij]	'family'	tranquillité	[trɑ̃kilite]	'tranquillity'
fille	[fij]	'daughter'	ville	[vil]	'town'
fusiller	[fyzije]	'to shoot'	village	[vilaʒ]	'village'
gentille	[ʒɑ̃tij]	'nice'			
outiller	[utije]	'to equip'			
pillage	[pijaʒ]	'plunder'			
quille	[kij]	'pin'			

Table 7.7. Pronunciations of final *il*

il after V			*il after C*				
[j]			[ɪ]			[i]	
deuil	[dœj]	'mourning'	avril	[avril]	'April'	fusil	[fyzi]	'gun'
fauteuil	[fotœj]	'armchair'	Brésil	[brezil]	'Brazil'	gentil	[ʒɑ̃ti]	'nice'
œil	[œj]	'eye'	civil	[sivil]	'civilian'	outil	[uti]	'tool'
soleil	[sɔlɛj]	'sun'	fil	[fil]	'thread'	persil	[persi]	'parsley' (but
soupirail	[supiʀɑj]	'air hole'	péril	[peril]	'peril'	*Persil* [persil], as a detergent
travail	[travaj]	'work'	subtil	[syptil]	'subtle'	brand)

Table 7.8. Pronunciation of *VyV* sequences

*ay*V [ejV]/[ɛjV]			*oy*V [wajV]/[wɑjV]			*uy*V [ɥijV]		
balayer	[baleje]	'to sweep'	croyant	[krwɑjɑ̃]	'believer'	bruyant	[brɥijɑ̃]	'noisy'
essayage	[esejaʒ]	'fitting'	royal	[rwɑjal]	'royal'	ennuyer	[ɑ̃nɥije]	'to bore'
payant	[pejɑ̃]	'paying'	soyeux	[swajø]	'silky'	tuyau	[tɥijo]	'pipe'
*ay*V [ajV]			*oy*V [ɔjV]			*uy*V [yjV]		
Bayard	[bajar]	(surname)	coyote	[kɔjɔt]	'coyote'	bruyère	[bryjɛr]	'heath'
Bayonne	[bajɔn]	(town)	Goya	[gɔja]	(surname)	gruyère	[gryjɛr]	'Swiss cheese'
cobaye	[kɔbaj]	'guinea pig'						
La Fayette	[lafajɛt]	(surname)						
mayonnaise	[majɔnɛz]	'mayonnaise'						

Table 7.9. Glides and orthography (summary)

[j]		[ɥ]		[w]	
i before [V]	lion [ljõ]	*u* before [V] nuit [nɥi]		*ou* before [V]	jouer [ʒwe]
y before [V]	Lyon [ljõ]			*oi* = [wa]/[wɑ]	loi [lwa]
ill = [ij]	fille [fij]			*oin* = [wɛ̃]	loin [lwɛ̃]
= [j]	faille [fɑj]			*w*	kiwi [kiwi]
Vil#	œil [œj]				

The spelling *y* for [j] presents interesting properties when *y* occurs between two vowels. In general, this letter then plays a dual role. It can be thought of as two consecutive *i*s. The first is associated with the preceding vowel to give the following sounds:

-with *a*: [ɛ]/[e]   (= *ai*)
-with *o*: [wa]/[wɑ]   (= *oi*)
-with *u*: [ɥi]   (= *ui*)

The second *i* represents the glide [j]. In the end, the types of pronunciation illustrated in the upper portion of Table 7.8 obtain. There are, however, a few words where the letter *y* does not behave in this way; the preceding vowel remains independent and the *y* serves only to indicate the presence of a [j] (see the lower portion of Table 7.8). For some words containing the sequence *uyV*, the *y* may or may not play a dual role, depending on the speaker (*bruyant*: [brɥijã] ~ [bryjã] 'noisy'; *tuyau*: [tɥijo] ~ [tyjo] 'pipe'). But pronunciations where *y* plays a dual role are always possible (thus, *bruyère* 'heath' and *gruyère* 'Swiss cheese' may be found pronounced [brɥijɛr] and [grɥijɛr]).

Table 7.9 summarizes the main correspondences between the spelling and the pronunciation of glides in French (the symbol # indicates word-final position).

7.4. The distribution of glides

Glides typically occur in slots where consonants occur, although not necessarily in all such slots. French [j] may occupy virtually any basic position where a consonant is possible. Thus, [j] is found in syllable-initial position (*hiérarchie* [jerarʃi] 'hierarchy', *yéti* [jeti] 'yeti'), in syllable-final position (*paye* [pɛj] 'paycheck', *travail* [travaj] 'work'), and after a consonant (*pièce* [pjɛs] 'coin', *rien* [rjɛ̃] 'nothing'). By contrast, French [ɥ] and [w] have defective distributions; these two glides are found only in syllable-initial position (*huit* [ɥit] 'eight'; *ouistiti* [wistiti] 'marmoset') and after a consonant (*nuit* [nɥi] 'night'; *bouée* [bwe] 'buoy'), but not in syllable-final position.

Table 7.10. *CLiV* = [CLijV]

crier	[krije]	'to shout'
peuplier	[pœplije]	'poplar'
plier	[plije]	'to fold'
ouvrier	[uvrije]	'worker'
sucrier	[sykrije]	'sugar bowl'

Table 7.11. Pronunciation of *CLuV* sequences

CLui = [CLɥi]			*CLuV* = [CLyV] (V ≠ i)		
bruit	[brɥi]	'noise'	cruauté	[kryote]	'cruelty'
fluide	[flɥid]	'fluid'	fluet	[flyɛ]	'slim'
truite	[trɥit]	'trout'	truand	[tryã]	'gangster'

Table 7.12. [CLwV] vs [CLuV]

CLoi (*n*) = [CLwa]/ [CLwɑ]([CLwɛ̃])			*CLouV* = [CLuV]		
cloison	[klwazõ]	'partition'	clouer	[klue]	'to nail'
croire	[krwɑr]	'to believe'	prouesse	[pruɛs]	'prowess'
trois	[trwɑ]	'three'	troua	[trua]	'(he) made a hole'
droit	[drwɑ]	'straight'	éblouir	[ebluir]	'to dazzle'
groin	[grwɛ̃]	'snout'	brouhaha	[bruaa]	'pandemonium'

There are special restrictions on the occurrence of glides after sequences composed of a stop or fricative followed by a liquid. As already seen in the preceding chapter (see pp. 95–8), [CLjV] sequences are in general impossible in the same syllable, and spelling sequences of the form *CLiV* are thus typically pronounced [CLijV], in two syllables ([CLi.jV]) (see Table 7.10).

CLɥV] sequences are also impossible, unless [V] is [i]. Spellings of the *CLui* type are thus generally pronounced [CLɥi], in one syllable, whereas spellings of the *CLuV* type where *V* is not [i] are pronounced [CLyV], in two syllables ([CLy.V]) (see Table 7.11).

Finally, [CLwV] sequences are impossible, unless [wV] corresponds to the spellings *oi* and *oin*. Spellings of the form *CLoi* and *CLoin* are thus pronounced [CLwa]/[CLwɑ] and [CLwɛ̃], in one syllable. Otherwise (that is, corresponding to a spelling of the type *CLouV*), only [CLuV] is found, pronounced in two syllables ([CLu.V]) (see Table 7.12).

In considering the restrictions on [CLGV] sequences (where G stands for glides), the question arises as to why some sequences are allowed and others not. A possible answer to this question comes from an examination of the behavior of word-initial glides with respect to liaison and elision.

Table 7.13. Word-initial glides and liaison/elision

	no liaison			*no elision*	
les yétis	[lejeti]	'the yetis'	le yéti	[lœjeti]	'the yeti'
les whiskys	[lewiski]	'the whiskeys'	le whisky	[lœwiski]	'the whiskey'
	liaison			*elision*	
les oiseaux	[lezwazo]	'the birds'	l'oiseau	[lwazo]	'the bird'
les huîtres	[lezɥitr]	'the oysters'	l'huître	[lɥitr]	'the oyster'

We saw in the preceding chapter (pp. 95–6) that there are glides which behave exactly like consonants, in that they allow neither liaison nor elision; but there are also word-initial glides which behave like vowels, in that they do allow liaison and elision (see Table 7.13). These two sets of examples show that there exist in French two types of [GV] sequences, one which behaves like a 'consonant + vowel' sequence and the other which behaves like a vowel. This difference can be captured by representing a [GV] sequence which behaves like a vowel as a rising diphthong constituting a (complex) *syllable nucleus* ('noyau syllabique'), in the same way that a monophthong constitutes a (simple) syllable nucleus. By contrast, [GV] sequences which behave like 'consonant + vowel' sequences can be analyzed as being composed of separate elements in the syllable: the glide constitutes the *consonantal onset* ('attaque consonantique') and the vowel constitutes the (monophthongal) nucleus. Given this double identity of glides in French, the paradox of their apparently contradictory behavior with respect to both liaison and elision can be resolved if the formulation of these two phenomena is refined to saying that they occur before a word-initial syllable nucleus (rather than before a word-initial vowel). For example, *yéti* [jeti] would have a syllable structure parallel to that of *képi* [kepi], and *oiseau* [wazo] a syllable structure parallel to that of *ami* [ami], as shown in Figure 7.1. In the two cases on the left, the presence of a word-initial syllable onset blocks liaison and elision; but in the two cases on the right, liaison and elision do take place, as the words begin with a syllable nucleus.

In this analysis, then, glides can be either in the onset of a syllable or in its nucleus (together with a vowel). Seen from this perspective, the restrictions on [CLGV] sequences can be expressed as a generalization of the constraint on [CLjV] already mentioned in the preceding chapter (p. 97): [CLGV] sequences are prohibited in the same syllable, unless the substring [GV] constitutes a (complex) syllable nucleus. In other words, what is not permitted is a syllable onset composed of the sequence

Figure 7.1. The place of glides in the syllable

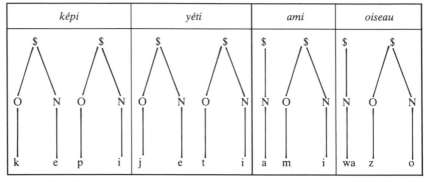

$ = syllable; O = onset; N = nucleus.

Figure 7.2. The structure of [CLGV] sequences in the syllable

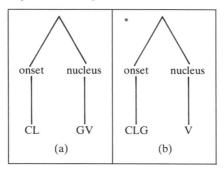

[CLG]. To summarize, in a given syllable, a configuration such as that of Diagram (a) in Figure 7.2 is possible, but not one like that of Diagram (b).

Note that the constraint in question is not, strictly speaking, of a phonetic nature, but rather of a functional nature. Indeed, what prevents the phonetic realization of certain [CLGV] sequences is not truly an articulatory unwillingness or incapability on the part of speakers to pronounce these sounds one after the other (since such sequences do, after all, occur); it is, in a more abstract way, the manner in which the elements of a [GV] group can be structurally distributed in the syllable.

7.5 Correspondences between closed vowels and glides

As a rule, when a vowel-initial suffix is added to a word ending in a closed vowel, the closed vowel changes into the corresponding glide by a process called *gliding* ('semi-vocalization') (see Table 7.14). This principle may also affect the word *y*, which is thus pronounced [i] before a consonant

Table 7.14. Alternations of closed vowels and glides

[i]~[j]	sci*e*	[si]	sci*er*	[sje]	'saw'	– 'to saw'
	défi	[defi]	défi*er*	[dcfjc]	'challenge'	– 'to challenge'
[y]~[ɥ]	tu*e*	[ty]	tu*er*	[tɥe]	'kills'	– 'to kill'
	mu*e*	[my]	mu*er*	[mɥe]	'shedding'	– 'to shed'
[u]~[w]	seco*ue*	[sœku]	seco*uer*	[sœkwe]	'shakes'	– 'to shake'
	lo*ue*	[lu]	lo*uer*	[lwe]	'rents'	– 'to rent'

Table 7.15. Cases of no gliding

(i)	anti-aérien	[ãtiaerjẽ]	'anti-aircraft'	à demi-enterré	[adœmiãterc]	'half-buried'
	semi-aride	[sœmiarid]	'semi-arid'	mi-octobre	[miɔktɔbr]	'mid-October'

(i)
(but note the special case of *demi* in the expression *une demi-heure* [yndœmijœr]~[yndœmjœr] 'a half-hour')

(ii) Marie-Anne   [marian]   (cf. *Marianne* [marjan])
      Marie-Antoinette [mariãtwanɛt] (cf. *mariage* [marjaʒ] 'wedding')

(iii) si adorable   [siadɔrabl]   'so cute'   (cf *scia* [sja] '(he) sawed')
       il su*e* à grandes eaux [ilsyagrãdzo] 'he sweats buckets' (cf. *sua* [sɥa] '(he) sweated')
       il lo*ue* à qui?   [illuaki]   'he rents to whom?' (cf. *loua* [lwa] '(he) rented')

(*elle y parviendra* [ɛliparvjẽdra] 'she'll do it') and usually [j] before a vowel (*elle y arrivera* [ɛljarivra] 'she'll get there'; *il y a* [ilja] 'there is/are', often simply reduced to [ja]). But gliding does not apply in other situations, for instance (i) in prefixes like *anti-*, *demi-*, *mi-*, *semi-*, (ii) in compounds, or (iii) across words (see Table 7.15).

The application of the gliding rule is also blocked when the closed vowel is preceded by a [CL] sequence. If the rule applied, the glide thus created could not form a rising diphthong (i.e. a complex syllable nucleus) with the following vowel, because it originated as a unit independent from the following vowel; it would therefore have to be part of the syllable onset, along with the sequence [CL]; but as we have just seen in the preceding section, this type of structure is prohibited in French (see Diagram (b) in Figure 7.2). Gliding is thus blocked under these circumstances, since its application yields no possible outputs. Gliding does not occur either when the closed vowel is itself preceded by a glide. The basic reason here is that sequences of glides are not permissible in the same syllable.

The question now is to determine what actually happens to the pronunciation of words where gliding is blocked by these constraints. It all depends on the nature of the vowel prevented from gliding. If the vowel is [i], then instead of [i] changing to [j], [j] is inserted between the [i] and the following vowel; if the vowel is [y] or [u], no change is made at all (see Table 7.16).

Table 7.16. Absence of gliding after [CL] sequences

(i) The vowel prevented from gliding is [i]: [j]-insertion				
plier	'to fold':	[pli+e]	→ [plije]	(from the noun *pli* [pli] 'fold')
ennuyer	'to bore':	[ãnɥi+e]	→ [ãnɥije]	(from the noun *ennui* [ãnɥi] 'boredom')
(ii) The vowel prevented from gliding is [y] or [u]: status quo				
gluant	'sticky':	[gly+ã]	→ [glyã]	(from the noun *glu* [gly] 'birdlime')
clouer	'to nail':	[klu+e]	→ [klue]	(from the noun *clou* [klu] 'nail')

Table 7.17. [j]-insertion after [ɛ] and [wa]/[wɑ]

balai	[balɛ]	'broom'	balayer	[baleje]	([balɛ+e])	'to sweep'
paiement	[pɛmã]	'payment'	payer	[peje]	([pɛ+e])	'to pay'
joie	[ʒwɑ]	'happiness'	joyeux	[ʒwajø]	([ʒwɑ+ø])	'happy'
soie	[swa]	'silk'	soyeux	[swajø]	([swa+ø])	'silky'
nettoie	[netwa]	'(he) cleans'	nettoyage	[netwajaʒ]	([netwa+aʒ])	'cleaning'
Savoie	[savwa]	(region)	savoyard	[savwajar]	([savwa+ar])	'from Savoie'
voit	[vwa]	'(he) sees'	voyons	[vwajõ]	([vwa+õ])	'let's see'

Notice that [j]-insertion also occurs when a vowel-initial suffix is added to a word ending in [ɛ] or in [wa]/[wɑ] (see Table 7.17; for the changes in vowel quality between [ɛ] and [e] and between [ɑ] and [a], cf. Chapter 4). These particular types of 'word + suffix' combinations do not, then, phonetically result in two consecutive vowels, as is the case, for example, in *créer* [kree] 'to create' and *création* [kreasjõ] 'creation' ([kre + e], [kre + asjõ]). Whether a [j] is inserted between two vowels brought together by suffixation depends, as noted, on the quality of the first vowel.

7.6. Remarks on pronunciation variations with glides

Glides in French give rise to numerous pronunciation variations across speakers, some of which are briefly mentioned here in the final section of this chapter.

The process of suffixation can theoretically create sequences of [j]s. This is the case, for instance, in imperfect and subjunctive verb forms like *cueilliez* (from *cueillir* 'to pick') and *habillions* (from *habiller* 'to dress'), which are composed of stems ending in [j] ([kœj], [abij]) and of suffixes beginning with [j] ([je], [jõ]): [kœj + je], [abij + jõ] (cf. *chantiez* [ʃãt + je] and *chantions* [ʃãt + jõ], from *chanter* 'to sing'). Similarly, there is a potential sequence of [j]s in the noun *groseillier* 'red-currant bush', which is formed by adding to the word *groseille* [grozɛj] 'red currant' the suffix *-ier* [-je]: [grozɛj + je] (cf. *poirier* [pwar + je] 'pear tree'). With some speakers, the double [j] is kept in the verb forms ([kœjje], [abijjõ]), but not elsewhere ([grozeje]). With other speakers, the double [j] is reduced everywhere ([kœje], [abijõ], [grozeje]); these speakers, then, do not make a phonetic distinction between the forms of the present *cueillez* and *habillons* on the one hand, and those of the imperfect and subjunctive *cueilliez* and *habillions* on the other hand.

Another type of variation concerns the constraint against [CLjV] sequences (see above and Chapter 6, p. 97). It turns out that a number of speakers actually allow such sequences, not tolerated by others, but under very specific and restricted conditions; they allow them only in verb forms where [CL] corresponds to the end of the verb stem and [jV] to the verb ending. For instance, the verb form *boucliez* (as in *il faudrait que vous boucliez votre ceinture* 'you should buckle your seatbelt') may be pronounced [buklje] (rather than [buklije]) by such speakers, whereas the noun *bouclier* 'shield' must be pronounced [buklije] (and not *[buklje]). By the same token, the verb form *oubliez* 'forget' must be pronounced [ublije] (rather than *[ublje]), as the *i* belongs to the verb stem, not to the verb ending. It may be that in the cases where [CLjV] is allowed, the [jV] sequence, which constitutes a grammatical ending, is analyzed by such speakers as a phonetic unit as well, so that the [j] is viewed as forming, together with [V], a rising diphthong constituting a possible syllable nucleus, rather than as an independent unit which would have to be placed, together with [CL], into an impossible syllable onset (cf. Figure 7.2). However, the nature of the consonant [L] in [CLjV] sequences also seems important. Thus, under the conditions just described, some speakers allow such sequences only if [L] is [l] (as in *boucliez* [buklje]), but not if [L] is [r] (as in *rentriez* [rãtrije], *[rãtrje], from *rentrer* 'to return'), while others allow them whether [L] is [l] or [r] (*boucliez* [buklje]; *rentriez* [rãtrje]).

In a perhaps related way, it is worth noting that the vowel [i] of the verb stem for *rire* 'to laugh' relatively rarely turns into the corresponding glide [j] when followed by a vowel-initial ending. Thus, for *riant* 'cheerful', *rieur* 'merry', and *rions* '(we) laugh', for instance, the pronunciations [rijã], [rijœr], and [rijõ] are much more common than [rjã], [rjœr], and [rjõ]; that is, while no speaker will find the first set impossible, many speakers will find the second odd. But the town name *Riom* (a single morpheme) is usually pronounced [rjõ]. If we now consider the case of the verb stem for *lier* 'to link', we also find two similar patterns of pronunciation for words like *liant* 'sociable', *lieur* 'binder', *lions* '(we) link': (i) [lijã], [lijœr], [lijõ], and (ii) [ljã], [ljœr], [ljõ]; except that this time, the second series is probably more generally accepted than the first. In sum, it seems that the consonant [l] more readily accepts gliding next to it than does the consonant [r]. These examples then underscore the importance of word structure in the phenomenon of gliding (compare

Figure 7.3. Propensity to gliding across
closed vowels

	nier	nouer	nuée	
(a)	[nje]	[nwe]	[nɥe]	gliding
(b)	[nje]	[nwe]	[nye]	no gliding
(c)	[nje]	[nue]	[nye]	

rions [rijõ] vs *Riom* [rjõ]), the relevance of the nature of the consonants preceding the gliding site ([r] vs [l]), and how speakers may vary in subtle ways in their consideration of such factors.

The nature of the closed vowel may itself introduce variations in gliding patterns across speakers (or even in the same speaker using different styles), for it seems that closed vowels do not actually all glide with the same ease. Everything else being equal, of the three closed vowels of French, [i] is the one that glides the most generally, next comes [u], and last, [y]. For instance, if we compare the three words *nier* 'to deny', *nouer* 'to make a knot', and *nuée* 'cloud', gliding is more likely to occur in the first case than in the second, and in the second than in the third; in other words, the pronunciation patterns (a–b–c) schematized in Figure 7.3 seem to hold, whereby for a given speaking style, [y]-gliding implies [i]- and [u]-gliding, and [u]-gliding implies [i] gliding, but not vice versa. The pronunciation of such sound sequences in one syllable (when gliding applies) is technically known as 'synaeresis' ('synérèse'), their pronunciation in two syllables (when gliding does not apply) as 'diaeresis' ('diérèse'). These terms often occur in discussions of French poetry, when the use of synaeresis or diaeresis in a given word can make the difference as to whether a line will conform to the required number of syllables.

Our final observation concerns a very common word, *hier* 'yesterday'. Some speakers say [ijɛr] (two syllables), others [jɛr] (one syllable). But *avant-hier* 'the day before yesterday' is quite generally pronounced [avɑ̃tjɛr], with the component *hier* yielding one syllable.

Part Three
Consonants

8
Consonantal systems

8.1. Introduction

This chapter is devoted to a comparative survey of the French and English consonantal systems, and to an examination of the most important articulatory differences between phonetically close consonants in these systems. The fundamentally distinct properties of *l* and *r* in the two languages warrant a separate chapter for these two consonants (Chapter 9). In Chapter 10, we shall consider questions internal to French regarding the pronunciation of double consonants and final consonants. Finally, in Chapter 11, we shall examine the phenomenon of liaison, which was already touched on in the discussion of nasal vowels in Chapter 5.

8.2. Consonant inventories and comparative overview

Tables 8.1–2 present the consonant inventories of French and English, together with the main articulatory parameters necessary to their description, with examples.

As these tables indicate, English uses a slightly larger consonant inventory than French: there are 22 consonants in English, compared to 17 in French. The stop systems closely resemble each other; however, the nasal series differ in that English has the velar [ŋ], whereas French has the palatal [ɲ]. The existence of the velar nasal [ŋ] in English does not create great difficulties for French speakers learning English. As a matter of fact, this consonant tends to enter into the French consonantal system; thus, some speakers use it in the ending *-ing* often found in words borrowed from English (see the first group of examples in Table 8.3), as well as in pseudo-borrowings (see the second group of examples). Sometimes [ŋg] is heard instead of [ŋ]; other speakers use the palatal nasal [ɲ] rather than [ŋ]; but the pronunciation [ɛ̃ʒ] for *-ing* is facetious. [ŋ] may also appear in French as a realization of [g] in a nasal context (for example in *longuement* [lõŋmã] 'at length' and *langue maternelle* [lãŋmatɛrnɛl] 'native language').

The palatal nasal [ɲ] is a new sound for English-speaking students. This sound (represented by the digraph *gn* in the orthography) commonly appears intervocalically and in word-final position; it appears in initial

Table 8.1. French consonants

Manner of articulation		bilabial	labiodental	dental	alveolar	alveopalatal	palatal	velar	uvular	Examples			
nasal		m		n			ɲ			mou	nous	gnon	(soft, we, blow)
stops	voiceless	p		t				k		pou	tout	cou	(louse, all, neck)
oral	voiced	b		d				g		bout	doux	goût	(end, mild, taste)
fricatives	voiceless		f		s	ʃ				fou	sous	chou	(mad, under, cabbage)
	voiced		v		z	ʒ				vous	zou	joue	(you, [interjection], cheek)
approximants	lateral				l						loup		(wolf)
	central								ʁ			roue	(wheel)

Place of articulation

Table 8.2. English consonants

Place of participation / Manner of articulation			bilabial	labiodental	(inter)dental	alveolar	alveopalatal	velar	glottal	Examples
stops	nasal		m			n		ŋ		*me* *kn*ee *si*ng
	oral	voiceless	p			t		k		*pea* *tea* *key*
		voiced	b			d		g		*bee* *deep* *geese*
fricatives	voiceless			f	θ	s	ʃ		h	*fee* *thin* *she* *he*
	voiced			v	ð	z	ʒ			*vee* *thee* *zee* mea*s*ure
affricates	voiceless						tʃ			*ch*eat
	voiced						dʒ			*J*eeves
approximants	lateral					l				*l*ead
	central					r				*r*ead

Table 8.3. French words in *-ing*

(i)	camping	[kɑ̃piŋ]	'camping'
	living	[liviŋ]	'living room'
	marketing	[markɛtiŋ]	'marketing'
	meeting	[mitiŋ]	'meeting'
	parking	[parkiŋ]	'parking-lot'
	pressing	[prɛsiŋ]	'pressing'
	shopping	[ʃɔpiŋ]	'shopping'
(ii)	caravaning	[karavaniŋ]	'camping (in a trailer)'
	footing	[futiŋ]	'jogging'
	smoking	[smɔkiŋ]	'tuxedo'

position in just a few words (see Table 8.4). [ɲ] is perceptually very close to the sequence [nj]. In fact, some speakers always pronounce [nj] rather than [ɲ], and thus do not make a distinction, for example, between *peignons* (from the verb *peindre* 'to paint') and *peinions* (from the verb *peiner* 'to toil'): the two words are both pronounced [penjõ], rather than [peɲõ] and [penjõ] respectively. Other speakers keep [ɲ] only word-finally, a position where, in fact, the sequence [nj] (more generally any [Cj] sequence) normally never occurs in French (except, obviously, in the speech of those who pronounce [nj] instead of [ɲ] in all circumstances). Note finally that in some words, the spelling *gn* represents the phonetic sequence [gn], not the sound [ɲ] (see Table 8.5).

Table 8.4. French words with [ɲ]

(i) [ɲ] *intervocalically*					
agneau	[aɲo]	'lamb'	se baigner	[sœbeɲe]	'to go swimming'
peigner	[peɲe]	'to comb'	oignon	[ɔɲõ]	'onion'

(ii) [ɲ] *word finally*					
digne	[diɲ]	'worthy'	ligne	[liɲ]	'line'
montagne	[mõtaɲ]	'mountain'	pagne	[paɲ]	'loin-cloth'

(iii) [ɲ] *word-initially*					
gnangnan	[ɲãɲã]	'namby-pamby'	gnognote	[ɲɔɲɔt]	'trash'
gnole	[ɲol]	'booze'	gnon	[ɲõ]	'blow'

Table 8.5. *gn* as [gn]

agnostique	[agnɔstik]	'agnostic'
diagnostique	[diagnɔstik]	'diagnosis'
gneiss	[gnɛs]	'gneiss'
gnome	[gnom]	'gnome'
stagnant	[stagnã]	'stagnant'

Concerning the fricatives, English has three sounds which do not exist in French and which create definite problems for French speakers learning English; these are [θ], [ð], and [h]. In general, French speakers tend to replace the (inter)dental fricatives [θ] and [ð] with the alveolar fricatives [s] and [z] (more rarely with the labiodentals [f] and [v]), and they tend to eliminate the glottal [h] altogether. The acquisition of these three fricatives, particularly [θ] and [ð], usually requires much effort on the part of French speakers. English speakers learning French should keep in mind the fact that these three consonants do not exist in French. In particular, they should not let themselves be fooled by the spelling *th*, which simply represents the sound [t] (see Table 8.6), nor by the spelling *h*, which does not represent any sound at all (see Table 8.7; but consult also Appendix D for a summary of the values of *h*). However, note that the sound [h] does exist in some French dialects, for example in the eastern part of France (where a word such as *haute* 'high' may be pronounced [hot], rather than [ot] as in standard French). In some regions of Canada, the sound [h] appears in place of initial [ʒ] (for example, *la jupe* 'the skirt' is pronounced [lahYp] rather than [laʒyp]).

The affricates which exist in English have no real counterparts in French. Affricates in French are found only in borrowed words, such as (from Spanish) *gaucho* [gotʃo] 'gaucho' (also pronounced [goʃo]) and

Table 8.6. *th* = [t]

a*th*ée	[ate]	'atheist'	or*th*ographe	[ɔrtɔgraf]	'orthography'
a*th*lète	[atlɛt]	'athlctc'	ry*th*me	[ritm]	'rhythm'
ba*th*	[bɑt]	'good'	syn*th*èse	[sɛ̃tɛz]	'synthesis'
ma*th*	[mat]	'math'	*th*éâtre	[teɑtr]	'theater'

Table 8.7. Silent *h*

de*h*ors	[dœɔr]	'outside'	men*h*ir	[menir]	'menhir'
*h*âte	[ɑt]	'haste'	Pan*h*ard	[pɑ̃ar]	(car make)
*h*omme	[ɔm]	'man'	tra*h*ir	[trair]	'to betray'

(from English) *bridge* [bridʒ] 'bridge' (dental prosthesis and card game), *catch* [katʃ] 'wrestling', *match* [matʃ] 'match', and *sandwich* [sɑ̃dwitʃ] 'sandwich' (also pronounced [sɑ̃dwiʃ]).

English and French both have the consonants *l* and *r*, but thcsc consonants have extremely different phonetic realizations in the two languages. For this reason, they are the subject of a scparate chapter (see Chapter 9).

8.3. Contrastive study

Aside from *l* and *r*, English consonants and their French counterparts are on the whole relatively close, phonetically speaking. There exist, however, several differences of detail which play determining characteristic roles in the two languages and which must be the focus of particular attention for the acquisition of a good pronunciation in the foreign tongue.

8.3.1. Voiceless stops

The most important phonetic distinction is probably that which separates the realization of the voiceless stops ([p, t, k]) in the two languages. In syllable-initial position, English [p, t, k] are said to be 'aspirated'. What this means is that a puff of air immediately follows the release of the occlusion. The degree of 'aspiration' is directly dependent on the force of the stress falling on the syllable. In French, [p, t, k] are not aspirated. Thus, if we compare the initial consonants in the English words *pair*, *tear*, and *care* with those in the French words *père* 'father', *terre* 'ground', and (*le*) *Caire* 'Cairo' while pronouncing these words a few inches away from the flame of a match, we observe that the flame tends to flicker during the production of the English words, whereas it hardly moves during the production of the French words. The difference may also be observed by

Figure 8.1. English vs French [p, t, k]

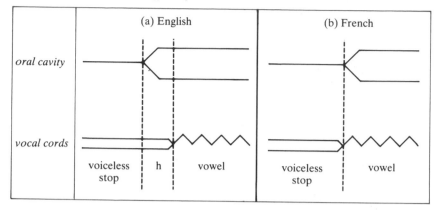

placing the palm of the hand in front of one's mouth; a puff of air is felt more strongly at the moment of production of the English consonants than during the production of the French consonants. French [p, t, k] resemble the unaspirated English [p, t, k] that occur, for example, after [s] in words such as *spare*, *stare*, and *scare*. In detailed phonetic transcriptions, the presence of aspiration in English is generally indicated by a small superscript *h*: [p^h, t^h, k^h].

The distinction between the presence of aspiration in English and its absence in French is due to a difference in synchronization in the two languages between the release of the occlusion of the voiceless stop and the beginning of the voicing for the following sound (see Figure 8.1). The two diagrams in Figure 8.1 represent what occurs at the level of the oral cavity and at the level of the vocal cords during the production of a voiceless stop followed by a vowel. We see that in the two languages, the sequences of movements are the same. The oral cavity is characterized by a complete occlusion (for the consonant) followed by an opening (for the production of the vowel). As for the vocal cords, they are first apart and allow air to pass freely; then they come together and begin to vibrate. What differentiates the two languages is the synchronization of these movements. In French, the release of the stop and the onset of the voicing are for all intents and purposes simultaneous (Diagram (b)); in English, by contrast, several hundredths of a second elapse between these two actions, hence the 'aspiration' (Diagram (a)).

In sum, it is important to remember that the elimination of all traces of aspiration in the pronunciation of the French consonants [p, t, k] constitutes one of the most basic requirements that must be met by any English speaker eager to approximate a native-like French pronunciation. The task is relatively easy to accomplish and the results are well worth the effort.

Figure 8.2. English vs French [b, d, g]

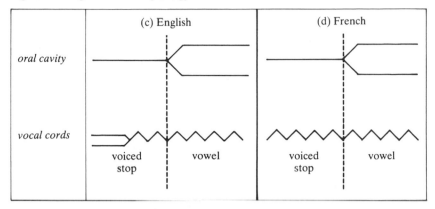

8.3.2. Voicing

We have just seen that the aspiration of syllable-initial voiceless stops in English is due to a delay in the onset of voicing, relative to what occurs in French. The same parameter also explains why the voiced stops [b, d, g] have a tendency to be only partially voiced in English (at least when they are not preceded by another voiced sound), whereas they are completely voiced in French. Figure 8.2 illustrates the relative delay in the onset of voicing in English voiced stops (Diagram (c)), in comparison to what occurs in French, where the vocal cords vibrate during the entire time these consonants last (Diagram (d)).

In the same way that the French stops [b, d, g] are more completely voiced than their English counterparts, the French voiced fricatives [v, z, ʒ] are more completely voiced than the corresponding voiced fricatives in English.

A comparison of the diagrams in Figures 8.1–2 shows that with regard to the time lag between the release of the occlusion and the onset of the voicing (technically known as VOT, Voiced Onset Time), English [pʰ, tʰ, kʰ] and French [b, d, g] are at the ends of the spectrum, with French [p, t, k] and English [b, d, g] occupying intermediate positions. This accounts for the confusions which sometimes arise when French speakers using English resort to their own voiceless stops instead of the aspirated ones (English listeners may perceive their own [b, d, g]) and conversely when English speakers using French resort to their own voiced stops (French listeners may perceive their own [p, t, k]).

It should also be noted that, in word-final position, English voiced consonants tend to lose their voicing, whereas this is not at all the case in French. This tendency towards devoicing in English may reach such a degree in some dialects that the phonetic difference between words like *bet* and *bed* is not, as one might expect, a voicing distinction between *t* and *d* (since they are both pronounced voiceless), but rather a length distinction between the vowels that precede: the [ɛ] is longer in *bed* ([bɛːt]) than in *bet* ([bɛt]). The devoicing of word-final consonants is a natural phenomenon encountered in numerous languages (in German and Russian, to cite just two well-known cases), as well as, quite generally, in the speech of children acquiring their native language (French included). The process is also attested in some French dialects (thus, in Belgium, for the word *garage* 'garage', for example, the pronunciation [garaʃ] is found instead of [garaʒ]). This type of devoicing is not, however, characteristic of standard French.

To conclude this section on voicing, let us simply emphasize, on a practical level, the necessity for English speakers to concentrate on fully voicing voiced consonants in French.

8.3.3. Release

The production of a consonant usually involves three distinct phases: (i) the positioning ('la mise en place') of the articulators, (ii) the holding in place ('la tenue') of the articulation, and (iii) the release ('la détente') of the articulators. In word-final position, or before another stop, the release of a stop may or may not be present. In English, it is generally absent, whereas in French it is usually audible, that is, one can hear some sort of reduced vocalic sound after the consonant. Let us take as an illustration the sequence of sounds [kt], which is found in the French and English words *acteur* and *actor*. In the transition from [k] to [t], the release of the articulation of [k] may be produced either before the positioning of the articulators for the emission of [t], or it may be produced afterwards (or simultaneously). The release of [k] will be audible in the first case, but not in the second case, where it will be drowned, as it were, in the production of [t]. As already indicated, the first pronunciation is characteristic of French, the second of English. Similarly, at the end of a word, the release of stops normally occurs quite audibly in French, whereas in English, in most instances, it is in some sense withheld, giving rise to unreleased consonants. In detailed phonetic transcriptions, to indicate that a consonant is unreleased, the superscript diacritic marks ˺ or ° are placed after it. The release of French consonants can be indicated by a small superscript schwa after the consonant. The examples in Table 8.8 illustrate the difference in the release of stops in English and in French.

Table 8.8. Unreleased English stops vs released French
stops

English		French		
cap	[kæp˺]	cape	[kapᵊ]	'cape'
bat	[bæt˺]	bath	[batᵊ]	'good'
sack	[sæk˺]	sac	[sakᵊ]	'bag'
crab	[kræb˺]	crabe	[krɑbᵊ]	'crab'
sad	[sæd˺]	Sade	[sadᵊ]	(surname)
bag	[bæg˺]	bague	[bagᵊ]	'ring'
actor	[æk˺tɔr]	acteur	[akᵊtœr]	'actor'

8.3.4. The place of articulation of [t, d, n]

As Tables 8.1–2 indicate, the stops [t, d, n] do not have exactly the same place of articulation in French and in English: these consonants are dental in French, but alveolar in English; in other words, the occlusion with the tip of the tongue is produced a little further front in French than in English (behind the upper front teeth rather than at the alveolar ridge). To gain a concrete feel for the dental articulation of these French consonants and for the difference from the usual alveolar articulation of the corresponding English consonants, consider how in some English words the phonetic context in fact imposes on [t, d, n] a dental, rather than an alveolar, articulation. For example, pronounce the word *ten* and focus on the place of articulation for *n*; clearly the *n* is alveolar, like the initial *t*. Pronounce next the word *tenth*; you will probably be able to feel that now the occlusion for this same *n* is produced a little further front than in *ten* (and than for the initial *t*), just in back of the upper teeth rather than at the alveolar ridge: the *n* is dental in *tenth*. This change in place of articulation is due to the presence of the suffix *-th* [θ], an (inter)dental consonant: during the production of the *n* of *tenth*, the tip of the tongue anticipates the (inter)dental articulation of the [θ] and the *n* itself becomes dental. The same type of assimilation can be observed, for instance, with the *n* of *in*, the *t* of *at*, and the *d* of *add* in sequences such as *in the kitchen*, *at the market*, and *add them up*: in these cases, the (inter)dental [ð] causes the assimilations.

In summary of this section on the articulation of [t, d, n], what is important to remember is that whereas in English these consonants are generally alveolar (they are dental only in the presence of a subsequent [θ] or [ð]), in French they always have a dental articulation. In a precise phonetic transcription, dental [t, d, n] are distinguished from alveolar [t, d, n] by the placement of the diacritic mark ̩ under the phonetic symbols: [t̪, d̪, n̪].

8.4. Practical concluding remarks

With the exception of *l* and *r* (see next chapter), the actual articulation of French consonants does not generally pose great problems for English speakers – in any case, far fewer than does the pronunciation of vowels. The main difficulty rests essentially in the necessary suppression of aspiration for syllable-initial voiceless stops ([p, t, k]). By comparison, the mastery of the other distinctions between English and French consonants (the voicing in voiced consonants, the release in final stops, and the place of articulation for [t, d, n]) merely constitutes refinements of details.

9
L and *R*

9.1. Introduction

In the languages of the world, there exists a great variety of sounds collectively called liquids, with two subcategories (the *l*-type and the *r*-type). From one language to another, the sounds in each of the two subcategories may be extremely different phonetically, as is the case for the French and English *r*s. In addition, in a given language, more than one kind of *l* or *r* may be found; such phonetic distinctions may correspond to meaning distinctions, as is the case for the two kinds of *r* which are found in Spanish *pero* 'but' and *perro* 'dog'. They may also simply depend on the phonetic context, as is the case for the two kinds of *l* which appear in the speech of many English speakers (compare, for example, the initial *l* in *leave* and the final *l* in *veal*). Finally, the phonetic differences may be dialectal variations or, for a given speaker, free variations, as is the case for certain kinds of *r* in French.

This chapter is mainly concerned with explaining and resolving the difficulties which the sounds *l* and *r* pose for English speakers learning French, but at the same time it offers an overview of the main varieties of *l* and *r* which are commonly found in the languages of the world.

9.2. *l*, *r*, and syllabicity

Before considering the articulatory differences which separate the consonants *l* and *r* in English and in French, it is appropriate to note the distinct functional roles which these consonants can play with respect to syllabification in the two languages.

In English, the words *table* and *sugar* each have two syllables. In French, the (corresponding) words *table* and *sucre* each have only one syllable. What separates the two languages here is the difference in the functioning of *l* and *r* in the syllable. In an English word such as *table*, the *l* constitutes a syllable nucleus, just as the vowel [e] does, hence the two syllables (see Diagram (a) in Figure 9.1; note that in phonetic transcriptions, the syllabicity of a consonant is generally indicated by means of a short vertical subscript line: [tebl]). In the French word *table*, there is only one syllable nucleus, the vowel [a]; the other sounds in the word,

Figure 9.1. Liquid syllabicity

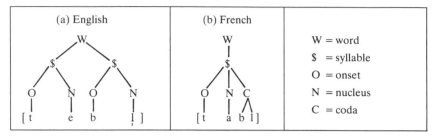

Table 9.1. Word-final liquids in French

| une tab*l*e de travail | [yntabdœtravaj] ~ [yntablœdœtravaj] | 'a work table' |
| du suc*r*e de canne | [dysykdœkan] ~ [dysykrœdœkan] | 'cane sugar' |

Figure 9.2. French *l* and *r* in syllable onsets

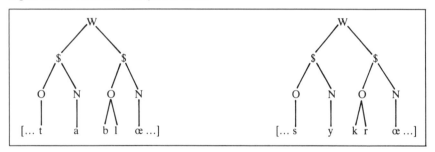

including the *l*, are linked to this nucleus to form the margins of a single syllable (the [t] constitutes the onset of the syllable and the [b] and the [l] its coda; see Diagram (b) in Figure 9.1). Roughly speaking, English *l* and *r* are syllabic when they are found at the end of a word and are preceded by a consonant (*table* [tebl̩], sugar [ʃɷgr̩]). In French, *l* and *r* are never syllabic (*table* [tabl], *sucre* [sykr]).

As already seen in Chapter 6 (pp. 103–4), word-final *l* and *r* may disappear in French when they are preceded by a stop or a fricative, especially if a consonant-initial word follows; and if the *l* or *r* are not dropped, then an [œ] generally appears between the two words (see Table 9.1). In the latter case, it may be said that the words *table* and *sucre* have two syllables, but note that the second syllable has [œ] as its nucleus, not *l* or *r*. (With the stop that precedes each of them, *l* and *r* form the onset of the second syllable; see Figure 9.2.)

To sum up, English *l* and *r* may, as it were, play the role of a vowel (and constitute a syllable nucleus, as in *table* [tebl̩] and *sugar* [ʃɷgr̩]) or they may behave as a consonant (and constitute or be part of a syllable margin, as in *lull*, *rare*, *please*, and *cry*). By contrast, in French, these two sounds may play only the role of a consonant (and constitute or be part of a syllable margin, as in *table* [tabl], *sucre* [sykr], *Lille* [lil] (town), *rare* [rɑr] 'rare', *pli* [pli] 'fold', and *cri* [kri] 'shout').

9.3. The articulation of *l*

In English, many speakers produce two varieties of *l*: one is said to be *clear* or *light* ('l clair') and the other is said to be *dark*, or *velar*, or *velarized* ('l sombre' or 'l vélaire'). The distribution of these two types of *l* depends on the phonetic context, more precisely on the position of *l* in the syllable. In general, clear *l* occurs in the onset of the syllable and dark *l* occurs elsewhere, that is, in the syllable nucleus or in coda position. Table 9.2 provides some examples of each sort.

These two types of *l* have in common the fact that they are produced by an alveolar occlusion created by the tongue tip and allowing air to escape without friction on one or both sides of the tongue (depending on the speaker). The difference between these two *l*s lies in the placement of the rest of the tongue. For clear *l*, the front part of the dorsum of the tongue is raised toward the hard palate, as for a relatively closed front vowel. For dark *l*, the front part of the dorsum of the tongue forms a hollow, and the back part of the tongue is raised toward the velum (velarization), as for a relatively closed back vowel. Usually, when one wishes to indicate the distinction between these two *l*s in a phonetic transcription, clear *l* is represented by the phonetic symbol [l] and dark *l* by means of an *l* barred with a tilde: [ɫ].

With some speakers, the occlusion which occurs during the production of dark *l* may be retroflex rather than alveolar; this means that the underside of the tongue tip, rather than the tip itself, enters into contact with the alveolar ridge. With yet other speakers, there is no occlusion at all during the production of dark *l*, and the result is the production of a closed back vowel or glide; this is what is called *vocalization* ('la

Table 9.2. Clear *l* vs dark *l* in English

clear l	*dark l*
*l*ook	coo*l*
*l*eaf	fee*l*
*l*eft	fe*l*t
*l*ark	Car*l*
p*l*ane	app*l*e

Table 9.3. Memories of Old French dark *l*

autre	[otr]	'other'	(cf. a*l*truisme	[altrᵹism]	'altruism')
hauteur	[otœr]	'height'	(cf. a*l*titude	[altityd]	'altitude')
beaux	[bo]	'beautiful'	(cf. be*ll*es	[bɛl]	'beautiful' fem.)
chevaux	[ʃœvo]	'horses'	(cf. cheva*l*	[ʃœval]	'horse')
cheveux	[ʃœvø]	'hair'	(cf. cheve*l*ure	[ʃœvlyr]	'hair')

vocalisation') of dark *l* (compare, for example, the pronunciations [pæɫ] and [pæ̃] for the word *pal*). In American English, the distinction between clear *l* and dark *l* is often blurred, and with many speakers, a dark *l* is found in all positions. In general, the degree of velarization of a dark *l* may vary from one context to another and from one speaker to another.

In modern French, there is only one type of *l*; regardless of its position in the syllable, French *l* is a clear (non-retroflexed) *l*. The main task of the English speaker, then, is to avoid pronouncing a dark *l* in French, in particular in word-final position and in preconsonantal position, since these positions are especially favorable to the appearance of dark *l* in English. For the pronunciation of French *l*, it is therefore necessary to stretch the tongue tip toward the front of the oral cavity (to avoid retroflexion) and to try not to bunch up the dorsum of the tongue toward the soft palate (to avoid velarization). English-speaking students should pay particularly close attention to the pronunciation of the *l* in common words such as *il*(*s*) 'he/they', *elle*(*s*) 'she/they', *quel* 'which' (and its derivatives), *belle* 'beautiful', etc.

Dark *l* existed in Old French in preconsonantal position, but it vocalized before the twelfth century. The resulting sound, transcribed in the spelling by means of the letter *u*, generally combined with the preceding vowels to form diphthongs and triphthongs which later became monophthongs. Today, traces of these linguistic changes may still be found in the pronunciation and spelling of many words (see Table 9.3).

Old French also had a palatal *l* ('l palatal' or 'l mouillé'), as is still found today in Italian (*figlio* 'son') and in Castilian Spanish (*calle* 'street'). This sound, which is perceptually close to the sequence [lj], is generally transcribed by means of the Greek letter lambda ([λ]): [fiλo], [kaλe]. As is the case in the varieties of Spanish spoken in the Americas, French palatal *l* generally reduced to [j], as in the examples of Table 9.4. This reduction began in the seventeenth century. In his dictionary of 1881, Littré still indicates some pronunciations with a palatal *l*, but today these pronunciations have completely disappeared in standard French. It is interesting to note that today, by a similar process of reduction, some speakers of modern French pronounce [lj] sequences as [j]. Such pro-

Table 9.4. Memories of Old French palatal *l*

famille	[famij]	'family'
fille	[fij]	'girl'
meilleur	[mejœr]	'better'
œil	[œj]	'eye'
paille	[pɑj]	'straw'
travail	[travaj]	'work'

Table 9.5. Reduction of [lj] to [j] in popular French

	Standard French	Popular French	
esca*l*ier	[ɛskalje]	[ɛskaje]	'staircase'
mi*ll*ion	[miljõ]	[mijõ]	'million'
sou*l*ier	[sulje]	[suje]	'shoe'

nunciations are characteristic of popular French and tend to be socially stigmatized (see Table 9.5).

In French, as in English, *l* is normally voiced, but it is devoiced after a voiceless consonant in the same word. The devoicing is partial if a vowel follows (as in *la plaine* [laplɛn] 'the plain') and complete otherwise (as in *le peuple* [lœpœpl̥] 'the people'; recall that the small subscript circle serves to indicate devoicing in detailed phonetic transcriptions). The devoicing may be accompanied by a soft friction noise, caused by the fact that the opening of the glottis corresponding to the devoicing releases a greater volume of pulmonary air than if the vocal cords were vibrating; the presence of this surplus of air, moving in the same oral space situated between the upper teeth and the sides of the tongue, creates the friction.

9.4. The articulation of *r*

Contextual and dialectal variations give rise to numerous varieties of *r*s in French as well as in English. It is therefore useful to begin with a relatively systematic review of the main types of *r*s that the reader is likely to encounter or produce in the two languages.

Two main groups of *r*s can be distinguished according to their manner of articulation: occlusive *r*s and constrictive *r*s. The *r*s of the first category are produced by a closure in the oral cavity caused by a flexible articulator coming into contact with another articulator (for example, the tongue tip against the alveolar ridge). The *r*s of the second category are produced by some constriction in the oral–pharyngeal cavity, with or without concomitant friction noise.

9.4.1. Occlusive rs

Among the occlusive rs, once again two different types of rs can be distinguished: rs with successive closures and rs with a single closure. The rs with several successive closures are usually called *rolled* or *trilled* rs ('r roulés'). rs with a single closure are usually called *tapped* or *flapped* rs ('r battus').

9.4.1.1. Trilled rs

The closures in trilled rs are produced by the same principle which causes the vocal cords to vibrate (the Bernoulli effect; see Chapter 2, Section 2.3.2). For example, in the case of the trilled alveolar *r*, where the tongue tip hits the alveolar ridge several times in succession, the repeated closures are in fact vibrations of the tongue tip made mechanically possible by a combination of factors including the position of the tongue tip in relation to the alveolar ridge, the tension of the tongue tip, and the pressure of the air from the lungs. Thus the closures are not the consequence of a muscular action of the tongue in which the tongue tip would be voluntarily projected several times in quick succession against the alveolar ridge, in the way in which one taps one's fingers on a table. Usually, the inability of some people to produce a trilled alveolar *r* springs simply from the fact that they attempt to do something which is physiologically impossible: they try, by muscular impulse, to have the tongue tip hit the alveolar ridge very quickly many times in a row. To produce a trilled alveolar *r*, it is sufficient, in fact, to place the tongue tip in very light contact with the alveolar ridge, to maintain a certain flexibility to the tongue, and then to force the air from the lungs between the tongue tip and the alveolar ridge. Minor adjustments to these three parameters (placement of the tongue tip in relation to the alveolar ridge, tension of the tongue, and amount of air) should, little by little, lead to the production of a genuine trilled alveolar *r*.

The trilled alveolar *r* is generally transcribed with the phonetic symbol [r]. This type of *r* is found in many languages, for example, in Spanish (*perro* [pero] 'dog'), in Italian (*tirare* [tirare] 'to pull'), in Russian (*gorod* [gorat] 'city'), in some English dialects (Scotland), and in some French dialects (in Quebec and in many rural areas in France). Even though the trilled alveolar *r* has been part of the consonant inventory of French since the beginnings of the language, this is not the type of *r* that is found in modern standard French. The trilled alveolar *r* began to be replaced by a back constrictive *r* in the seventeenth century and in fact, today, it tends to be socially stigmatized, at least in France, especially in large cities.

Another form of trilled *r* is produced by vibrations of the uvula against the back part of the dorsum of the tongue. This trilled uvular *r*, sometimes known in French as 'r grasseyé', does not seem very common today, but examples particularly rich in vibrations can (or could) be found in some French actors and singers (Edith Piaf was a well-known case in point). The trilled uvular *r* is usually transcribed with the symbol [R].

9.4.1.2. Tapped rs

For the tapped *r*s, there is a single very rapid occlusive contact of the tongue tip against the alveolar ridge; this time, the occlusion is not due to the Bernoulli effect, but is triggered by a voluntary movement of the tongue muscles.

The alveolar tapped *r* is usually transcribed with the phonetic symbol [ɾ]; American linguists often represent it with the symbol [D]. This sound is found, for example, in Spanish (*pero* [peɾo] 'but') and in American English, where it is the phonetic realization of the consonants [t] and [d] in intervocalic position, when the following syllable nucleus is not stressed (*city, latter, petal, writer; Eddy, ladder, pedal, rider*). It should be noted that, in the same context, the consonant [n] is realized as a nasal tapped alveolar *r* (*dinner, manner, tanner*).

In American English, a retroflex tapped *r* is also found, where the tapping is obtained by a very rapid occlusive contact of the underside of the tongue tip against the post-alveolar region of the palate. The retroflex tapped *r* is very common for the pronunciation of *t* and *d* between a constrictive *r* and an unstressed vowel (*party, hardy*). Usually, this sound is transcribed by means of the phonetic symbol [ɽ] (an *r* with a vertical tail ending in a hook).

9.4.2. Constrictive rs

Several varieties of constrictive *r*s can be distinguished according to their place of articulation. Their production may take place with friction, with very little friction, or without any friction at all. If friction occurs, it is a fricative *r*; otherwise, it is an approximant *r*. We shall consider first English, and then French, varieties of constrictive *r*s. Basically, English constrictive *r*s are produced in the front of the oral cavity, whereas French constrictive *r*s are produced in the back of the oral cavity.

9.4.2.1. Front rs

The alveolar constrictive *r* found, for instance, in word-initial position in English (as in *red*) is produced by raising the tongue tip toward the alveolar ridge, while at the same time bunching up the dorsum of the tongue and holding it in a relatively high position in the oral cavity. This *r* is usually transcribed by means of the phonetic symbol [ɹ] (an inverted *r*).

The retroflex constrictive *r* found in American English is produced in the same way, except that it is the underside of the tongue tip which forms a constriction in the post-alveolar region of the palate. The phonetic symbol generally used to represent this sound is [ɻ] (an inverted *r* with a subscript dot).

The central constrictive *r* is equivalent to an alveolar or retroflex constrictive *r* having lost the raising of the tongue tip, which remains behind the lower teeth. The center part of the dorsum of the tongue is bunched up and touches the upper molars on each side of the oral cavity. The central constrictive *r* is found in American English, in particular after the velar stops (as in *crate* and *great*). There is no standard phonetic symbol reserved for this sound.

9.4.2.2. Back *r*s

The *r* found in standard French is a back constrictive *r*, but there actually exist several varieties of this type, as indicated by the different descriptive terms commonly used to refer to it ('dorsal *r*', 'velar *r*', 'uvular *r*', 'pharyngeal *r*'). Adding to the confusion is the fairly common use, for at least some of these *r*s, of the subjective term '*r* grasseyé' (which may also be found referring to the quite different trilled uvular *r*, as was mentioned at the end of Section 9.4.1.1.). It is this phonetic and terminological abundance which leads us to use the generic term of 'back' *r*.

The essential articulatory characteristic of the back *r* in standard French seems to be a pharyngeal constriction produced in part by drawing back the root of the tongue. But this constriction may occur in two different places, more toward the lower end of the pharynx or more toward the upper end. The *r* with a low pharyngeal constriction is almost always voiced and does not generally include any friction noise, because the passage between the root of the tongue and the pharyngeal wall remains relatively wide, which allows the air from the lungs to go through freely. In impressionistic fashion, but ultimately rather accurately, it is often said that this *r* comes from the depths of the throat ('du fond de la gorge'). This sound is characteristic of a variety of popular Parisian French stigmatized by some as 'vulgar'.

The *r* with a high pharyngeal constriction is produced by raising and withdrawing the back part of the tongue (dorsum and root), which, in addition to a pharyngeal constriction, creates a velar constriction and a uvular constriction. If the uvula happens to vibrate against the dorsum of the tongue, then the sound produced is not a constrictive *r*, but the trilled uvular [R] mentioned earlier (see Section 9.4.1.1). If the uvula does not vibrate, the resulting constrictive *r* is the one characteristic of standard French. The phonetic symbol generally used to represent this sound is [ʁ] (an inverted *R*). This type of *r* is generally voiced and non-fricative. However, just like the consonant *l* (see p. 139), it is devoiced when it immediately follows a voiceless stop or fricative in the same word. The devoicing is partial if the *r* precedes a vowel (as in *quatre ans* 'four years' and *présent* 'present'), complete otherwise (as in the sentence *ils sont quatre* 'there are four of them'). The devoicing is usually accompanied by friction, because more pulmonary air is released due to the absence of vocal cord vibrations (the glottis is open). The phonetic symbol of the IPA corresponding to this voiceless *r* is [χ], but in practice, [ʁ] is often used instead (ʁ with a small subscript zero for devoicing).

All else being equal, a voiced [ʁ] is more likely to be pronounced with some friction noise itself when the adjacent vowel in the same syllable has a relatively back or open articulation. This is because vowels with a relatively front and closed articulation do not favor the raising and backing of the dorsum and root of the tongue, thereby diminishing the chances of obtaining friction for the [ʁ]. A small friction noise may thus accompany the *r* in words such as *sourd* 'deaf' and *Sarre* 'Saar', in contrast to words such as *cire* 'wax' and *sûr* 'sure'. Obviously, adjustments in the degree of constriction and/or in the quantity of air coming from the lungs may eliminate, or on the contrary produce, friction noise. For example, if *j'en suis sûr* 'I am sure of it' is said with strong emphasis on the adjective *sûr*, a fricative *r* will easily be obtained because of the large volume of air released for the added stress. In southwestern France, a voiceless and very fricative back *r* is commonly found; the very strong friction is due to a constriction narrower than that which is normally found in standard French.

Another variety of back *r* is found in the speech of some French speakers from Africa and Haiti. Strictly speaking, this *r* does not have a pharyngeal constriction, but rather a velar constriction without much noticeable friction noise. It is voiced. This type of *r* seems in fact equivalent to the intervocalic realization of the letter *g* in Spanish (a voiced velar approximant or fricative), as in *pagar* [paɣar] 'to pay'.

9.5. English and French *r*: contrastive study

As we have just seen, English and French *r*s are extremely different from an articulatory point of view. English *r* is formed in the front of the oral cavity, whereas French *r* is formed in the back. For English *r*, the tongue tip generally plays an active role and is directed upward. With French *r*,

Figure 9.3. English *r* vs French *r* (adapted from Pierre Delattre, *Comparing the Phonetic Features of English, French, German, and Spanish*, 1965, pp. 72, 74–5)

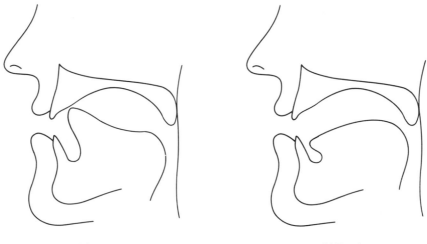

(a) English *r*   (b) French *r*

the tongue tip is always inactive and remains behind the lower teeth in a resting position; it is the back part of the tongue and its root which play an active role (see Figure 9.3).

To these extremely marked articulatory differences correspond equally dramatic perceptual differences, so that the pronunciation of an English *r* in French and the pronunciation of a French *r* in English immediately create the impression of a strong foreign accent.

In addition, it is important to note that English *r* strongly influences the quality of a preceding vowel which it places in a closed syllable (compare, for instance, the quality of the vowels in words such as *hair* and *head*), whereas in French, it is more the vowels which influence the *r* by having an effect on the constriction of its articulation, thereby making it more or less fricative (cf. the difference described earlier between *sourd* and *cire*, for example).

9.6. Learning the French back *r*

When learning to produce the *r* of standard French, it is useful for English speakers to keep in mind two essential points: (i) Do not involve the tongue tip in the articulation of this sound, but simply allow it to rest behind the lower teeth (attached with scotch tape or held in this position with a pencil if need be); (ii) Move the bulk of the tongue toward the back (toward the uvula and the pharynx), rather than toward the top (toward the hard palate).

The throat noise made by some people prior to spitting is quite similar to the French back *r*: both noises are produced by means of a radico-pharyngeal constriction (root of the tongue and pharyngeal wall). The difference is that the noise caused by 'throat clearing' is very 'hard', as it carries with it a lot of friction noise, whereas the back *r* is relatively 'soft', since it is essentially frictionless. By beginning with the noise of 'throat clearing', one thus approximates the right place of articulation for the back *r*; it is then a matter of adjusting the constriction and the air flow in such a way that the friction is practically eliminated; the resulting noise corresponds to the French back *r* and one can practise combining it with vowels, as in *iris* [iʁis] 'iris', *errer* [eʁe] 'to wander', *heureux* [øʁø] 'happy', *à ras* [aʁɑ] 'to the brim', *gourou* [guʁu] 'guru', *oraux* [oʁo] 'oral' (plural).

Another method for learning French *r* consists in starting with a back [ɑ] as in the French word *âme* 'soul' or in the English word *father*, and to exaggerate the radico-pharyngeal constriction which already exists for this type of vowel (as in gargling). A sound close to the desired goal may thus be obtained. Students may find it useful to practise this method with sequences of the form [ɑʁɑ].

A third approach to the production of this sound is to begin with the voiced velar stop [g], go to the corresponding fricative [ɣ], and finally draw the tongue toward the back to get to [ʁ]. Those who know some Spanish may find this method useful (cf. *pagar* [paɣar] 'to pay'), but it might be even easier for them to choose to start from the Spanish jota (the sound written *j* in words like *hoja* 'leaf', *jinete* 'horseman', and *reloj* 'clock') and 'soften' this sound (i.e. make it less fricative and voice it).

Once the English speaker succeeds in producing a back *r*, it frequently happens that this *r* is too 'hard' (too fricative and incorrectly voiceless). When this type of sound follows a voiced consonant, it even tends to devoice it by assimilation, which causes, for example, *grand* [grɑ̃] 'tall', *drain* [drɛ̃] 'drain', and *broc* [bro] 'pitcher' to resemble phonetically *cran* [krɑ̃] 'notch', *train* [trɛ̃] 'train', and *pro* [pro] 'pro', respectively. The latter problem is naturally compounded by the fact that voiced consonants in English are usually less completely voiced than in French (see Chapter 8, Section 8.3.2). There seem to be three main causes to such excess friction and lack of voicing, and three possible remedies can be tried. First, it may be that the constriction produced is too narrow; the solution here is to bring the tongue toward the front very slightly. Second, it may be that too much air is allowed to go through at once; in this case, the answer is to try not to give it such a big push from the lungs when the *r* is pronounced. Third, it is also possible that too much muscular tension is applied around the throat at the moment of production of the uncooperative sound; the remedy for this problem is simply to relax.

9.7. Conclusion

l and *r* are the consonants which usually present the most difficulties for English speakers learning French. Acquiring the appropriate articulations for these sounds is well worth the effort, however, for a bad pronunciation of these consonants has particularly salient effects on a speaker's overall perceived accent. To sum up, for French *l*, it is mainly a matter of avoiding the production of a dark *l*, and for French *r*, it is mainly a matter of producing a back *r*.

10
Double consonants and final consonants

10.1 Introduction

The preceding two chapters were essentially devoted to the articulatory differences separating English and French consonants. In this chapter and the next one, we shall focus on some specific properties of French regarding the presence or absence of pronounced consonants in certain contexts. This chapter is concerned with the relation between pronunciation and spelling as far as double consonants and final consonants are concerned when words are produced in isolation. The next chapter deals with liaison, that is, roughly speaking, the question of the pronunciation of word-final consonants when words are strung together in phrases and sentences.

10.2. Double consonants

In this section, we shall first consider the question of the pronunciation of double consonant-letters. We shall see that this type of spelling corresponds to a double pronunciation of the consonant only in relatively rare and very specific cases. Secondly, we shall survey the cases (also well defined) where a double consonant is found in the pronunciation, but without any indication of such a pronunciation in the orthography.

10.2.1. The pronunciation of the double consonants of the orthography

French orthography comprises numerous cases of double consonants; the following examples illustrate the possible doublings: a*bb*é 'abbot', o*cc*uper 'to occupy', a*dd*ition 'addition', a*ff*ectueux 'affectionate', a*gg*raver 'to aggravate', co*ll*er 'to glue', ho*mm*age 'homage', a*nn*ée 'year', a*pp*orter 'to bring', a*rr*êt 'stop', a*ss*ez 'enough', a*tt*aque 'attack', ja*zz* 'jazz'. There are in fact only seven consonant-letters (out of the twenty in the French alphabet) which are never double in the spelling: *h*, *j*, *k*, *q*, *v*, *w*, and *x*. As a rule, the appearance of a double consonant in the spelling of a French word does not signal anything special with regard to its pronunciation; with few exceptions, a double consonant simply has the

Table 10.1. Double consonants = single consonants

ab*b*é	[abe]	'abbot'	abeille	[abɛj]	'bee'
o*cc*uper	[ɔkype]	'to occupy'	oculiste	[ɔkylist]	'oculist'
a*dd*ition	[adisjõ]	'addition'	a*d*ipeux	[adipø]	'fat'
a*ff*ectueux	[afɛktɥø]	'affectionate'	a*f*in de	[afɛ̃dœ]	'in order to'
a*gg*raver	[agrave]	'to aggravate'	agrafer	[agrafe]	'to staple'
co*ll*er	[kɔle]	'to glue'	co*l*ère	[kɔlɛr]	'anger'
ho*mm*age	[ɔmaʒ]	'homage'	ho*m*ard	[ɔmar]	'lobster'
a*nn*ée	[ane]	'year'	a*n*éantir	[aneãtir]	'to wipe out'
a*pp*orter	[apɔrte]	'to bring'	a*p*ogée	[apɔʒe]	'apogee'
a*rr*êt	[arɛ]	'stop'	a*r*ête	[arɛt]	'fish bone'
a*tt*aque	[atak]	'attack'	a*t*avisme	[atavism]	'atavism'
ja*zz*	[dʒɑz]	'jazz'	ga*z*	[gɑz]	'gas'

phonetic value of a single consonant, as the examples in Table 10.1 illustrate.

Having established this general principle of correspondence between spelling and pronunciation, let us now examine the few cases which depart from it. They can be divided into four groups: (i) *ll* = [j], (ii) *ss* = [s], (iii) *cc* = [ks] and *gg* = [gʒ], and finally (iv) consonants written double which are actually pronounced double.

(i) The spelling *ll*. As already mentioned in Chapter 7 (Section 7.3.3), after the letter *i*, the sequence *ll* often contributes to the representation of the glide [j] (e.g. *juillet* [ʒɥijɛ] 'July', *fouiller* [fuje] 'to search', *briller* [brije] 'to shine'); but the sequence *ill* may also straightforwardly denote the sequence of sounds [il] after a consonant (compare, for example, *fille* [fij] 'daughter' and *ville* [vil] 'city'), as is always the case at the beginning of a word (e.g. *illustré* [ilystre] 'illustrated').

(ii) The spelling *ss*. As already observed in Chapter 1 (Section 1.2), the letter *s* between two vowel-letters usually represents the sound [z], not the sound [s] (*poison* [pwazõ] 'poison'). Elsewhere, the letter *s* (if pronounced) always has its basic phonetic value [s] (e.g. *sac* [sak] 'bag', *as* [ɑs] 'ace', *astérisque* [asterisk] 'asterisk', *psychologue* [psikɔlɔg] 'psychologist'). The intervocalic doubling of *s* in the orthography is a way to preserve this basic phonetic value in cases where a single *s* would ordinarily have its positional phonetic value [z] (*poisson* [pwasõ] 'fish'). There are, however, some instances where a single intervocalic *s* has the phonetic value [s]: *impresario* [ɛ̃presarjo] 'agent', *susurrer* [sysyre] 'to whisper', and words constructed on the pattern 'prefix with a final vowel-letter + word with initial *s*' (see Table 10.2).

(iii) The spellings *cc* and *gg*. These two spellings generally have the phonetic values [k] and [g] (*occuper* [ɔkype] 'to occupy', *aggraver* [agrave] 'to aggravate'), except in the following cases: *cc* represents the sequence [ks] before the vowel-letters *e* and *i* (as in *accent* [aksã] 'accent'

Table 10.2. Cases where intervocalic *s* = [s]

asymétrie	[asimetri]	'asymmetry'	(cf.	Asie	[azi]	'Asia')
antisocial	[ãtisɔsjal]	'antisocial'	(cf.	isoler	[izɔle]	'to isolate')
cosinus	[kɔsinys]	'cosine'	(cf.	cosaque	[kɔzak]	'cossack')
contresens	[kõtrœsãs]	'misinterpretation'	(cf.	trésor	[trezɔr]	'treasure')
désolidariser	[desɔlidarize]	'to disassociate'	(cf.	désolé	[dezɔle]	'sorry')
entresol	[ãtrœsɔl]	'entresol'	(cf.	résolu	[rezɔly]	'determined')
monosyllabe	[mɔnɔsilab]	'monosyllable'	(cf.	oser	[oze]	'to dare')
parasol	[parasɔl]	'parasol'	(cf.	rasoir	[rɑzwar]	'razor')
présupposer	[presypoze]	'to presuppose'	(cf.	présumer	[prezyme]	'to presume')
resaler	[rœsale]	'to salt again'	(cf.	résumé	[rezyme]	'summary')
résection	[resɛksjõ]	'resection'	(cf.	réserver	[rezɛrve]	'to reserve')
vraisemblable	[vrɛsãblabl]	'plausible'	(cf.	aisance	[ɛzãs]	'ease')

Table 10.3. [rr] vs [r]

[rr]		[r]
future	*conditional*	*imperfect*
il courra [ilkurra]	il courrait [ilkurrɛ]	il courait [ilkurɛ]
il mourra [ilmurra]	il mourrait [ilmurrɛ]	il mourait [ilmurɛ]

and *accident* [aksidã] 'accident'), and *gg* represents the sequence [gӡ] before the vowel-letter *e* (e.g. *suggérer* [sygӡere] 'to suggest'); this is in accordance with the general rules determining the basic and positional values of *c* and *g* (see Chapter 1, Section 1.3.1, and Appendix D).

(iv) Finally, there are a few cases where double consonants in the orthography may correspond in the pronunciation to double (or *geminate*, or *long*) consonants ('consonnes doubles' or 'géminées' or 'longues'). Geminate consonants differ from single consonants by a longer duration of their articulation, without intervening release. French geminate consonants reflected in the spelling can be classified into four categories, depending on the nature of the consonants, word structure, and speakers' styles.

(a) The geminate consonant [rr] (corresponding to the double consonant *rr* of the spelling) is found in the conjugation of the verbs *courir* 'to run' and *mourir* 'to die' in the future and conditional. The stems of these verbs end with *r* and the endings for the future and conditional themselves begin with *r*, hence the gemination. The pronunciations of these forms may be contrasted, for instance, with those of the imperfect of the same verbs, which have a single [r] (see Table 10.3). Note that the verb *pouvoir* 'to be able to' also takes two *r*s in the future and conditional, but that there is only one [r] in the pronunciation (e.g. *il pourra* [ilpura], *il pourrait* [ilpurɛ]).

(b) A similar case of gemination occurs with the prefix *in-* and its

Table 10.4. Geminates with the prefix *in-* and
its variants

*inn*é	[inne]	~	[ine]
*imm*ortel	[immɔrtɛl]	~	[imɔrtɛl]
*ill*isible	[illizibl]	~	[ilizibl]
*irr*esponsable	[irrɛspõsabl]	~	[irɛspõsabl]

Table 10.5. Other cases of orthographic and phonetic
double consonants

Ho*ll*ande	[ɔllɑ̃d]	~	[ɔlɑ̃d]	'Holland'
i*ll*usion	[illyzjõ]	~	[ilyzjõ]	'illusion'
sy*ll*abe	[sillab]	~	[silab]	'syllable'
gra*mm*aire	[grammɛr]	~	[gramɛr]	'grammar'
so*mm*et	[sɔmmɛ]	~	[sɔmɛ]	'peak'

variants *im-*, *il-*, and *ir-*, when these forms are added to words which
themselves begin with *n*, *m*, *l*, and *r*, hence, for example, *inné* 'innate',
immortel 'immortal', *illisible* 'illegible', and *irresponsable* 'irrespon-
sible'. Here, however, contrary to the preceding case, gemination is not
obligatory; two pronunciations are thus possible (see Table 10.4).

(c) A third case concerns a number of words such as those of Table
10.5, which may or may not, depending on the speaker, contain a
geminate consonant corresponding to the double consonant of the
spelling.

The three cases of geminate consonants examined up until now
illustrate the fact that the double consonant-letters susceptible to being
pronounced double without any particular stylistic effect are actually
circumscribed to the nasals *m* and *n* and the liquids *l* and *r*. Let us repeat in
addition that gemination is obligatory only in the first case cited (the
future and conditional of *courir* and *mourir*). From a practical point of
view, it is useful to observe then that the geminate pronunciation of
double consonant-letters is extremely restricted in French.

(d) With some speakers, the geminate pronunciation of double consonant-letters can be observed in a larger number of cases than those just
mentioned, but it is then a matter of pronunciations generally considered
affected or pedantic (for example, *addition* 'addition' pronounced
[addisjõ] instead of [adisjõ]). Nasals and liquids may also be the object of
stylistically marked geminate pronunciations (for example, *intelligence*
'intelligence' pronounced [ɛ̃tɛlliʒɑ̃s] instead of [ɛ̃teliʒɑ̃s]).

10.2.2. Other cases of geminate consonants

Besides pronounced geminate consonants correlating with written double consonants, there also exist in the pronunciation geminate consonants which do not correspond to double consonant-letters in the orthography. Here we shall distinguish three separate cases: (i) gemination of the elided personal pronoun *l'*, (ii) gemination resulting from the deletion of a vowel, and (iii) gemination due to emphatic stress.

(i) The personal pronoun *l'*. In rather idiosyncratic fashion, the elided personal pronoun *l'* 'him/her/it' is often geminated when preceded by a pronounced vowel (see Table 10.6). The gemination does not occur when the pronoun is not elided. Thus, *tu l'apprendras* 'you will learn it' may be pronounced with the *l* geminated or not, but *tu la prendras* 'you will take it' only with a single [l]. If *l'* represents the definite article *le* or *la*, the gemination does not take place either. Thus, *nous voulons l'envoyer* 'we want to send it' has two possible pronunciations, but *nous voulons l'envoyé* 'we want the envoy' has only one (see Figure 10.1).

(ii) The deletion of an *e* between two identical consonants also creates geminate consonants in the pronunciation (on *e*-deletion see Chapter 6). Note that, as opposed to the previous case, the gemination is then obligatory (see Table 10.7). This case is comparable with the case of the

Table 10.6. The gemination of the pronoun *l'*

je *l'*ai vu	[ʒœllɛvy]	~ [ʒœlɛvy]	'I saw it'
Henri *l'*a su	[ãrillasy]	~ [ãrilasy]	'Henry knew it'
il faut *l'*attraper	[ifollatrape]	~ [ifolatrapɛ]	'it must be caught'

Figure 10.1. Contrastive contexts and the gemination of *l*

Gemination possible	*No gemination*
tu *l'*apprendras ———————[tyllaprãdra]	
[tylaprãdra]————————tu *la* prendras	
nous voulons *l'*envoyer ——[nuvulõllãvwaje]	
[nuvulõlãvwaje]———— nous voulons *l'*envoyé	

Table 10.7. Gemination as a result of *e*-deletion

il s'aventu*rera*	[ilsavãtyrra]	'he'll venture'	(cf. il s'aventu*ra*	[ilsavãtyra]	'he ventured')
là-*dedans*	[laddã]	'inside'	(cf. la *dent*	[ladã]	'the tooth')
l'honnê*teté*	[lɔnɛtte]	'honesty'	(cf. *été*	[ete]	'summer')
mê*mement*	[mɛmmã]	'similarly'	(cf. mais *ment*!	[mɛmã]	'but lie!')

Table 10.8. Geminate consonants across words

une pure ration	[ynpyrrasjõ]	(cf. une pure action	[ynpyraksjõ])	'a pure ration' / 'a pure action'
une grande dame	[yngrãddam]	(cf. une grande âme	[yngrãdam])	'a great lady' / 'a great soul'
un honnête tome	[ɛ̃nɔnɛttɔm]	(cf. un honnête homme	[ɛ̃nɔnɛtɔm])	'an honest volume' / 'an honest man'
il aime m'en voler	[ilɛmmãvɔle]	(cf. il aime en voler	[ilɛmãvɔle])	'he likes to steal some from me' / 'he likes to steal some'

Table 10.9. Gemination as a result of vowel deletion

à *tout* à l'heure	[atutalœr]	→	[attalœr]	'see you later'
*mam*an	[mamɑ̃]	→	[mmɑ̃]	'mom'
*pap*a	[papa]	→	[ppa]	'dad'

Table 10.10. Gemination and emphatic stress

*f*ormidable	[ffórmidábl]	'terrible'
*é*pouvantable	[eppǔvɑ̄tábl]	'horrible'

geminate consonants found at the boundary between two words, the first of which phonetically ends in a consonant identical to that which begins the second word (see Table 10.8). The sporadic deletion of word-internal vowels other than *e* (see Chapter 6, Section 6.4) may also result in the creation of geminate consonants (see Table 10.9).

(iii) Finally, let us mention the case of the geminate consonants due to *emphatic stress* ('l'accent d'insistance'). As will be seen in more detail in Chapter 12, there exists in French, in addition to word-final stress, another type of stress, appropriately called 'emphatic' stress, which affects syllable prominence at the *beginning* of words. Roughly speaking, emphatic stress reinforces the first syllable with an initial consonant. One of the possible phonetic manifestations of the reinforcement is the gemination of this syllable-initial consonant. In the examples given in Table 10.10, the double acute accent is used to indicate emphatic stress, while the single acute accent marks regular word-final stress.

10.2.3. Double consonants: summary

While double consonants abound in the spelling of French words, they are rare in the pronunciation. Pronounced double consonants are obligatory on only two occasions: (i) in the future and conditional of the verbs *courir* and *mourir* and (ii) following the deletion of a vowel between identical consonants (e.g. *honnêteté* [ɔnɛtte] 'honesty'). Double consonants must also be pronounced between two words abutting with identical pronounced consonants (e.g. *une bonne nageuse* [ynbɔnnaʒøz] 'a good swimmer'). Otherwise, possible geminate consonants in the language are not indispensable, as their existence is linked to dialectal and stylistic variations.

10.3. Final consonants

This section focuses on the problem of the pronunciation of word-final consonants. We exclude for now the phenomenon of liaison, which concerns variations in the pronunciation of words when they are strung together in phrases (see Chapter 5, Section 5.7, and Chapter 11). Our concern here will thus be the pronunciation of words spoken in isolation; specifically, we shall try to determine when word-final consonant-letters are silent and when they are pronounced. As we shall see in Chapter 11, the pronunciation of words produced in isolation is also, for the most part, that which is found in a spoken chain of words.

10.3.1. General considerations

From the point of view of an English speaker learning French, the situation with final consonants is, from the beginning, almost a constant source of difficulties. Paradoxically, the perplexity and the confusion of students over this problem often grow in proportion to the growth of their knowledge of French. Why? First, since word-final written consonants are almost always pronounced in English (for example, the *s* of the plural), the natural tendency is to do the same thing in French. Usually informed very early that written final consonants are not pronounced in French, students generally make every effort to stop pronouncing them; in hypercorrective zealousness, some may even sometimes proceed to eliminate a good number of *phonetic* final consonants. In addition, students quickly find themselves confronted with words where written final consonants (which they strove so diligently not to pronounce) must, in fact, be pronounced. At a more advanced stage of acquisition, and to their great frustration and dismay, students may even discover a few words where French speakers differ among themselves with respect to their pronunciation of written final consonants (or perhaps worse, where individual French speakers have both pronunciations in their repertory).

The preceding description is very schematic and, no doubt, somewhat of a caricature of the stages through which English speakers come to grips with final consonants in French. Nevertheless, it contains a certain degree of truth reflective of a very thorny situation. In order to establish some general principles, specify certain tendencies, and recognize where things really seem unpredictable, we shall consider here the case of each consonant separately and systematically.

At the outset, let me say clearly, so as to nip a myth in the bud, that the existence of final consonants is not phonetically aberrant in French. Statistics show that there is about the same number of words which end in a vowel as which end in a consonant, with even a slight numerical advantage for the consonants (cf. *Dictionnaire inverse de la langue française*, by Alphonse Juilland, Appendix 1, pp. 437–456, 1965). It is therefore not at all exceptional for a word to be pronounced with a final consonant, and native speakers in no way feel that such pronunciations go against their native linguistic intuitions. Note in addition that of the 17 consonants and 3 glides which occur in French, only the two glides [ɥ] and [w] never appear in word-final position.

In relation to spelling, a pronounced final consonant will always be found if the word ends in at least one written consonant followed by the letter *e* (which, as seen in Chapter 6, Section 6.2, is usually silent). Exceptions to this principle are simply the result of *optional* simplifications in the pronunciation. For instance, as already indicated in Chapter 6 (see pp. 103–4), at the end of words, the liquids [l] and [r] preceded by a stop or a fricative may be omitted under certain conditions (e.g. *quatre murs* [katrœmyr] ~ [katmyr] 'four walls'). It can also be noted that some speakers do not always pronounce the [l] of the pronoun *elle* [ɛl] 'she' when the following word begins in a consonant (e.g. *elle veut venir* [ɛlvøvnir] ~ [ɛvøvnir] 'she wants to come'). Finally, in some dialects (for example, in Quebec French), a final consonant may be deleted if it is preceded by a consonant other than [l] or [r]: thus, *journalisme* 'journalism' and *journaliste* 'journalist' are usually pronounced in the same way: [ʒurnalis], instead of [ʒurnalism] and [ʒurnalist]. But again, remember that these pronunciations where a written consonant followed by a final *e* is not pronounced are merely options, not requirements.

If the presence of a final *e* is an infallible sign of the possibility of pronouncing the preceding consonant-letter, its absence does not mean that conversely, a written final consonant is necessarily silent. This is exactly where the real difficulties begin and where it is useful to proceed to a systematic examination of each of the consonants. Keep in mind that in the following, all my remarks apply only to *written consonants in word-final position* and that we are considering *words as pronounced in isolation* (i.e. liaison cases are excluded from our perspective).

10.3.2. *Individual study of final consonants*

10.3.2.1. B
 (i) relatively rare spelling
 (ii) always pronounced, except after *m* (*plomb* [plõ] 'lead'):

baoba*b*	[baɔbab]	'baobab'
clu*b*	[klœb]	'club'
sno*b*	[snɔb]	'snob'
toubi*b*	[tubib]	'doc' (also [tubi])

10.3.2.2. C

(i) usually pronounced in words in *-Vc* and *-Cc* (*V* = vowel; *C* = oral consonant) (see Chapter 1, p. 10):

cogna*c*	[kɔɲak]	'cognac'
ave*c*	[avɛk]	'with'
trafi*c*	[trafik]	'traffic'
fro*c*	[frɔk]	'monk's gown'
cadu*c*	[kadyk]	'deciduous'
par*c*	[park]	'park'
Mar*c*	[mark]	'Mark'
tal*c*	[talk]	'talcum powder'
fis*c*	[fisk]	'Internal Revenue Service'
tur*c*	[tyrk]	'Turkish'

Exceptions:

estoma*c*	[ɛstɔma]	'stomach'
taba*c*	[taba]	'tobacco'
accro*c*	[akro]	'hindrance'
escro*c*	[ɛskro]	'swindler'
caoutchou*c*	[kautʃu]	'rubber'
mar*c*	[mar]	'coffee grounds'
cler*c*	[klɛr]	'clerk'
por*c*	[pɔr]	'pork'

(ii) silent after a nasal vowel:

ban*c*	[bɑ̃]	'bench'
blan*c*	[blɑ̃]	'white'
fran*c*	[frɑ̃]	'franc/frank'
jon*c*	[ʒɔ̃]	'furze'
tron*c*	[trɔ̃]	'trunk'
vain*c*	[vɛ̃]	'(he) defeats'

Exceptions:

don*c*	[dɔ̃k]	'therefore'
zin*c*	[zɛ̃g]	'zinc'

Note: the word *donc* may be pronounced [dɔ̃], but only inside a verb group and with a weak meaning (*il est donc venu/arrivé* [ilɛdɔ̃vny/arive] 'so he came').

10.3.2.3. D

(i) usually silent

(ii) pronounced in the following words:

Alfre*d*	[alfrɛd]	'Alfred'
ble*d*	[blɛd]	'boondocks', 'godforsaken hole'
oue*d*	[wɛd]	'watercourse'
ze*d*	[zɛd]	(the letter *z*)

raid	[rɛd]	'raid'
caïd	[kaid]	'chief'
celluloïd	[selylɔid]	'celluloid'
David	[david]	'David'
yod	[jɔd]	'yod'
sud	[syd]	'south'
Talmud	[talmyd]	'Talmud'
week-end	[wikɛnd]	'week-end'

10.3.2.4. F

(i) usually pronounced
(ii) silent in the following words:

clef	[kle]	'key' (also spelled *clé*)
cerf	[sɛr]	'deer' (also pronounced [sɛrf])
nerf	[nɛr]	'nerve'
serf	[sɛr]	'serf' (more often pronounced [sɛrf])

10.3.2.5. G

(i) silent after *r*:

bourg	[bur]	'market town'
faubourg	[fobur]	'suburb'

(ii) usually silent after *n*:

étang	[etɑ̃]	'pond'
rang	[rɑ̃]	'rank'
sang	[sɑ̃]	'blood'
hareng	[arɑ̃]	'herring'
long	[lõ]	'long'
poing	[pwɛ̃]	'fist'

Exceptions:

bang	[bɑ̃g]	'bang'
gang	[gɑ̃g]	'gang'
boumerang	[bumrɑ̃g]	'boomerang'
gong	[gõg]	'gong'

Borrowed words in *-ing* such as *parking* [parkiŋ] 'parking lot' (cf. Chapter 8, pp. 125, 127) (but *shampooing* [ʃɑ̃pwɛ̃] 'shampoo').

(iii) pronounced after an oral vowel:

gag	[gag]	'gag'
zigzag	[zigzag]	'zigzag'
grog	[grɔg]	'grog'
joug	[ʒug]	'yoke' (also pronounced [ʒu])

10.3.2.6. H

(i) rare spelling after a vowel and always silent (*Allah* [ala] 'Allah')

(ii) after consonants, occurs only after *c* (see Chapter 1, pp. 10–12) and *t* (see Chapter 8, pp. 128–9):

-*ch*: (a) usually pronounced [k] (*varech* [varek] 'seaweed')
　　　(b) silent in *almanach* [almana] 'almanac' (also pronounced [almanak])
　　　(c) [ʃ] in *Auch* [oʃ] (town) and *Foch* [fɔʃ] (surname)
　　　(d) note also borrowed words:

cat*ch*	[katʃ]	'wrestling'
mat*ch*	[matʃ]	'match'
sandwi*ch*	[sãdwi(t)ʃ]	'sandwich'

-*th*: always pronounced [t]

ba*th*	[bat]	'good'
ma*th*	[mat]	'math'
mammou*th*	[mamut]	'mammoth'
zéni*th*	[zenit]	'zenith'

10.3.2.7. J

(non-existent spelling)

10.3.2.8. K

always pronounced:

bifte*ck*	[biftɛk]	'steak'
te*k*, tec*k*	[tɛk]	'teak'
do*ck*	[dɔk]	'dock'
mar*k*	[mark]	'(German) mark'

10.3.2.9. L

(i) always pronounced

(ii) except in *cul* [ku] 'ass' and *soûl* [sul] 'drunk', and in some words in -*il*, of which the following are the most common (see pp. 112–13):

fusi*l*	[fyzi]	'rifle'	genti*l*	[ʒɑ̃ti]	'nice'
outi*l*	[uti]	'tool'	nombri*l*	[nõbri]	'navel'
persi*l*	[pɛrsi]	'parsley'	sourci*l*	[sursi]	'eyebrow'

Note that the brand of laundry detergent *Persil* is pronounced [pɛrsil]; *nombril* and *sourcil* are also pronounced [nõbril] and [sursil].

10.3.2.10. M

(i) always pronounced

(ii) except in the following words, where *m* combines with the preceding vowel-letters to form a digraph or a trigraph representing a nasal vowel (see Chapter 5, Section 5.6):

Ada*m*	[adɑ̃]	'Adam'	fai*m*	[fɛ̃]	'hunger'
parfu*m*	[parfɛ̃]	'perfume'	dai*m*	[dɛ̃]	'deer'
no*m*	[nõ]	'name'	reno*m*	[renõ]	'fame'

10.3.2.11. N

(i) usually combines with the preceding vowel-letters to form a digraph or trigraph representing a nasal vowel (see Chapter 5, Section 5.6):

| bo*n* | [bõ] | 'good' | divi*n* | [divɛ̃] | 'divine' |
| plei*n* | [plɛ̃] | 'full' | paysa*n* | [peizã] | 'peasant' |

(ii) but, with only two exceptions (*Agen* [aʒɛ̃] (town), *examen* [egzamɛ̃] 'examination'), endings in -*Cen* (*C* = consonant-letter) are always pronounced [-Cɛn] (see Chapter 5, pp. 79–81):

| abdom*en* | [abdɔmɛn] | 'abdomen' |
| poll*en* | [pɔlɛn] | 'pollen' |

(iii) the same type of pronunciation [Vn] is also found in words borrowed from English:

| gi*n* | [dʒin] | 'gin' |
| blue-jea*n* | [bludʒin] | 'bluejeans' |

10.3.2.12. P

(i) usually silent

(ii) but pronounced in interjections and borrowings:

he*p*	[ɛp]	(interjection)
ho*p*	[ɔp]	(interjection)
sto*p*	[stɔp]	'stop sign'
to*p*	[tɔp]	(time signal)
ca*p*	[kap]	'cape'
handica*p*	[ãdikap]	'handicap'
crou*p*	[krup]	'croup'
sli*p*	[slip]	'underwear'

10.3.2.13. Q

(i) rare spelling

(ii) always pronounced:

| cin*q* | [sɛ̃k] | 'five' | co*q* | [kɔk] | 'rooster' |

10.3.2.14. R

(i) always pronounced

(ii) except in the word *monsieur* [məsjø] 'sir' and in the sequence -*er*, which may be pronounced [e], [ɛr], or [œr] (see (iii) below)

(iii) the sequence -*er*:

    (a) pronounced [e] in the following cases:
        infinitive ending (*chanter* [ʃãte] 'to sing')
        suffix -*ier* or -*er*:

| banqu*ier* | [bãkje] | 'banker' |
| bouch*er* | [buʃe] | 'butcher' |

the following adjectives:

dern*er*	[dɛrnje]	'last'
enti*er*	[ɑ̃tje]	'entire'
premi*er*	[prœmje]	'first'
lég*er*	[leʒe]	'light'

(b) elsewhere, *-er* is pronounced [ɛr], in particular in the following words:

adjectives:

am*er*	[amɛr]	'bitter'
ch*er*	[ʃɛr]	'expensive'
fi*er*	[fjɛr]	'proud'

the adverb *hier* [ijɛr] 'yesterday'

nouns:

canc*er*	[kɑ̃sɛr]	'cancer'
cuill*er*	[kɥijɛr]	'spoon'
enf*er*	[ɑ̃fɛr]	'hell'
hiv*er*	[ivɛr]	'winter'
f*er*	[fɛr]	'iron'
m*er*	[mɛr]	'sea'

Note: *cuiller* is also spelled *cuillère*.

borrowings:

gangst*er*	[gɑ̃gstɛr]	'gangster'
pok*er*	[pɔkɛr]	'poker'
report*er*	[rœpɔrtɛr]	'reporter'
revolv*er*	[revɔlvɛr]	'revolver'

(c) Note: some borrowings in *-er* end in [œr]:

lead*er*	[lidœr]	'leader'
speak*er*	[spikœr]	'announcer'

10.3.2.15. S

The situation is complex. As a first approximation, one can say that final *s* is usually silent, although there exist numerous cases where it is pronounced.

(i) Cases where *s* is always silent.

(a) plural endings:

joli*s*	[ʒɔli]	'pretty'
écureuil*s*	[ekyrœj]	'squirrels'

(b) verb endings:

tien*s*	[tjɛ̃]	'hold'
prend*s*	[prɑ̃]	'take'

(c) adverbs and prepositions:

alor*s*	[alɔr]	'then'
mai*s*	[mɛ]	'but'
toujour*s*	[tuʒur]	'always'
volontier*s*	[vɔlɔ̃tje]	'gladly'
dan*s*	[dɑ̃]	'in'
san*s*	[sɑ̃]	'without'
sou*s*	[su]	'under'
ver*s*	[vɛr]	'toward'

Note: *jadis* 'formerly' is pronounced [ʒadis].

(d) nouns ending in -*Vis*:

engr*ais*	[ãgrɛ]	'fertilizer'
Franç*ais*	[frãsɛ]	'French'
camb*ouis*	[kãbwi]	'grease'
L*ouis*	[lwi]	'Lewis'
b*ois*	[bwɑ]	'wood'
Chin*ois*	[ʃinwɑ]	'Chinese'

(e) adjectives:

ba*s*	[bɑ]	'low'
gra*s*	[grɑ]	'fat'
gri*s*	[gri]	'gray'
préci*s*	[presi]	'precise'
épai*s*	[epɛ]	'thick'
mauvai*s*	[mɔvɛ]	'bad'
clo*s*	[klo]	'closed'
gro*s*	[gro]	'large'
confu*s*	[kõfy]	'confused'
obtu*s*	[ɔpty]	'obtuse'
absou*s*	[apsu]	'absolved'
dissou*s*	[disu]	'dissolved'
épar*s*	[ɛpar]	'scattered'
retor*s*	[rœtɔr]	'twisted'

(ii) Cases where *s* is almost always silent:

(a) pronouns and nouns ending in -*ous*:

n*ous*	[nu]	'we'
v*ous*	[vu]	'you'
rendez-v*ous*	[rãdevu]	'appointment'

But note *couscous* [kuskus] 'couscous' and the pronoun *tous* [tus] 'all' (cf. *ils sont tous là* [ilsõtuslɑ] 'they are all here' vs *tous les ans* [tulezã] 'every year').

(b) nouns ending in -*rs*:

recou*rs*	[rœkur]	'recourse'
secou*rs*	[sœkur]	'help'
velou*rs*	[vœlur]	'velvet'

Exceptions:

ma*rs*	[mars]	'March'
ou*rs*	[urs]	'bear'
moeu*rs*	[mœrs]	'manners' (also [mœr])

(c) nouns ending in -*ns*:

dépe*ns*	[depã]	'expense'
ence*ns*	[ãsã]	'incense'
guet-ape*ns*	[gɛtapã]	'ambush'

Exceptions:

ce*ns*	[sãs]	'census'
se*ns*	[sãs]	'meaning'

(d) nouns ending in -*as*:

b*as*	[bɑ]	'bottom'
c*as*	[kɑ]	'case'

embarr*as*	[ãbara]	'trouble'
fatr*as*	[fatra]	'jumble'
lil*as*	[lila]	'lilac'
p*as*	[pɑ]	'step'
rep*as*	[rœpɑ]	'meal'
t*as*	[tɑ]	'pile'

Exceptions:

as	[ɑs]	'ace'
atl*as*	[atlas]	'atlas'
anan*as*	[ananas]	'pineapple' (also [anana])
pancré*as*	[pãkreas]	'pancreas'
vasist*as*	[vazistas]	'skylight'

(iii) Cases where *s* is always pronounced:

(a) words ending in -*ss*:

busine*ss*	[biznɛs]	'business'
expre*ss*	[ɛksprɛs]	'express'
gnei*ss*	[gnɛs]	'gneiss'
stre*ss*	[strɛs]	'stress'

(b) words ending in -*ps*:

bice*ps*	[bisɛps]	'biceps'
force*ps*	[fɔrsɛps]	'forceps'
trice*ps*	[trisɛps]	'triceps'
la*ps*	[laps]	'lapse'

(iv) Cases where *s* is almost always pronounced:

nouns ending in -*us*:

autob*us*	[ɔtɔbys]	'bus'
cact*us*	[kaktys]	'cactus'
camp*us*	[kãpys]	'campus'
détrit*us*	[detritys]	'garbage'
hiat*us*	[jatys]	'hiatus'
laps*us*	[lapsys]	'slip' (error)
process*us*	[prɔsesys]	'process'
vir*us*	[virys]	'virus'

Exceptions:

ab*us*	[aby]	'abuse'
j*us*	[ʒy]	'juice'
ob*us*	[ɔby]	'shell'
p*us*	[py]	'pus'
ref*us*	[rœfy]	'refusal'
tal*us*	[taly]	'slope'

(v) Difficult cases (lists of contrastive examples)

(a) nouns ending in -*Cis*:

	[-Cis]	
b*is*	[bis]	'encore'
cass*is*	[kɑsis]	'blackcurrant'

ibis	[ibis]	'ibis'
iris	[iris]	'iris'
maïs	[mais]	'corn'
métis	[metis]	'hybrid'
myosotis	[mjɔzɔtis]	'forget-me-not'
oasis	[ɔazis]	'oasis'
tennis	[tenis]	'tennis'
tournevis	[turnœvis]	'screwdriver'
vis	[vis]	'screw'
volubilis	[vɔlybilis]	'convolvulus'

	[-Ci]	
avis	[avi]	'opinion'
débris	[debri]	'debris'
fouillis	[fuji]	'jumble'
gâchis	[gɑʃi]	'mess'
gazouillis	[gazuji]	'warbling'
hachis	[aʃi]	'hash'
panaris	[panari]	'whitlow'
parvis	[parvi]	'parvis'
salsifis	[salsifi]	'salsify'
souris	[suri]	'mouse'
taudis	[todi]	'slum'
tapis	[tapi]	'carpet'

(b) nouns ending in -ès:

	[-ɛs]	
aloès	[alɔɛs]	'aloe'
cacatoès	[kakatɔɛs]	'cockatoo'
Jaurès	[ʒɔrɛs]	(surname)
kermès	[kɛrmɛs]	'kermes'
palmarès	[palmarɛs]	'prize list'
pataquès	[patakɛs]	'false liaison'
xérès	[gzerɛs]	'sherry wine'

	[-ɛ]	
abcès	[apsɛ]	'abscess'
accès	[aksɛ]	'access'
cyprès	[siprɛ]	'cypress'
décès	[desɛ]	'decease'
progrès	[prɔgrɛ]	'progress'
succès	[syksɛ]	'success'
très	[trɛ]	'very'

(c) nouns ending in -os:

	[-ɔs]/[-os]	
albinos	[albinos]	'albino'
albatros	[albatros]	'albatross'
cosmos	[kosmos]	'cosmos'
os	[ɔs]	'bone'
rhinocéros	[rinɔserɔs]	'rhinoceros'
tétanos	[tetanos]	'tetanus'

	[-o]	
d*os*	[do]	'back'
cha*os*	[kao]	'chaos'
encl*os*	[ãklo]	'enclosure'
hér*os*	[ero]	'hero'
prop*os*	[propo]	'remark'
rep*os*	[rœpo]	'rest'

Note: *os* 'bone' is pronounced [o] or [ɔs] in the plural.

10.3.2.16. T

The situation is complex here too. Again, as a rough approximation, one can say that final *t* is generally silent, with, however, exceptions.

(i) Cases where *t* is always silent:

third person verb endings:

il veu*t*	[ilvø]	'he wants'
ils veul*ent*	[ilvœl]	'they want'
il chantai*t*	[ilʃãtɛ]	'he was singing'
ils chanter*ont*	[ilʃãtrõ]	'they will sing'

(ii) Cases where *t* is almost always silent:

(a) words in: -*ait* (*souhait* [swɛ] 'wish'); but *fait* [fɛ(t)] 'fact'
          -*aut* (*défaut* [defo] 'defect')
          -*uit* (*fruit* [frᵾi] 'fruit'); but *huit* [ᵾit] 'eight'
          -*oit* (*droit* [drwa] 'right')
          -*et* (*garçonnet* [garsɔnɛ] 'little boy'); but *net* [nɛt] 'clean'
          -*ot* (*sot* [so] 'stupid'); but *dot* [dɔt] 'dowry'
          -*at* (*chat* [ʃa] 'cat'); but *mat* [mat] 'mat'; *fat* [fa(t)] 'vain'
(b) after a nasal vowel (*gant* [gã] 'glove')
(c) after *r* (*art* [ar] 'art'); but *flirt* [flœrt] 'flirt', *yaourt* [jaur(t)] 'yogurt'
(d) adjectives ending in -*it* (*petit* [pœti] 'little')

(iii) Cases where *t* is almost always pronounced:

(a) after *c*:
adjectives

compa*ct*	[kõpakt]	'compact'
corre*ct*	[kɔrɛkt]	'correct'
stri*ct*	[strikt]	'strict'

nouns

conta*ct*	[kõtakt]	'contact'
intelle*ct*	[ɛ̃telɛkt]	'intellect'
verdi*ct*	[vɛrdikt]	'verdict'

Note: In some cases, there is hesitation between a pronunciation with or without [kt]:

exa*ct*	[egza(kt)]	'exact'
suspe*ct*	[syspɛ(kt)]	'suspect'

Pronunciation generally without [kt]:

distin*ct*	[distɛ̃]	'distinct'
succin*ct*	[syksɛ̃]	'succinct'

(b) after *l*:

coba*lt*	[kɔbalt]	'cobalt'

co*lt*	[kɔlt]	'pistol'
vo*lt*	[vɔlt]	'volt'

(c) after *p*:

abru*pt*	[abrypt]	'abrupt'
ra*pt*	[rapt]	'abduction'
conce*pt*	[kõsɛpt]	'concept'
transe*pt*	[trãsɛpt]	'transept'

Note: *sept* 'seven' is pronounced [sɛt].

(d) after *s*:

e*st*	[ɛst]	'east'
le*st*	[lɛst]	'ballast'
oue*st*	[wɛst]	'west'
te*st*	[tɛst]	'test'
ze*st*	[zɛst]	'zest'
tru*st*	[trœst]	'trust'

Note: *est* (from *être* 'to be') is pronounced [ɛ].

(iv) Difficult cases (lists of contrastive examples)

(a) nouns ending in -*it*:

	[-it]	
access*it*	[aksesit]	'merit award'
défic*it*	[defisit]	'deficit'
gran*it*	[granit]	'granite'
prétér*it*	[preterit]	'preterite'
trans*it*	[trãzit]	'transit'

	[-i]	
band*it*	[bãdi]	'bandit'
espr*it*	[ɛspri]	'mind'
hab*it*	[abi]	'clothes'
prof*it*	[prɔfi]	'profit'
réc*it*	[resi]	'story'

(b) nouns ending in -*out*:

	[-ut]	
knock-*out*	[knɔkut]	'knockout'
kn*out*	[knut]	'knout'
sc*out*	[skut]	'scout'
verm*out*	[vɛrmut]	'vermouth'

	[-u]	
b*out*	[bu]	'end'
deb*out*	[dœbu]	'standing'
égo*ut*	[egu]	'sewer'
go*ût*	[gu]	'taste'

Note: *août* 'August' is pronounced [ut] or [u].

(c) words ending in -*ut*:

	[-yt]	
azim*ut*	[azimyt]	'azimuth'
br*ut*	[bryt]	'rough'
ch*ut*	[ʃyt]	'hush'
occip*ut*	[ɔksipyt]	'occiput'

rut	[ryt]	'rut'
scorbut	[skɔrbyt]	'scurvy'
ut	[yt]	'do' (music)

	[-y]	
attribut	[atriby]	'attribute'
bahut	[bay]	'trunk'
début	[deby]	'beginning'
institut	[ɛ̃stity]	'institute'
rebut	[rœby]	'waste'
salut	[saly]	'salute'
statut	[staty]	'statute'

Note: *but* 'goal' is pronounced [byt] or [by].

10.3.2.17. V

(i) very rare spelling

(ii) always pronounced:

| Kie*v* | [kjɛv] | 'Kiev' |
| Tel-Avi*v* | [tɛlaviv] | 'Tel Aviv' |

10.3.2.18. W

(non-existent spelling)

10.3.2.19. X

(i) silent as a grammatical marker:

   (a) plural marker (*hiboux* [ibu] 'owls')
   (b) verb ending (*je peux* [ʒœpø] 'I can')

(ii) silent also after:

   -i (*prix* [pri] 'prize'), except *phénix* [feniks] 'phenix' and (iii) below
   -ai (*paix* [pɛ] 'peace')
   -oi (*choix* [ʃwɑ] 'choice')
   -u (*flux* [fly] 'flow')
   -au (*faux* [fo] 'false')
   -eu (*deux* [dø] 'two')
   -ou (*doux* [du] 'soft')

(iii) pronounced [s] in *six* [sis] 'six' and *dix* [dis] 'ten'

(iv) pronounced [ks] elsewhere, in particular in the following cases:

   after: *-a* (*thorax* [tɔraks] 'thorax')
   -e (*silex* [silɛks] 'flint')
   -in (*sphinx* [sfɛ̃ks] 'sphinx')
   -yn (*larynx* [larɛ̃ks] 'larynx')

10.3.2.20. Z

(i) silent in the verb ending *-ez*

(ii) silent in the following words:

asse*z*	[ase]	'enough'
che*z*	[ʃe]	'at'
re*z*-de-chaussée	[retʃɔse]	'ground floor'
ra*z* de marée	[rɑdmare]	'tidal wave'

(iii) pronounced [z] in the following words:

fe*z*	[fɛz]	'fez'
ga*z*	[gɑz]	'gas'
ja*zz*	[dʒɑz]	'jazz'

(iv) note also *quartz* [kwarts] 'quartz'

10.3.3. Final consonants: conclusion

In French, word-final consonant-letters are silent to a point probably unsurpassed in any other written language. It is, nonetheless, true that French allows pronounced final consonants, and that a good number of these phonetic final consonants are also written final consonants. Today's spelling is thus a system of undeniable ambiguity in its phonetic representation of the language. From the classification laid out in the preceding section, it is difficult to draw exceptionless generalizations across consonants. Nevertheless, in addition to the regularities specific to each consonant already mentioned in the course of our survey, certain overall tendencies seem to emerge which may be helpful to the language learner:

(i) Consonants which are markers for grammatical endings such as plural (in nouns and in adjectives) or person (in the conjugation of verbs) are silent.

(ii) With only a few exceptions, final consonants are silent in adjectives.

(iii) Even though all consonant-letters occurring in word-final position (except, of course, *h*) may in fact be pronounced in one case or another, some among them have, from a statistical point of view, a more marked propensity than others to appear phonetically. These are *b, c, f, k, l, m, q,* and *r*.

(iv) In borrowed words, final consonants are usually pronounced.

(v) The greatest difficulties concern *s* and *t*, but essentially in a few groups of nouns identifiable by the preceding vowel. Elsewhere, various clues are generally available and sufficient to help determine whether or not the consonant is pronounced.

11
Liaison

11.1. Introduction

Liaison in French is comparable to certain phenomena which occur in English. For example, the English indefinite article is *a* before a word beginning with a consonant (*a book*) and *an* before a word beginning with a vowel (*an old book*). In some English dialects (for instance British English), words which end in a 'vowel + r' sequence in the orthography (for example, *far*, *never*) are pronounced without a final [r], unless the next word begins in a vowel (compare *far* [fɑ:] and *far away* [fɑ:rəwe], *never* [nɛvə] and *never again* [nɛvərəgen]). The absence/presence of these consonants [n] and [r] in English is, on a reduced scale, similar to the pervasive phenomenon of liaison in French, where ordinarily silent word-final consonants may be pronounced before vowel-initial words (see Table 11.1).

In Chapter 5 (Section 5.7), liaison was briefly considered in its interaction with nasal vowels. The goal of this chapter is to take a closer and more comprehensive look at liaison. We shall first present a cursory history of the phenomenon, and then a fairly detailed examination of the conditions under which liaison (or linking) consonants may occur. We shall close the chapter on a set of practical rules which foreign students can use as convenient guidelines for their own speech.

11.2. Brief history of liaison

Consider again the English examples given at the beginning of this chapter. Historically, the definite article *a* comes from the form *an* (itself derived from the word *one*) by deletion of the [n] in preconsonantal position (but not before a vowel). Today, however, English speakers generally make the following reinterpretation: *a* is the basic form of the indefinite article; *an* results from the addition of a linking [n] before vowel-initial words.

Similarly, in the history of British English, postvocalic [r] deleted everywhere, except before a vowel; in word-final position, it now occurs as a linking [r] when the next word begins with a vowel. It is interesting to note that, by extension, some British speakers pronounce an [r] before

Table 11.1. French liaison

il est peti*t*	[ilɛpti]	'he is little'
un peti*t* curé	[ɛ̃ptikyre]	'a little priest'
un peti*t* abbé	[ɛ̃ptitabe]	'a little abbot'

vowel-initial words not only when the preceding word ends in an *r* in the spelling, but also when it ends in a vowel (e.g. *the idea-r-of it*, *I saw-r-it there*). The reason for this phenomenon is that linking [r] has ended up being interpreted by these speakers not as a word-final consonant which can delete everywhere except before vowels, but rather as the result of an intervocalic insertion at the boundary between two words. In those cases where the presence of a linking [r] is not justified by the etymology (or, equivalently here, by the spelling), one usually talks about an 'intrusive' [r], i.e. a type of 'false' liaison, historically speaking.

The phenomenon of liaison in contemporary French has arisen from the same processes of linguistic change, but on a much more extensive scale, as more words and more consonants are involved. In Old French, final consonants were pronounced, but from the twelfth to the sixteenth centuries, they progressively disappeared, first in preconsonantal position and then at the pause, leaving them to appear only in prevocalic position. Later, other restrictions came to reduce even more the contexts in which these consonants could appear, so much so that liaison today occurs far less than it used to (but probably more than tomorrow).

French speakers sometimes make false liaisons, i.e. they use a linking consonant which is incorrect with respect to the norm, whose main guide is spelling. False liaisons are usually referred to as 'pataquès'. Two types of pataquès can be distinguished: the 'cuirs' (literally 'leather'), which are inappropriate liaisons with [t], and the 'velours' (literally 'velvet'), which are inappropriate liaisons with [z]. The word 'pataquès' [patakɛs] comes from the sentence *je ne sais pas-t-à qu'est-ce* [ʒœnœsɛpatakɛs] (for *je ne sais pas à qui c'est* 'I don't know to whom it belongs'); the sentence itself comes from the following anecdote, told by the grammarian Urbain Domergue around 1800 and cited by Philippe Martinon in his 1913 book, *Comment on prononce le français* (pp. 60–1):

> 'Un beau diseur était au spectacle dans une loge, à côté de deux femmes, dont l'une était l'épouse d'un agioteur, ci-devant laquais; l'autre d'un fournisseur, ci-devant savetier. Tout à coup le jeune homme trouve sous sa main un éventail: Madame, dit-il à la première, cet éventail est-il à vous? – Il n'est poin-z-à moi. – Est-il à vous, en le présentant à l'autre? – Il n'est pa-t-à moi. – Le beau diseur, en riant: Il n'est poin-z-à vous, il n'est pas-t-à vous, je ne sais pa-t-à qu'est-ce. Cette plaisanterie a couru dans les cercles, et le mot est resté.

(A twaddler was attending a play in a theater box, next to two
women, one wife to a former footman turned speculator, the other
to a former cobbler turned supplier. All of a sudden the young
man's hand finds a fan: Madam, he says to the first, is this fan
yours? – It is not mine. – Is it yours, showing it to the second? – It
is not mine. – The twaddler, laughing: It is neither yours, nor yours,
I do not know whose it is. This joke spread quickly in society, and
the word has remained.) [This translation is intended only to relate
the general meaning of the French quote; for obvious reasons, it
does not capture the phonetic characteristics of the verbal exchanges
which ultimately yielded the word 'pataquès'.]

False liaisons with [z] are called 'velours' and false liaisons with [t] are
called 'cuirs', presumably because [z] (a voiced fricative) is subjectively
softer than [t] (a voiceless stop), just as velvet is softer than leather. An
example of an extremely widespread velours is liaison with [z] in a plural
'numeral adjective + noun' sequence (see Table 11.2). [z] being the
plural linking consonant par excellence (cf. next section), such word
sequences provide a particularly natural context for its occurrence.
Nevertheless, with the exception of the expression *entre quat'zyeux*
[ɑ̃trœkatzjø] 'between you and me', whose existence is usually acknow-
ledged in dictionaries and grammars, this velours remains outside the
norm. But that is not to say that a pataquès may never be officially
accepted in the language. For example, the linking [t] which is found
today in constructions like *aime-t-il?* [ɛmtil] 'does he love?' and *dîne-t-
elle?* [dintɛl] 'is she having dinner?' is an old sixteenth-century cuir. In
those days, such phrases were still written without the *t*, but began to be
pronounced with a [t]: [ɛmti] and [dintɛl] (the *l* of *il* was not pronounced).
It had, however, been about four centuries since the old verb ending [t]
had completely disappeared from both the pronunciation and the spelling
as the marker for the present indicative third person singular of first group
verbs (and a few other verbs such as *avoir* and *aller*). Its reintroduction
into the pronunciation was followed by its reintroduction into the
orthography; a cuir was thus integrated into the norm. In the same group
of verbs, the orthographic *s* found in the imperative second person
singular when the pronouns *en* and *y* follow immediately is an example of
velours accepted as the norm and integrated into the orthography (see
Table 11.3).

False liaisons are not generally made haphazardly. I have already
alluded to the motivations behind the intrusive [r] in English and behind
the linking [z] used in French with numeral adjectives. The linking [z] and
[t] just mentioned in connection with some French verb forms in the
second and third person singular are also motivated within the language;

Table 11.2. Examples of false liaison (velours)

	velours	*norm*	
quatre officiers	[katzɔfisje]	[katrɔfisje]	'four officers'
huit épreuves	[ɥizeprœv]	[ɥiteprœv]	'eight tests'
neuf oeufs	[nœfzø]	[nœfø]	'nine eggs'
vingt-cinq années	[vɛ̃tsɛ̃kzane]	[vɛ̃tsɛ̃kane]	'twenty-five years'
trois mille évêques	[trwɑmilzevɛk]	[trwɑmilevɛk]	'three thousand bishops'

Table 11.3. Cases of integrated velours

manges-en	[mɑ̃ʒzɑ̃]	'eat some'	(cf. mange un peu [mɑ̃ʒɛ̃pø] 'eat a little')
vas-y	[vazi]	'go there'	(cf. va à Paris [vaapari] 'go to Paris')

Table 11.4. Liaison with verb endings

viens avec moi	[vjɛ̃zavɛkmwa]	'come with me'
tu chantais encore	[tyʃɑ̃tɛzɑ̃kɔr]	'you were still singing'
vit-il à Paris?	[vitilapari]	'does he live in Paris?'
elle sortirait avec eux	[ɛlsɔrtirɛtavɛkø]	'she would go out with them'

these two consonants systematically mark second and third persons when they appear in liaison elsewhere in the verb system (see Table 11.4).

11.3. Conditions for the occurrence of linking consonants

The phonetic appearance of linking consonants is subject to various conditions that can be divided into four groups of factors: phonetic, syntactic, morphological, and stylistic.

There is really only one absolute constraint concerning the appearance of linking consonants; it is of a phonetic nature. Liaison may occur only before a vowel-initial or a glide-initial word. Apart from this, liaison is an extremely variable phenomenon where stylistic factors combine with other factors to yield a considerable range of possibilities going from an extremely limited liaison system to a very dense one. As a rule, the more elevated the style, the more often liaison occurs; the more colloquial the style, the less often liaison occurs. Liaison also depends on syntactic cohesion between words; the tighter the syntactic link between contiguous words, the more likely liaison is to occur; the looser the syntactic link, the less likely liaison is to occur. Finally, liaison tends to occur more readily if it signals a precise morphological mark (for example, the plural) than if it represents no particular grammatical information.

Table 11.5. The basic phonetic factor in liaison

liaison			no liaison		
un peti*t* igloo	[ε̃ptitiglu]	'a little igloo'	un peti*t* vélo	[ε̃ptivelo]	'a little bike'
les gros arbres	[legrozarbr]	'the big trees'	les gros camions	[legrokamjɔ̃]	'the big trucks'
o*n* arrive	[ɔ̃nariv]	'we are coming'	o*n* part	[ɔ̃par]	'we are leaving'
u*n* oiseau	[ε̃nwazo]	'a bird'	u*n* livre	[ε̃livr]	'a book'
les huîtres	[lezɥitr]	'the oysters'	les coquillages	[lekɔkijaʒ]	'the seashells'
de beaux yeux	[dœbozjø]	'beautiful eyes'	de beaux dessins	[dœbodesε̃]	'beautiful drawings'

We shall now consider the most important of these phonetic, syntactic, and morphological factors and see how they interface with stylistic levels. Clearly, foreign students cannot be expected to absorb and integrate immediately into their spontaneous speech all the following details. The goal of the present section is mainly to offer a fairly systematic description and classification of the facts of liaison. The last section of the chapter provides a simple pedagogical framework within which the more complex elements of this section can be progressively incorporated.

11.3.1. Phonetic factors

As already indicated, liaison may occur only with a following vowel-initial (or glide-initial) word; it does not take place before a consonant-initial word (see Table 11.5).

H-aspiré words (cf. Chapter 6, pp. 93–5, and Appendix E) constitute an exceptional class of vowel-initial words, because linking consonants may not in principle appear before them (see Table 11.6). It is not rare, however, for some of these words to be regularized in spontaneous speech (for example, *les haricots* 'the beans' will be pronounced [lezariko] instead of [leariko]). One can also observe interesting variations in a given speaker in certain cases; for instance, in the conjugation of h-aspiré verbs such as *hocher* (*la tête*) 'to shake (one's head)', or *hacher* (*la viande*) 'to grind (the meat)', liaison will often not occur with *nous* 'we' and *vous* 'you', but it will with *ils/elles* 'they'.

As was mentioned in Chapter 6 (pp. 95–6), there are also glide-initial words which do not allow liaison (see Table 11.7). We saw in Chapter 7 (Section 7.4) that by conceiving the phenomenon of liaison as the

Table 11.6. No liaison with h-aspiré words

un peti*t* hibou	[ɛ̃ptiibu]	'a little owl'
les gro*s* haricots	[legroariko]	'the big beans'
o*n* hurlait	[õyrlɛ]	'we were yelling'
u*n* héros	[ɛ̃ero]	'a hero'
le*s* hors-d'œuvre	[leɔrdœvr]	'the hors d'œuvres'
de beau*x* hêtres	[dœboɛtr]	'beautiful beech trees'

Table 11.7. No liaison with certain glide-initial words

un peti*t* yéti	[ɛ̃ptijeti]	'a little yeti'
le*s* yaourts	[lejaurt]	'the yogurts'
un bo*n* whisky	[ɛ̃bõwiski]	'a good whiskey'
u*n* ouistiti	[ɛ̃wistiti]	'a marmoset'

Figure 11.1. Glides and liaison

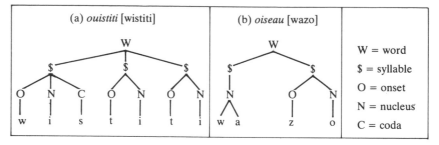

appearance of a consonant before a word-initial syllable nucleus, the absence of liaison with these glide-initial words is automatically explained if it is assumed that the glide occupies the onset position in the initial syllable (see Diagram (a) in Figure 11.1). By contrast, for words such as *oiseau* [wazo] 'bird', with which liaison does occur (cf. Table 11.5 above), it is sufficient to assume that the initial syllable of the word does not contain an onset and that the glide, together with the following vowel, constitutes a diphthong which forms the (complex) nucleus of this syllable (see Diagram (b) in Figure 11.1).

A very small group of consonants may actually serve as linking consonants; these are [z, t, n, r, p, g]. Among these consonants, just three ([z, t, n]) are frequently used as linking consonants.

Liaison in [g] is used with only one word, the adjective *long* followed by a noun (*un long été* [ɛ̃lõgete] 'a long summer'). Liaison in [k] with *long* ([ɛ̃lõkete]), instead of [g], is archaic. Some speakers do not link at all with *long* ([ɛ̃lõete]). Note, simply as a matter of curiosity, that liaison with [k] is sometimes heard in the expression *sang impur* [sɑ̃kɛ̃pyr] 'impure blood'. This is an old pronunciation which has become fixed in the context of the French national anthem. Today, such a pronunciation sounds artificial and one would normally say [sɑ̃ɛ̃pyr], with no liaison at all.

[p] is also rare as a linking consonant. It is used with two words only, the adverbs *trop* 'too much' and *beaucoup* 'many' (see Table 11.8). Sometimes, liaison with *trop* is accompanied by the opening of [o] to [ɔ] (*trop aimé* [trɔpeme]).

Liaison with [r] is frequent only with the adjectives *léger* 'light', *premier* 'first', and *dernier* 'last' followed by a noun (see Table 11.9). This linking consonant is also used, but rarely, with infinitives of first conjugation verbs (*aimer un peu* [emerɛ̃pø] 'to love a little'). Such liaison is characteristic of a very formal style, possibly pedantic or even pompous. By an interesting phenomenon of hypercorrection, the past participles of first conjugation verbs (which are homophonous with the infinitives)

Table 11.8. Liaison with [p]

tro*p* aimé	[tropeme]	'too much loved'
beaucou*p* aimé	[bokupeme]	'much loved'

Table 11.9. Liaison with [r]

un lége*r* incident	[ε̃leʒerε̃sidã]	'a slight mishap'
au premie*r* étage	[oprœmjereta3]	'on the second floor'
un dernie*r* avertissement	[ε̃dεrnjeravεrtismã]	'a last warning'

Table 11.10. Liaison with [t]

(i)	chantera-*t*-elle?	[ʃãtratεl]	'will she sing?'
	il fau*t* en parler	[ilfotãparle]	'we have to talk about it'
	ils se plaignen*t* encore	[ilsœplεɲtãkɔr]	'they are complaining again'
(ii)	extrêmemen*t* important	[εkstrεmmãtε̃pɔrtã]	'extremely important'
	aveuglémen*t* amoureux	[avœglemãtamurø]	'blindly in love'
(iii)	un peti*t* avion	[ε̃ptitavjõ]	'a little plane'
	un gran*d* homme	[ε̃grãtɔm]	'a great man'

sometimes enter into false liaison in [r] with the following word (for example, *nous avons terminé ensemble* 'we finished together' pronounced [nuzavõtεrminerãsãbl] instead of [nuzavõtεrmineãsãbl]). With some speakers, the [e] which precedes the linking [r] may open to [ε] (*au premier étage* [oprœmjεreta3], *aimer un peu* [emεrε̃pø]).

The truly frequent linking consonants are [z, t, n]. Liaison with [n] occurs only with words ending in a nasal vowel (see Chapter 5, Section 5.7). But the reverse is not true: all the words which end in a nasal vowel do not necessarily link with [n]. Thus, *en* [ã] does link with [n] (*en Autriche* [ãnotriʃ] 'in Austria'), but *dans* [dã] links with [z] (*dans un mois* [dãzε̃mwa] 'in a month'), *tant* [tã] links with [t] (*tant admiré* [tãtadmire] 'so admired'), and *selon* [sœlõ] is not supposed to link (*selon eux* [sœlõø] 'according to them').

[t] is also an important linking consonant. It is the linking consonant for verbs conjugated in the third person (singular and plural) (see Table 11.10, Part i). It also characterizes liaison with adverbs in *-ment* (see Table 11.10, Part ii). And it is very common with prenominal adjectives such as *petit* and *grand* (see Table 11.10, Part iii).

As a rule, spelling indicates precisely the phonetic nature of the linking consonants (for example, [g] with *long*, [p] with *trop* and *beaucoup*, [n] with *en*, [t] with *petit*). But note that words ending in the letter *d* and

Table 11.11. Liaison with [z]

(i)	les étudiants	[lezetydjã]	'the students'
	ces arbres	[sezarbr]	'these trees'
	leurs habits	[lœrzabi]	'their clothes'
	deux petits animaux	[døptizanimo]	'two little animals'
	de grands enfants	[dœgrãzãfã]	'tall children'
	des maisons ensoleillées	[demezõzãsɔleje]	'sunny houses'
	les soldats américains	[lesɔldazamerikẽ]	'the American soldiers'
(ii)	je suis arrivé	[ʒœsɥizarive]	'I arrived'
	nous comprenons enfin	[nukõprœnõzãfẽ]	'we finally understand'
	tu viens à Paris	[tyvjẽzapari]	'you are coming to Paris'
	vous chantez encore	[vuʃãtezãkɔr]	'you are still singing'
(iii)	un gros éléphant	[ẽgrozelefã]	'a big elephant'
	joyeux anniversaire	[ʒwajøzanivɛrsɛr]	'happy birthday'

linking with the following word use the consonant [t] in liaison (even if the *d* is pronounced [d] in a related word). Thus, the following words have liaison with [t]:

– the conjunction *quand*, like the word *quant* (*quand il arrivera* [kãtilarivra] 'when he arrives'; *quant à eux* [kãtaø] 'as to them');

– the adjectives *grand* and *second* (*un grand avion* [ẽgrãtavjõ] 'a large plane'; *un second arrivage* [ẽsœgõtarivaʒ] 'a second delivery'), in spite of *grande* [grãd] 'large' (feminine), *grandeur* [grãdœr] 'size', *grandir* [grãdir] 'to grow', and *seconde* [sœgõd] 'second' (feminine), *secondaire* [sœgõdɛr] 'secondary', and *seconder* [sœgõde] 'to second';

– verb forms such as *attend* and *vend* (*attend-on?* [atãtõ] 'do we wait?', *vend-on?* [vãtõ] 'do we sell?'), in spite of *attendons* [atãdõ] 'let's wait' and *vendons* [vãdõ] 'let's sell'.

The most frequent linking consonant is [z] (its pervasiveness probably accounts for the fact that it is also the most widespread linking consonant in pataquès). It is the plural marker for determiners, adjectives, and nouns (see Table 11.11, Part i). It is the first and second person marker for both singular and plural conjugated verbs (see Table 11.11, Part ii). And it occurs frequently with adjectives like *gros*, *heureux*, *joyeux* in prenominal position (see Table 11.11, Part iii). This linking consonant generally appears as *s* in the spelling; but *x* and *z* are also found, *x* in some plural forms and in the words *six* and *dix*, in spite of their pronunciations [sis] and [dis] at the pause (see Table 11.12, Part i), *z* in *chez* and in the second person plural of verbs (see Table 11.12, Part ii).

The occurrence of a linking consonant is restricted when the preceding word already ends in a pronounced consonant (which frequently happens to be [r]). The restriction, however, is not uniform. Syntactic and

Table 11.12. *x* and *z* as linking [z]

(i)	de nouveaux arrivants	[dœnuvozarivã]	'newcomers'
	six amis	[sizami]	'six friends'
	dix exercices	[dizɛgzɛrsis]	'ten exercises'
(ii)	chez un professeur	[ʃezɛ̃prɔfɛsœr]	'at a professor's home'
	vous arrivez à point	[vuzarivezapwɛ̃]	'you come just in time'

morphological factors play an important diversifying role and the stylistic effects vary accordingly.

As we shall see later, liaison is generally obligatory between an adjective and a noun. But the adjectives *court* [kur] 'short', *fort* [fɔr] 'strong', and *lourd* [lur] 'heavy' do not link with a following singular noun (no liaison with [t]) (see left-hand side of Table 11.13). By contrast, liaison usually occurs in the plural (liaison with [z]) (see right-hand side of Table 11.13). Note, however, that liaison with [z] between plural adjectives and nouns is sometimes omitted in spontaneous speech if the adjective already ends in a consonant; the omission of this liaison is particularly frequent with the adjective *autre* [otr] 'other' (e.g. *les autres années* 'the other years' [lezotrane] instead of [lezot(rœ)zane]).

With the adverbs *fort* [fɔr] 'very' and *toujours* [tuʒur] 'always', liaisons with [t] and [z] are possible (*fort intéressant* [fɔrtɛ̃teresã] 'very interesting', *toujours intéressant* [tuʒurzɛ̃teresã] 'always interesting'), but they are the mark of a very formal style. Liaison with *fort* is actually frequent, but that is because the use of this word as an adverb characterizes a rather affected vocabulary and a corresponding style accommodating a maximum number of liaisons.

Liaisons in [z] with the prepositions *vers* [vɛr] 'toward', *envers* [ãvɛr] 'toward', and *à travers* [atravɛr] 'through' do not generally occur, but they may sometimes be heard in a style seeking to be elevated.

Concerning singular verb forms such as *cours, dors, meurs*, and *court, dort, meurt* ([kur], [dɔr], [mœr], from *courir* 'to run', *dormir* 'to sleep', *mourir* 'to die'), liaison with [z] and [t] does not generally occur either, except in constructions with the postverbal pronouns *il, elle, on, en*, and *y*, where it is absolutely obligatory (cf. Section 11.3.3 below and see the contrasting examples in Table 11.14, Part i). Note that in contexts where liaison in [t] with the singular verbs *court* and *meurt* is not generally tolerated, liaison in [t] with the corresponding plural forms *courent* and *meurent* is possible (see Table 11.14, Part ii).

Table 11.13. Phonetic restriction on liaison with adjectives

no liaison		liaison		
un court entracte	[ɛ̃kurɑ̃trakt]	de courts entractes	[dœkurzɑ̃trakt]	'a short intermission' / 'short intermissions'
un très fort alibi	[ɛ̃trefɔralibi]	de très forts alibis	[dœtrefɔrzalibi]	'a very strong alibi' / 'very strong alibis'
un lourd objet	[ɛ̃lurɔbʒɛ]	de lourds objets	[dœlurzɔbʒɛ]	'a heavy object' / 'heavy objects'

Table 11.14. Phonetic restriction on liaison with verbs

(i)

no liaison			obligatory liaison		
tu dors encore	[tydɔrɑ̃kɔr]	'you're still sleeping'	dors-y	[dɔrzi]	'sleep there'
il court encore	[ilkurɑ̃kɔr]	'he is still running'	cours-en un	[kurzɑ̃ɛ̃]	'run one'
on y meurt encore	[ɔ̃nimœrɑ̃kɔr]	'one still dies there'	meurt-il?	[mœrtil]	'does he die?'

(ii) liaison possible

elles courent encore	[ɛlkur(t)ɑ̃kɔr]	'they are still running'
ils y meurent encore	[ilzimœr(t)ɑ̃kɔr]	'they are still dying there'

11.3.2. Morphological factors

As already emphasized, the phonetic nature of linking consonants depends on the preceding word. In many cases, morphological character-istics predict which linking consonant will be used, but there nevertheless exists a set of arbitrary cases where it is difficult to connect the particular nature of the linking consonant with anything other than etymology and orthography.

In the case of invariable words (for example, prepositions and adverbs), no general prediction can be made: from a synchronic point of view, the linking consonant is arbitrary and every French speaker must learn the appropriate linking consonant word by word. Only with adverbs in *-ment* can speakers establish a generalization: they all link with [t].

Given the arbitrary character of the linking consonants used with invariable words, it is not surprising that false liaison occurs. False liaison is particularly frequent with the adverb *trop*, whose linking consonant [p] does not have wide currency. *Trop* is often heard to link with [z], especially when the following word is in the plural. The extension of the plural linking [z] was noted, earlier in this chapter, with normatively invariable numeral adjectives (cf. pp. 170–1). To the examples cited then can be added the cases of *vingt* [vɛ̃] 'twenty' and *cent* [sɑ̃] 'one hundred', which theoretically link with [t] (*vingt étudiants* [vɛ̃tetydjɑ̃] 'twenty students', *cent arbres* [sɑ̃tarbr] 'one hundred trees'), but are often heard entering into liaison with [z].

Concerning singular masculine adjectives, their linking consonants are phonetically related to the endings found in the corresponding feminine forms. The existing correlations are given in Table 11.15, with some examples.

In the plural, liaison with determiners, adjectives, and nouns is always made with [z] (*nos anciens étudiants américains* [nozɑ̃sjɛ̃zetydjɑ̃-zamerikɛ̃] 'our former American students'). Liaison with [z] is also found with the personal pronouns *nous*, *vous*, *ils*, *elles*, and *les* (see Table 11.16). Note that the plural possessive adjective *leurs* links with *z*, but the plural possessive pronoun *leur* does not: cf. *leurs amis* [lœrzami] 'their friends' vs *il leur a mis* (*un point*) [illœrami] 'he gave them (one point)'.

Linking consonants with conjugated verb forms are limited to two possibilities: [z] for first and second person, and [t] for third person. In the plural, there is no phonetic or morphological restriction concerning the use of these linking consonants (see Table 11.17).

In the singular, facts are more complicated. We have already seen that liaison here is subject to restrictions of a phonetic nature (cf. Table 11.14, Part i). There are in addition restrictions of a morphological nature:

Table 11.5. Correspondences between feminine and linking consonants

masculine	feminine consonant	linking consonant
joli	Ø ⟷	Ø
petit, haut, sot	t	
grand	d	t
heureux, joyeux	z	
gros	s	z
long	g ⟷	g
premier, dernier, léger	r ⟷	r
bon, plein, certain	n ⟷	n

Table 11.16. Liaison in [z] with personal pronouns

nous irons	[nuzirõ]	'we shall go'
vous écoutez	[vuzekute]	'you are listening'
ils arrivent	[ilzariv]	'they are coming'
elles en parlent	[ɛlzãparl]	'they are talking about it'
tu les as vus	[tylezavy]	'you saw them'

Table 11.17. Plural liaison with verbs

nous partirons ensemble	[nupartirõzãsãbl]	'we'll leave together'
pensez à vos parents	[pãsezavoparã]	'think of your parents'
ils chantèrent à Paris	[ilʃãtɛrtapari]	'they sang in Paris'

liaison does not occur in the present indicative, imperative, and simple past of first conjugation verbs; neither does it occur in the future or in the subjunctive for all verbs. However, as already mentioned (cf. again Table 11.14, Part i), and for reasons to be explained later, liaison with [t] is obligatory in all cases where the conjugated verb form is followed by an inverted subject pronoun (*il, elle, on*), and liaison with [z] is also general and obligatory when the verb is in the imperative and followed by the object pronouns *en* or *y*. The contrasting examples provided in Table 11.18 illustrate these facts.

In the present indicative and simple past of first conjugation verbs, and also in the future and subjunctive of all verbs, the final orthographic *s* found in the second person singular leads some speakers who are

Table 11.18. Morphological restrictions on singular verb liaison

no liaison		liaison		
on partira ensemble	[õpartiraɑ̃sɑ̃bl]	partira-*t*-on ensemble?	[partiratõɑ̃sɑ̃bl]	'we'll leave together' / 'shall we leave together?'
pense à tes parents	[pɑ̃sateparɑ̃]	penses-y	[pɑ̃szi]	'think of your parents' / 'think about it'
il chanta à Paris	[ilʃɑ̃taapari]	chanta-*t*-il à Paris?	[ʃɑ̃tatilapari]	'he sang in Paris' / 'did he sing in Paris?'

Table 11.19. Morphological restriction on liaison with prepositions, adverbs, and auxiliaries

dans un mois	[dɑ̃zɛ̃mwɑ]	'in a month'	depuis un mois	[dœpɥi(z)ɛ̃mwɑ]	'for a month'
très intéressant	[trezɛ̃teresɑ̃]	'very interesting'	assez intéressant	[ase(z)ɛ̃teresɑ̃]	'interesting enough'
il est amoureux	[ilɛtamurø]	'he is in love'	il était amoureux	[ilete(t)amurø]	'he was in love'

particularly avid fans of liaison to link these forms with [z], thereby eliminating some of the restrictions just stated.

As a final note on verbs, let us mention again the liaison with [r] that is sometimes found with the infinitives of first conjugation verbs (*chanter en chœur* [ʃãterãkœr] 'to sing together').

Word length also plays a role in liaison. The crucial distinction is between monosyllables and polysyllables. This distinction particularly affects prepositions, adverbs, and auxiliaries. All else being equal, monosyllabic prepositions, adverbs, and auxiliaries have a tendency to enter into liaison more readily than corresponding polysyllables (see Table 11.19). In a colloquial style, such liaisons may all be ignored, whereas in a formal style, they may all occur. But in between these two extremes, there is an intermediate style where the tendency is to have liaison with monosyllables and not with polysyllables. There is no natural style where the converse is true, that is, where liaisons are limited to polysyllables, to the exclusion of monosyllables.

It is necessary to qualify somewhat these general statements concerning monosyllables and polysyllables. First, even in a very colloquial style, liaison is obligatory in the expressions *chez eux/chez elle(s)* 'at their/her place' ([ʃezø]/[ʃezɛl]), and with the preposition *en* directly followed by a noun (*en argent* [ãnarʒã] 'in silver', *en Iran* [ãnirã] 'in Iran'). Liaison with the adverb *assez* [ase] 'enough' seems more common than with polysyllabic adverbs ending in *-ment*; this is perhaps due to the fact that *assez* links with [z], whereas *-ment* adverbs link with [t]. The same distinction seems valid with the prepositions *depuis* [dœpɥi] 'since' and *pendant* [pãdã] 'for': liaison in [z] with *depuis* is relatively more expected than liaison in [t] with *pendant*. In general, all else being equal, liaison with [z] seems to occur more readily than liaison with [t] (or any other consonant). Note in this respect that the adverb *trop* [tro] 'too much', even though monosyllabic, links relatively seldom, far less, for instance, than other monosyllabic adverbs like *très* [trɛ] 'very'; the fact is that the linking consonant of *trop*, [p], is a rare linking consonant, whereas the linking consonant of *très*, [z], is a pervasive linking consonant; as noted earlier, *trop* is often found to trigger false liaison with [z].

Plurality is another morphological factor favoring the occurrence of liaison. For example, as we shall see later, there is in principle no liaison between a noun and the following word. This rule is absolute if the noun is singular, even in the most formal styles (*un étudiant américain* [ɛnety-djãamerikɛ̃] 'an American student'). But, if the noun is in the plural, it is then possible to have liaison in [z] occur with a following adjective (*les étudiants américains* [lezetydjã(z)amerikɛ̃]). In a very formal style, liaison with [z] may even be found between a plural subject noun and its verb (*les soldats avancèrent* [lesɔlda(z)avɑ̃sɛr] 'the soldiers advanced'). Similarly, liaison in [t] between a third person verb and its complement or an adverb occurs relatively more readily in the plural (*ils viennent aux Etats-Unis* 'they come to the United States') than in the singular (*il vient aux Etats-Unis* 'he comes to the United States'). These examples illustrate how the morphological factor of plurality somehow breaks down the barrier set by certain syntactic constraints. We saw earlier how it also breaks down the barrier set by certain phonetic constraints: in the singular, liaison between an adjective and a noun does not occur if the adjective already ends in another pronounced consonant (*un court entracte* [ɛ̃kurɑ̃trakt] 'a short intermission'); but liaison usually occurs in the plural (*de courts entractes* [dœkurzɑ̃trakt] 'short intermissions').

11.3.3. Syntactic factors

We now consider the role played by syntactic structure in determining the possibilities of occurrence of liaison consonants. We have already alluded to some of these factors, but a more systematic presentation is in order. As a general principle, it can be stated that the stronger the syntactic tie between two words, the greater the tendency for liaison to occur; conversely, the weaker the syntactic tie, the lesser the tendency for liaison to occur. Syntactic relationships between words thus determine by themselves a wide gamut of possibilities, ranging from obligatory liaisons to prohibited liaisons, with intermediate series of optional liaisons whose absence or presence corresponds to differences in style.

Let us first illustrate the influence that syntax may have on liaison, with some clear examples. Consider the following sequence of words: *Allez + vous + écouter*. This group of words may be interpreted in two ways: (a) as a question, where *vous* is the inverted subject of *allez* ('Are you going to listen?'), or (b) as an imperative, where *vous* is the direct object of *écouter* ('Go listen to yourself!'). In the first case, *vous* is associated with *allez* (see Diagram (a) in Figure 11.2); in the second case, *vous* forms a unit with *écouter* (see Diagram (b) in Figure 11.2). A sentence, then, is not just a sequence of words; it is also a structure composed of syntactic units (or 'constituents') larger than the word. Figure 11.2 shows graphically that the syntactic solidarity between *vous* and *écouter* is tighter in Sentence (b), where the two words form a constituent, than in Sentence (a), where they do not. Correspondingly, liaison between *vous* and *écouter* is obligatory in Sentence (b) ([alevuzekute]), but not in Sentence (a) ([alevuekute]).

Considering now a sentence like *Ses anciens étudiants annoncèrent un grand exploit* 'His former students announced a great achievement', we can assign it a partial syntactic structure such as that given in Figure 11.3.

Figure 11.2. Contrasting syntactic groupings and liaison

(a) *Allez-vous écouter?*	(b) *Allez vous écouter!*
allez-vous écouter	allez vous écouter

Figure 11.3. Syntactic structure of a sentence

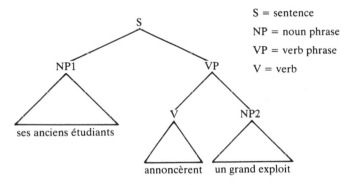

S = sentence
NP = noun phrase
VP = verb phrase
V = verb

The sentence, S, is divided into a subject noun phrase (NP1) and a verb phrase (VP). The verb phrase itself is subdivided into a verb (V) and an object noun phrase (NP2). This diagram (or 'tree') clearly indicates that the syntactic solidarity between words found within each of the two noun phrases is tighter than the syntactic solidarity between the verb V and the first word of the second noun phrase NP2. It is also clear that the syntactic solidarity between V and NP2 is itself tighter than that between the last word of the first noun phrase NP1 and V. The phenomenon of liaison respects this syntactic hierarchy: thus, liaison within the constituents NP1 and NP2 is obligatory ([sezãsjẽzetydjã], [ẽgrãtɛksplwɑ]), liaison between V and NP2 would only be made in a formal style, and liaison between NP1 and V would practically never occur.

We are now in a position to consider several common syntactic contexts and examine to what degree liaison is or is not favored in them. Syntactic solidarity is particularly tight between a number of small grammatical words and the words of which they may be considered satellites. Liaison in these cases is obligatory. This group of small grammatical words includes noun determiners (i.e. articles and possessive adjectives) and personal pronouns (which form an extremely compact unit with the verb of which they are either the subject or the object). Noun determiners link obligatorily with a following adjective or noun (see Table 11.20).

Table 11.20. Obligatory liaison with noun determiners

un ami	[ɛ̃nami]	'a friend'
les anciens murs	[lezɑ̃sjɛ̃myr]	'the old walls'
ses études	[sezetyd]	'his studies'
nos autres livres	[nozotrœlivr]	'our other books'

Table 11.21. Obligatory liaison between verbs and pronouns

nous arrivons	[nuzarivõ]	'we arrive'
achètes-en	[aʃɛtzɑ̃]	'buy some'
ils en auront	[ilzɑ̃nɔrõ]	'they will have some'
on y va	[õniva]	'we go there'
allons-y	[alõzi]	'let's go there'
vient-elle?	[vjɛ̃tɛl]	'is she coming?'

The syntactic combinations 'pronoun + verb' and 'verb + pronoun' also constitute favorable ground for liaison to occur; these combinations may not be interrupted by other words, except other pronouns, and liaison is obligatory between all the elements within these verbal constituents (see Table 11.21). It is essential to remember that liaison is obligatory only if pronouns and verbs are syntactically related; their simple juxtaposition is not sufficient (cf. Diagrams (a) and (b) in Figure 11.2 for the sequence *Allez + vous + écouter*).

The syntactic solidarity between a preposition or an adverb and the following constituent modified by the preposition or the adverb is sufficiently tight to make liaison possible. As mentioned earlier, liaison is much more likely to occur if the preposition or adverb is monosyllabic. Liaison with *chez, dans, en, sans, sous, très* is thus extremely common; its absence would actually denote a rather colloquial style (see Table 11.22). Liaison with *assez* [ase] 'enough' is not so common. Liaison with the other polysyllabic prepositions and adverbs (e.g. *depuis* [dœpɥi] 'since', *pendant* [pɑ̃dɑ̃] 'for', *extrêmement* [ɛkstrɛmmɑ̃] 'extremely') is even less common and characterizes a more formal style.

The syntactic solidarity within an 'adjective + noun' sequence usually guarantees an obligatory liaison, but in spontaneous speech, exceptions to this general principle may be found. As a rule, liaison can be considered obligatory with a small number of adjectives which are frequently placed before the noun, for instance *petit* 'small', *grand* 'tall', *bon* 'good' (see Table 11.23). But quite often liaison does not occur with other adjectives, for example *long* [lõ] 'long', *blond* [blõ] 'blond', *premier* [prœmje] 'first', *chaleureux* [ʃalørø] 'warm'. We also saw earlier that under certain phonetic conditions, particularly when the adjective

Table 11.22. Cases of frequent liaison with prepositions and adverbs

chez une amie	[ʃezynami]	'at a friend's home'
dans une semaine	[dɑ̃zynsœmɛn]	'in a week'
en un quart d'heure	[ɑ̃nẽkardœr]	'in a quarter of an hour'
sans un sou	[sɑ̃zẽsu]	'penniless'
sous un arbre	[suzẽnarbr]	'under a tree'
très intéressant	[trɛzẽteresɑ̃]	'very interesting'

Table 11.23. Cases of obligatory liaison with adjectives

un petit écureuil	[ẽptitekyrœj]	'a little squirrel'
un grand amour	[ẽgrɑ̃tamur]	'a great love'
un bon appétit	[ẽbɔnapeti]	'a good appetite'

ends in a pronounced consonant, liaison occurs less often (for example, liaison with *autres* [otr] 'other') and may even be completely blocked (for example, liaison with *court* [kur] 'short'). Finally, note that in some dialects (for instance in some regions of Belgium), liaison between an adjective and a noun has completely disappeared (even in cases such as those illustrated in Table 11.23).

The syntactic solidarity within a 'noun + adjective' sequence is much more lax. Liaison between singular nouns and adjectives never occurs (*un étudiant américain* [ẽnetydjɑ̃amerikẽ] 'an American student'). As noted earlier, however, this barrier can be broken down by the linking consonant [z] when it indicates plural (*des étudiants américains* [dezetydjɑ̃zamerikẽ] 'some American students'). Such liaison, however, characterizes a rather careful style.

The syntactic solidarity between a subject noun phrase and its verb is even more lax. There also, liaison never occurs, at least not in the singular (*l'étudiant écouta* [letydjɑ̃ekuta] 'the student listened'). In the plural, it is only found in an extremely elevated style (*les soldats avancèrent* [lesɔldazavɑ̃sɛr] 'the soldiers advanced').

The syntactic solidarity between a conjugated verb and its complement (*il buvait un bon vin* 'he was drinking a good wine') or an adverb (*il buvait encore* 'he was still drinking') is sufficiently lax for the presence of liaison to characterize a rather elevated style ([ilbyvɛtẽbõvẽ], [ilbyvɛtɑ̃kɔr]).

11.3.4. Additional remarks

The next few remarks add to the picture of liaison presented so far some details concerning frequently used constructions.

Liaison never occurs with the coordinating conjunction *et* [e] 'and'. The *t* in this word is nothing but an orthographic ornament.

The word *quand* [kɑ̃] 'when' may link with the following word when it corresponds to the subordinating conjunction (*Quand il arrivera, partez* [kɑ̃tilarivraparte] 'When he arrives, leave'), but in a colloquial style, liaison tends to be omitted. *Quand* does not link when it plays the role of an interrogative word in direct questions (*Quand arrivera-t-il?* [kɑ̃arivratil] 'When will he arrive?'), but liaison occurs, except in colloquial style, before the interrogative form *est-ce que* (*Quand est-ce qu'il arrivera?* [kɑ̃tɛskilarivra]). In indirect questions (*Je ne sais pas quand il arrivera* 'I don't know when he will arrive'), the situation seems intermediate: liaison occurs less readily than with *quand* used as a subordinating conjunction, but it is not as difficult as with *quand* used in a direct question without *est-ce que*.

The situation is similar with the interrogative word *comment* [kɔmɑ̃] 'how'. *Comment* does not link in direct questions (*Comment arriverez-vous?* [kɔmɑ̃arivrevu] 'How will you arrive?'), except with *est-ce que*, where liaison is possible (*Comment est-ce que vous arriverez?* [kɔmɑ̃tɛskœvuzarivre]', and in the fixed expression *Comment allez-vous?* 'How are you?', where liaison is obligatory ([kɔmɑ̃talevu]). Liaison is possible in indirect questions, at least in a somewhat formal style (*Savez-vous comment elles reviendront?* 'Do you know how they will come back?').

11.4. Practical advice

Liaison errors by foreign students naturally occur in the two logically possible directions: occurrence of liaison where it should not occur and absence of liaison where it should occur. However, in general, foreign students tend to sin with an overabundance rather than a dearth of liaisons. This asymmetry is probably due in part to the fact that linking consonants usually appear in the spelling as final consonants; English speakers beginning to learn French have a tendency to pronounce such written consonants, since written word-final consonants are pronounced in their native language. More advanced students may also have trouble resisting this natural temptation, especially when the following word begins with a vowel and they know that this context is one necessary for liaison (forgetting that it is not sufficient).

Rather than adopting the strategy viewing the acquisition of liaison as learning the contexts in which this phenomenon does not occur, it is preferable, from a practical standpoint, to make the base assumption that liaison occurs nowhere, and then to learn the general contexts where liaison is really necessary if one wishes to escape notice, linguistically speaking. If one follows this path, there are then only three very simple and very useful rules to remember:

(i) In a noun phrase, liaison occurs before the noun.
(ii) In a verb phrase, liaison occurs among the verb and the pronominal satellites around it.
(iii) Liaison occurs with monosyllabic prepositions, adverbs, and auxiliaries.

Observing these three golden rules will allow a student to go far in the correct use of liaison in standard French.

The following summary recapitulates, with illustrations, the main cases where it is indispensable or preferable to have liaison.

(a) Before a noun: Liaison within the noun phrase between the noun and a preceding word, and also between the preceding words themselves.

> Article + noun:
> les étudiants   [lezetydjã]   'the students'
> Article + adjective + noun
> mes anciens étudiants   [mezãsjẽzetydjã]   'my former students'

(b) Around the verb: Liaison between the verb and its satellite pronouns (subject and object), and also between the satellite pronouns themselves.

> Subject pronoun + verb:
> nous irons   [nuzirõ]   'we shall go'
> Subject pronoun + object pronoun + verb:
> nous en avons   [nuzãnavõ]   'we have some'
> Verb + subject pronoun:
> vient-il?   [vjẽtil]   'is he coming?'
> Verb + object pronoun
> allons-y   [alõzi]   'let's go there'
> Verb + object pronoun + object pronoun:
> allons-nous-en   [alõnuzã]   'let's leave'

(c) Adverbs and prepositions: Liaison with the following (monosyllabic) adverbs and prepositions.

très	très intéressant	[trɛzẽteresã]	'very interesting'
chez	chez eux/chez elle/	[ʃezø]/[ʃezɛl]/	'at their/her/a
	chez un ami	[ʃezẽnami]	friend's house'
dans	dans un mois	[dãzẽmwu]	'in a month'
en	en anglais, en une	[ãnãglɛ],	'in English', 'in a
	semaine	[ãnynsœmɛn]	week'
sans	sans intérêt, sans un	[sãzẽterɛ],	'without interest',
	sou	[sãzẽsu]	'penniless'
sous	sous un arbre	[suzẽnarbr]	'under a tree'

(d) Liaison with the auxiliary *est*:

c'es*t* impossible	[sɛtɛ̃pɔsibl]	'it's impossible'
elle es*t* ici	[ɛlɛtisi]	'she is here'

To these fundamental cases may be added a few stock phrases ('expressions figées') inside which liaison must occur, even though the conditions described above are not fulfilled.

accen*t* aigu	[aksɑ̃tegy]	'acute accent'
le ca*s* échéant	[lœkɑzeʃeɑ̃]	'if need be'
mo*t* à mot	[motamo]	'word by word'
nui*t* et jour	[nɥiteʒur]	'night and day'
Etat*s*-Unis	[etazyni]	'United States'
Champ*s*-Elysées	[ʃɑ̃zelize]	(street name)
peti*t* à petit	[ptitapti]	'little by little'
de plu*s* en plus	[dœplyzɑ̃plys]	'more and more'
de moin*s* en moins	[dœmwɛ̃zɑ̃mwɛ̃]	'less and less'
tou*t* à coup	[tutaku]	'all of a sudden'
tou*t* à fait	[tutafɛ]	'absolutely'
tou*t* à l'heure	[tutalœr]	'soon'
de temp*s* à autre	[dœtɑ̃zɑotr]	'from time to time'
de temp*s* en temps	[dœtɑ̃zɑ̃tɑ̃]	'from time to time'
de fon*d* en comble	[dœfɔ̃tɑ̃kɔ̃bl]	'from top to bottom'
de hau*t* en bas	[dœotɑ̃bɑ]	'from top to bottom'

Part Four
Suprasegmentals

12
Stress and intonation

12.1. Introduction

The preceding chapters dealt mainly with the study of the articulation of the sounds (or segments) which make up words in French and in English. But an utterance in any language does not simply consist of a succession of various articulations. Loudness and pitch are other parameters which inherently enter into the pronunciation of every utterance, and their own modulations play extremely important linguistic roles. Because variations in loudness and pitch are *super*imposed upon the spoken chain of sounds (or *segmental* chain), the term *suprasegmentals* ('traits suprasegmentaux') is used to refer to the linguistic manifestations of these particular parameters. The same concepts are also designated by the term 'prosody' ('la prosodie'), a word borrowed from poetics.

Two specific cases of suprasegmental phenomena were mentioned in previous chapters. In Chapter 2 (Section 2.3.2), we spoke briefly of *intonation* ('l'intonation'). Recall that intonation is determined by pitch variations (which are themselves dependent on the rate of vibration of the vocal cords), and that such pitch variations give sentences various melodic profiles which allow, for instance, to distinguish between a declarative sentence such as *Le petit chat est mort* 'The little cat is dead' (with a descending intonation) and a question made up of the same sequence of sounds, but with a rising intonation (*Le petit chat est mort?* 'Is the little cat dead?'). There is a multitude of possible intonation variations that natural languages can use to express a multitude of nuances of meaning which go well beyond the expression of simple declarative sentences or questions. Thanks to intonation effects, all sorts of feelings can be conveyed, such as surprise, indignation, mockery, doubt, etc. For example, as all speakers intuitively know, the intonation which accompanies a very short answer like *oui* 'yes' will often carry at least as much information as the sound sequence [wi] itself; thus, among many other possibilities, the intonation can carry with it the meaning of a definite 'yes' (enthusiastic or exasperated), or the meaning of just 'perhaps', or the meaning of a timid 'no' ('I'd rather not').

In Chapter 3 (Section 3.2), we discussed another suprasegmental phenomenon, *stress* ('l'accent'), which we defined as the effect of relative prominence which marks a given syllable as perceptually salient in relation to others. Thus, stress distinguishes the English verb *to insult*, where the second syllable is more salient than the first, from the noun *insult*, where the first syllable is more salient than the second. Stressed syllables are generally characterized by greater loudness, longer duration, and higher pitch. But languages may vary as to which of these three characteristics correlate most closely with the recognized presence of stress.

Vowel and consonant length is often included among suprasegmental features. We talked about vowel length in French in Chapter 4 (Section 4.2), and we shall not return to this feature in this chapter, except insofar as it is a manifestation of stress.

In closing this introduction, I shall add a very brief mention of an important suprasegmental phenomenon found in many languages (spoken mainly in Africa and the Far East), whereby relative pitch values function like consonant or vowel quality, and allow meaning differences between words. In these languages, called *tone languages* ('langues à tons'), different words may thus be composed of exactly the same sequences of segments; what differentiates them is their respective melodic profiles, their *tones*. For instance, in Chinese, the sequence [ma] means 'mother' when pronounced with a high and even tone; it means 'hemp' when pronounced with a rising tone; it means 'horse' when pronounced with a tone first descending and then rising; finally, it means 'to scold' when pronounced with a descending tone. Since English and French do not make use of pitch changes in this way, we shall not have anything further to say about tones.

In the rest of this chapter, then, we shall confine ourselves to stress and intonation, and without going into the same type of detailed coverage often provided in previous chapters for the sounds of French.

12.2. Stress

Depending on its function, stress is usually divided into two main categories, which we shall call *grammatical* stress ('l'accent grammatical') and *emphatic* stress ('l'accent d'insistance'). Grammatical stress is the type of stress that we talked about in Chapter 3 (calling it simply 'stress' there). It refers to the distribution of syllable prominence in words as determined by the grammar of the language, as opposed to speakers' choice. For example, English grammar specifies that in many bisyllabic noun/verb pairs such as *insult*, *present*, and *torment*, the noun receives (grammatical) stress on its first syllable and the verb on its second syllable; French grammar specifies that words receive (grammatical) stress on their last pronounced syllable, Swahili grammar on their next to the last syllable, and Czech grammar on their initial syllable. In order to sound like a native speaker (and in some cases simply to be understood at all), one must follow such stress specifications; there is no choice. Grammatical stress typically appears on the words of sentences spoken in a neutral manner (that is, without any particular emphasis on any constituent).

Emphatic stress, by contrast, comes as it were on top of grammatical stress to highlight a specific constituent of the sentence. Thus, when the English sentence *The hare chased the cat* is said in a neutral manner, grammatical stress normally falls on each of the three main words *hare*, *chased*, and *cat*. But to indicate, for example, that it is the hare, and not some other animal, which chased the cat, one can highlight the word *hare* by placing on it extra prominence (emphatic stress), clearly making it the most salient word of the sentence (*The HARE chased the cat*). In the French sentence *C'est épouvantable* 'It's terrible', grammatical stress normally falls on the last pronounced syllable of the adjective (*épouvan-TABLe*); but if one wishes to show with more vigor the horror of the situation, another stress (an emphatic stress) can be placed on the second syllable of the word (*C'est éPOUvanTABLe*). Emphatic stress thus corresponds to this extra prominence which a given syllable may receive when speakers wish to add some special effects in their speech: in our English example, the special effect has a contrastive purpose; in our French example, an augmentative purpose.

12.2.1. *Grammatical stress*

In Chapter 3 (Section 3.2), I pointed out some essential characteristics that distinguish grammatical stress in French and in English. I shall take them up again briefly here, and add additional information concerning certain kinds of stress adjustment which words typically undergo when they are assembled into phrases and sentences.

12.2.1.1. *The placement of grammatical stress*
Grammatical stress in French and grammatical stress in English differ first of all by the position they may hold in a word. In French, grammatical stress is fixed; it falls invariably on the last syllable of the word, excluding final *es*, whether these are pronounced or not (e.g. *voiture* 'car', *animál* 'animal', *épouvantáble* 'terrible'; *cultúre* 'culture', *culturél* 'cultural', *culturellemént* 'culturally'). In words of more than two syllables, weaker stresses (secondary stresses) may also be found to the left of the final (primary) grammatical stress, usually distributed in every other syllable.

In English, by contrast, the placement of grammatical stress is *variable*, in the sense that it may, for example, fall on the last, the second to the last, or the third to the last syllable of the word (e.g. *Japán, Scótland, América; divíne, habítual, prímitive*). It may or may not shift position depending on the grammatical category to which the word belongs (compare, for example, *to presént/a présent*, with two different stress patterns for the verb and the noun, and *to páttern/a páttern*, with the same stress pattern on both the verb and the noun). The type of suffix added to a word also determines whether stress variations will be produced in the original word: compare, for instance, the series *phótográph, photó-graphy, phòtográphic*, in which the stress pattern of the original word varies with suffixation, and the series *América, Américan, Américanìze*, where the stress pattern of the original word remains the same, regardless of suffixation. As is the case in French, a given English word may receive more than one grammatical stress, but in English secondary stresses are not distributed in as regular a fashion as they are in French; in particular, the distance between a primary grammatical stress and a secondary one may vary, and a secondary grammatical stress is not necessarily found to the left of the primary grammatical stress (e.g. *antìcipátion, fràternizá-tion, vètò, ánecdòte*).

The diversity of stress patterns in English should not make one believe that grammatical stress is distributed completely haphazardly in this language. The facts may appear disconcerting (and they certainly are for those who learn English as a foreign language), but there actually is some order to them. Thus, while a number of words are to a certain extent idiosyncratic, it has been established that general principles, dependent in part on the syllable structure of words, on their morphemic composition, and on their syntactic category, can provide a description of possible and impossible stress patterns in English. It nevertheless remains true that as owner of one of the most intricate stress systems among the languages of the world, English is in this respect much more complex than French, which only requires locating the last syllable of the word to ensure proper grammatical stress placement.

To conclude this section on the placement of grammatical stress in French and in English, it may be said that the task of the English speaker learning French is much easier than that of the French speaker learning English. Like French speakers, English speakers must nevertheless guard against automatically imposing upon the words of the foreign language stress patterns conforming to the principles internalized unconsciously during the acquisition of their native language.

12.2.1.2. The strength of grammatical stress

A second fundamental way in which French and English differ with respect to grammatical stress concerns its relative strength in the two languages. Grammatical stress is much weaker in French than it is in English; as a consequence, the prominence of stressed syllables is less evident in French than in English. The fact that in English the peaks of prominence are strongly marked gives to oral discourse a type of rhythm crucially determined by the regular return of these strong stresses. In French, by contrast, the basic rhythm is more dependent on the enunciation of each syllable at a level of prominence which is practically speaking equal to that of its neighboring syllables. English is said to have a *stress-timed rhythm* ('rythme accentuel'), whereas French is said to have a *syllable-timed rhythm* ('rythme syllabique').

The perceptual difference between the two stress systems is made even more evident by the fact (which is perhaps a consequence of grammatical stress strength) that unstressed vowels in English are usually reduced to schwa, whereas in French (at least in standard French) all vowels keep their full quality.

In sum, English speakers learning French should try to minimize the differences in prominence between stressed and unstressed syllables. They should also make every effort to preserve the specific quality of each vowel in each syllable. The task of French speakers learning English is naturally the reverse. They must, from their own point of view, exaggerate the prominence of stressed syllables in relation to unstressed syllables, and they must also try to neutralize and reduce the quality of unstressed vowels.

12.2.1.3. Grammatical stress in phrases and sentences

When words are grouped together to form phrases and sentences, they do not all keep their grammatical stresses to the same degree. This is true in both French and English. For example, we saw earlier that in the English sentence *The hare chased the cat* pronounced in a neutral manner, there is a grammatical stress on each of the words *hare*, *chased*, and *cat*. But it must also be noted that these three grammatical stresses are not all of equal strength; the strongest stress is on *cat*, the weakest stress is on *chased*, and the stress on *hare* is intermediate. Likewise, in the sequence of words *black + board + eraser*, the three grammatical stresses are not equally preserved; their respective strength varies according to the manner in which the words in the sequence are syntactically grouped to mean different things; Figure 12.1 provides a graphic illustration of the correlation between the distribution of degrees of stress and meaning. (The higher the block, the stronger the stress; the square brackets

Figure 12.1. Degrees of stress and the meaning of phrases

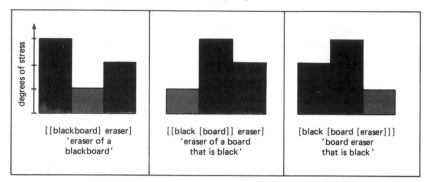

[[blackboard] eraser]	[[black [board]] eraser]	[black [board [eraser]]]
'eraser of a	'eraser of a board	'board eraser
blackboard'	that is black'	that is black'

indicate the syntactic groupings, which correlate with the paraphrases given within quotation marks.) As a third example, consider the written sentence *George has plans to leave.* This sentence is ambiguous between the two meanings 'George has plans which he intends to leave' and 'George is planning to leave'. But note that in speech, there is no ambiguity: for the first meaning grammatical stress is stronger on *plans* than on *leave*, and for the second meaning grammatical stress is stronger on *leave* than on *plans*.

Well-defined principles govern the phenomenon of stress subordination just illustrated. We shall not consider these principles here, however, as the goal of our examples is simply to show that grammatical stress in English usually undergoes prominence adjustments when words are grouped into phrases and sentences.

Similar adjustments affect grammatical stress in French. In general, one can say that in this language, the strength of the main grammatical stress carried by each word is proportional to the importance of the following syntactic break. Let us examine a few examples. Consider first sentences (a) and (b):

    (a) J'ai besoin de pâte   'I need dough'
    (b) J'ai besoin de pâte à tarte   'I need pie dough'

The main grammatical stress falls on *pâte* in (a) and on *tarte* in (b), in both cases right before the major syntactic break represented by the end of the sentences. The word *pâte* is stressed in both sentences, but the prominence of the stress is weaker in (b) than in (a), the syntactic break following *pâte* in (b) being very minor.

Let us now compare sentences (c) and (d):

    (c) Ceux qui savent leur souffleront   'Those who know will prompt
                                  them'
    (d) Ceux qui savent l'heure   'Those who know the time will
        souffleront   prompt'

We see that (c) and (d) are composed of the same sequences of sounds ([søkisavlœrsuflœrõ]), but that they are distinguished syntactically and semantically by the fact that the major internal break (that separating the subject noun phrase from the verb phrase) is between [sav] and [lœr] in (c), and between [lœr] and [suflœrõ] in (d). In the first case, [sav] (*savent*) receives a relatively strong grammatical stress, while the pronoun [lœr] (*leur*) is agglutinated to its verb [suflœrõ] (*souffleront*) and is as it were unstressed; in the second case, it is [lœr] (*l'heure*) which receives a relatively strong grammatical stress, whereas [sav] (*savent*) is much less stressed. In turn, in both sentences, the last word *souffleront* receives a stronger grammatical stress than *savent* (in (c)) and than *l'heure* (in (d)), since the end of a sentence represents a stronger syntactic break than any syntactic break within a sentence. In sum, for these two sentences, we have the approximate basic stress patterns given in (c') and (d') (vertical lines indicate major syntactic breaks):

(c') Ceux qui sàvent | leur soufflerónt ||
(d') Ceux qui savent l'hèure | soufflerónt ||

To sum up the facts about grammatical stress in French sentences, one can say that within each syntactically (and semantically) delimited portion of a sentence, it is normally the word furthest to the right which stands out, because of the presence of a primary grammatical stress which is not reduced (if the word occurs at the end of the sentence) or at any rate less reduced than those which precede (if the word is found at the end of a group that is not sentence-final).

In addition to the way in which words are grouped in phrases and sentences, there is another factor which leads to grammatical stress adjustments in the languages of the world, namely, a rather widespread tendency against having two strongly stressed syllables in a row across contiguous words. For example, in English, the word *thirteen* is ordinarily stressed on the second syllable, as in the phrase *thirteèn compúters*. But if *thirteen* is followed by a word stressed on its first syllable (such as *stúdents*), then the stress on *thirteen* is shifted to the first syllable of the word (*thìrteen stúdents*). The same rhythmic principle seems to apply in French, even though it is less perceptible because of the lesser strength of grammatical stress in this language than in English. For instance, in the phrases *l'ami de Pierre* [lamidpjɛr] 'Peter's friend' and *l'ami d'Alfred* [lamidalfrɛd] 'Alfred's friend', the main grammatical stress naturally falls on the last syllable in each case ([pjɛr] and [frɛd]), but whereas the secondary grammatical stress expectedly falls on the last syllable of the word *l'ami* in *l'ami d'Alfred*, it falls on the first syllable of the word *l'ami* in *l'ami de Pierre*, so that two contiguous stresses are avoided (*l'ami de*

Pierre [làmidpjɛ́r] vs *l'ami d'Alfred* [lamìdalfrɛ́d]). It is of interest to note that in a style where, in the first phrase, the *e* of the preposition *de* would be pronounced ([lamidœpjɛr]), the syllable [mi] would then receive the secondary grammatical stress ([lamìdœpjɛ́r]), exactly as in the second phrase.

12.2.1.4. *Grammatical stress: concluding remarks*

In these brief concluding remarks, we reiterate the three most important aspects of grammatical stress in French which English speakers often tend to forget:

(i) Grammatical stress in French occurs to the right (the right of words, the right of phrases, the right of sentences).
(ii) The differences in prominence which grammatical stress in French confers on syllables are, in comparison to English, almost negligible; from a practical standpoint, it is therefore not unreasonable to aim for equally weighted syllables.
(iii) In standard French, at least, vowels do not get reduced; they keep their full quality at all times and under all circumstances; this fact may be related to the preceding point, in the sense that one could say that French vowels always receive some stress, at least enough to preserve their integrity. This characteristic stands, of course, in very deep contrast with what occurs in English, where unstressed vowels are usually reduced to schwa.

12.2.2. *Emphatic stress*

Emphatic stress differs from grammatical stress not only in its function, but also in its realization. Its function is basically to call the attention of the listener to a particular word, with a view to contrasting it with another word, or in order to give it more force. Its presence is thus in direct relation to the semantics, rather than the syntax, of speech. Its realization is also different. Overall, one can say that it is more readily perceptible than grammatical stress (a characteristic made necessary by its function). First, emphatic stress is stronger than grammatical stress: it may, for instance, occur in the position of a grammatical stress and be as it were superimposed on it, as in the English sentence *The HARE chased the cat* or the French sentence *C'est aTROCe* 'It's atrocious'. Second, it obeys placement principles different from those governing grammatical stress, especially in French, and may thus be found in syllables where primary grammatical stress cannot occur, as in *C'est éPOUvantable* 'It's terrible'. The rest of this section focuses on the specific characteristics of emphatic stress in French.

Table 12.1. Emphatic stress

la canaille	(a) [lakanáj] (b) [lak(k)ǎnáj]	'the rat'
c'est parfaitement vrai	(a) [sɛparfɛtmãvrɛ́] (b) [sɛp(p)ǎrfɛtmãvrɛ́]	'it's perfectly true'
c'est épouvantable	(a) [sɛtepuvãtábl] (b) [sɛtep(p)ǔvãtábl] (c) [sɛtˀěpuvãtábl] (d) [sɛt(t)ěpuvãtábl]	'it's terrible'
c'est absolument faux	(a) [sɛtapsɔlymãfó] (b) [sɛtaps(s)ǒlymãfó] (c) [sɛtˀǎpsɔlymãfó] (d) [sɛt(t)ǎpsɔlymãfó]	'it's absolutely false'

In French, whereas grammatical stress normally falls on the last syllable of the word, emphatic stress generally falls on the first syllable with an initial consonant. In practice, this means that if a word begins with a consonant, it is the first syllable which receives the emphatic stress; if a word begins with a vowel, it is usually the second syllable which receives the emphatic stress. The first syllable of a vowel-initial word may, however, receive emphatic stress if a glottal stop is placed in front of the vowel, or if a linking consonant is present.

The syllable on which emphatic stress falls is modified in the following manner: the vowel is pronounced with greater loudness and on a higher pitch, and the initial consonant is usually reinforced by lengthening (gemination). In the illustrations presented in Table 12.1, the phonetic transcriptions given in (a) indicate pronunciations without emphatic stress (that is, with only grammatical stress); the other phonetic transcriptions indicate possible pronunciations with emphatic stress. (The single acute accent on a vowel represents grammatical stress, the double acute accent emphatic stress; the symbol ˀ, a question mark without its bottom dot, represents a glottal stop ('un coup de glotte'); the optional gemination of a consonant is expressed by repeating in parentheses the phonetic symbol for that consonant.)

12.3. Intonation

As everyone knows more or less consciously, and as good actors prove in their best performances, intonation has the property of being able to adorn the segmental chain of speech with innumerable semantic nuances. Various melodic profiles associated with words as brief as *oui* and *non*, *yes* and *no*, can, for instance, imply absolute certainty or uncertainty, surprise, enthusiasm, horror, disappointment, exasperation, etc. The

Figure 12.2.

L'animal qui s'enfuit en courant | a mordu le gros chien-loup du voisin

Figure 12.3.

L'animal | qui s'enfuit en courant | a mordu | le gros chien-loup du voisin

Figure 12.4.

L'animal | qui s'enfuit | en courant | a mordu | le gros chien-loup | du voisin

richness of *implicative* intonations is considerable, but their rigorous analysis is a delicate matter, and we shall not broach this topic here. Rather, we shall briefly consider a small number of relatively simple (and often simplified) intonation patterns which can characterize basic types of French sentences produced without any particular implication of the sort just mentioned.

Let us begin by considering the case of a rather long declarative sentence such as *L'animal qui s'enfuit en courant a mordu le gros chien-loup du voisin* 'The animal that's running away bit the neighbor's big German shepherd dog'. From both the syntactic and the semantic standpoints, this sentence can be divided into two main constituents: the noun phrase *L'animal qui s'enfuit en courant* and the verb phrase *a mordu le gros chien-loup du voisin*. This syntactico-semantic division has intonation correlates: the first phrase is pronounced with a globally rising intonation, whereas the second is pronounced with a globally descending intonation, as illustrated in Figure 12.2. However, one cannot say that in these two major phrases, the pitch goes first up and then down absolutely regularly. Actually these two constituents can themselves be subdivided into two phrases (*L'animal* and *qui s'enfuit en courant*; *a mordu* and *le gros chien-loup du voisin*) to yield the more precise intonation curve given in Figure 12.3. In turn, the constituents *qui s'enfuit en courant* and *le gros chien-loup du voisin* can be decomposed into smaller phrases (*qui s'enfuit* and *en courant*; *le gros chien-loup* and *du voisin*) to provide an even more detailed intonation curve (see Figure 12.4). On a syntactic basis, one could, of course, continue to break down the phrases which we have just isolated into smaller elements, but note that whereas it is possible to have a natural pause after each of the phrases shown in Figure 12.4, it would not be possible to do so with the smaller elements (one cannot really stop, however briefly, after *qui, en, a, le, gros,* or *du*).

The types of phrases at which we ultimately arrived in our example are usually called *rhythmic groups* or *phonological groups* ('groupes ryth-miques', 'groupes phonologiques'). Rhythmic groups often correspond to syntactic or semantic constituents, but not necessarily so. Thus, in a simple sentence such as *L'animal s'enfuit*, which is composed of two rhythmic groups (*L'animal* and *s'enfuit*), the division into rhythmic groups does correspond to the syntactic and semantic division into subject and verb. However, this type of isomorphy may not obtain in more complex sentences such as the one we have been considering. For instance, the last division we made separated *le gros chien-loup* and *du voisin*; but semantically what is 'gros' is not strictly speaking 'le chien-loup', but more accurately 'le chien-loup du voisin'. Thus, *chien-loup* forms a syntactic and semantic constituent with *du voisin*, but the division into rhythmic groups separates it from *du voisin*, and places it instead with *le gros*. We see then that there is not necessarily an absolute isomorphy between syntactico-semantic structures and rhythmic struc-tures. General principles determine precisely the correspondences between the two types of structures, but we shall stay here at the level of an intuitive perception of these correspondences. Let us simply add about rhythmic groups that they are the domains where the main grammatical stresses in a sentence are assigned and where the basic components of a sentence's intonation are grafted.

A sentence may have a single rhythmic group. For instance, a sentence composed of a subject pronoun and a verb without a complement will form a single rhythmic group, which, if the sentence is declarative, will have a descending intonation (see Figure 12.5). If we add a rhythmic group by adding a complement, we then get back to the global rising–falling intonation pattern presented at the beginning of this section (compare Figure 12.6 with Figure 12.2).

Figure 12.5.

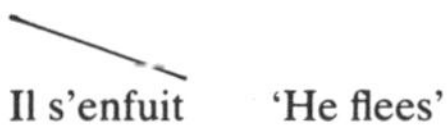

Il s'enfuit   'He flees'

Figure 12.6.

Il s'enfuit   en courant   'He runs away'

Figure 12.7.

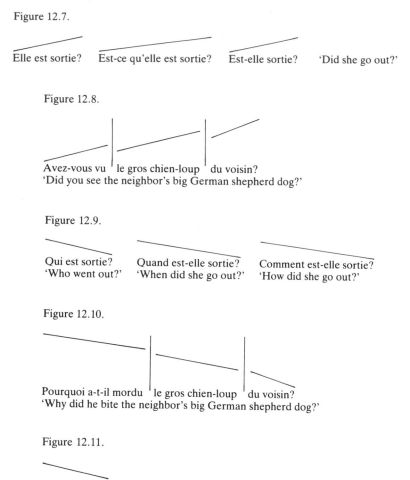

Elle est sortie?   Est-ce qu'elle est sortie?   Est-elle sortie?   'Did she go out?'

Figure 12.8.

Avez-vous vu 'le gros chien-loup ' du voisin?
'Did you see the neighbor's big German shepherd dog?'

Figure 12.9.

Qui est sortie?   Quand est-elle sortie?   Comment est-elle sortie?
'Who went out?'   'When did she go out?'   'How did she go out?'

Figure 12.10.

Pourquoi a-t-il mordu 'le gros chien-loup 'du voisin?
'Why did he bite the neighbor's big German shepherd dog?'

Figure 12.11.

Allez au labo!   'Go to the lab!'

So far, we have only considered examples of declarative sentences. What happens with other types of sentences? Interrogative sentences exhibit two main types of intonation, depending on whether they are 'yes/ no' questions (i.e. questions which can be answered by either 'yes' or 'no') or 'question-word' questions (i.e. questions beginning with an interrogative word such as *qui* 'who', *quand* 'when', *où* 'where', *comment* 'how', etc.). In the first case, the overall intonation pattern is rising, no matter the exact syntactic form chosen to express the question (see Figure 12.7). This intonation curve is different from the rising portion of a declarative sentence's intonation (e.g. that of *Elle est sortie* in *Elle est sortie sous la pluie* 'She went out in the rain'): it reaches a higher pitch at the end and thus, all else being equal, represents a more accelerated rise. Just like a declarative sentence, a 'yes/no' question may, of course, contain several rhythmic groups; there will then be several rising groups, as shown in Figure 12.8.

In the case of 'question-word' questions, the overall intonation is by contrast descending (see Figure 12.9). Here again, the intonation curve is different from the descending portion of a declarative sentence's intonation (e.g. that of *qui est sortie* in *Il se demande qui est sortie* 'He wonders who went out'): it starts on a higher pitch and thus, all else being equal, falls more rapidly. If several rhythmic groups are present, there will be several descending groups (see Figure 12.10). A descending intonation comparable to that of 'question-word' questions may also characterize imperative sentences (see Figure 12.11).

We have merely skimmed the complex topic of French intonation in this section. Informative practical exercises, available on tape, can be found in the second part of Monique Léon's *Exercices systématiques de prononciation française* (1976, pp. 129–83).

Part Five
Appendices

Appendix A
The International Phonetic Association

The following text is taken from the pamphlet entitled *The Principles of the International Phonetic Association*, published by the International Phonetics Association (1949 edition).

A short history of the Association Phonétique Internationale

The *Association Phonétique Internationale* (in English, *International Phonetic Association*, in German, *Weltlautschriftverein*) was inaugurated in 1886, under the title of *The Phonetic Teachers' Association*, by a small group of language teachers in France who had found phonetic theory and phonetic transcription of value in connexion with their work, and who wished to popularise the methods that they had found so useful. A journal entitled *Dhi Fonètik Tîtcer* was started in May of that year, under the editorship of Paul Passy. It was a unique periodical, in that its contents were printed entirely in phonetic transcript.

At first the Association concerned itself mainly with phonetics as applied to the teaching of English, but the membership was international from the very start. (Incidentally, Otto Jespersen became a member in June, 1886, Wilhelm Viëtor in July, 1886, Henry Sweet and J. A. Lundell in September, 1886.) Soon a demand arose for phonetic texts in languages other than English, and for articles dealing with general phonetic problems. The first of these texts (French and German) were published in the May, 1887, issue of the journal, the title of which was then printed for the first time as *dh∂ fɔnetik tîtc∂r*.[1]

The administration of the Association was at first left in the hands of a Committee of members resident in Paris. It became clear, however, after a short time, that it would be preferable to elect an International Council to look after the Association's affairs. The Committee was accordingly replaced by an International Council in 1888, and the policy and work of the Association have been guided by such a council ever since.

During the first two years of the Association's activity a tentative system of phonetic transcription was employed by the editor. This gave place to another tentative scheme in January, 1888. During

---

[1] From September, 1887, to July, 1888, the title was printed as *ð∂ fɔnetik tîtc∂r* and from August to December, 1888, as *ðe fonetik tîtc∂r*.

those years the Association had no particular policy in regard to transcription, and contributors to the journal used various systems in their articles. The idea of establishing a phonetic alphabet which should be applicable to all languages was first put forward by Otto Jespersen in a letter to Paul Passy which was reproduced in *Dhi Fonètik Tîtcer*, June, 1886. This idea was taken up with enthusiasm by other members, and after consultations extending over more than two years the first version of the International Phonetic Alphabet was drawn up. It was published in *ðə fonetik tîtcər*, August, 1888, together with a set of principles regarding its construction and its use. These were as follows:

(1) There should be a separate letter for each distinctive sound, that is, for each sound which, being used instead of another, in the same language, can change the meaning of a word.
(2) When any sound is found in several languages, the same sign should be used in all. This applies also to very similar shades of sound.
(3) The alphabet should consist as much as possible of the ordinary letters of the alphabet, as few new letters as possible being used.
(4) In assigning values to the roman letters, international usage should decide.
(5) The new letters should be suggestive of the sounds they represent, by their resemblance to the old ones.
(6) Diacritic marks should be avoided, being trying for the eyes and troublesome to write.

It will be seen that with the exception of (5) and some special cases coming under (2), those principles still hold good to-day. (In regard to (5) it is now considered that letters should have unmistakable forms, and be as unlike each other as possible.) It will be observed that (1) is an early statement of what we now call the "phonemic" principle of writing.

In 1888, when the international character of the Association was formally recognized and when the first international alphabet had been designed, it was decided, as from January, 1889: (1) to adopt French as the official language of the Association; (2) to change the name of the society to *L'Association Phonétique des Professeurs de Langues Vivantes*; (3) to change the title of the journal to *Le Maître Phonétique* – the title which it has borne ever since. In 1897 the name of the society was altered once more, and it became known by its present title *L'Association Phonétique Internationale*.

The original International Phonetic Alphabet of 1888 contained quite a number of the special letters used to-day, but it was imperfect in various respects. The Council has accordingly, since 1889, worked unremittingly to remedy defects, improving upon signs which proved unsatisfactory and extending the alphabet to provide for languages which had not received consideration at the outset. The result is that we now have a system which, though doubtless capable of still further improvement, is a very effective instrument for transcription on international lines, and one which can be used both in "broad" and in "narrow" forms for the phonetic representation of all the principal languages of the world, and as a basis for orthographic reform for all languages needing it.

It is satisfactory to find that the work of the Association, extending as it does over more than seventy years, has met with considerable success. Its alphabet is now used for indicating pronunciation not only in the association's official publications, but also in numerous dictionaries and textbooks by authors unconnected with the Association in many countries. And even more important, some of the Association's special letters are beginning to find their way into the common orthographies of some languages.[2]

The Association considers that by encouraging the use of internationally recognised phonetic symbols for all languages its work contributes seriously to the creation and maintenance of cordial relations between peoples of different countries.

---

[2] They are officially authorized for several languages of Africa. See *Practical Orthography of African Languages* (published by the Oxford University Press for the International African Institute).

Appendix B
Diacritic marks in French orthography

In addition to the letters of the alphabet, French orthography makes use of diacritic marks, i.e. special signs which can be combined with certain letters of the alphabet to form additional graphic symbols. There are five of these diacritic marks: the *cedilla* ('la cédille'), the *acute accent* ('l'accent aigu'), the *grave accent* ('l'accent grave'), the *circumflex accent* ('l'accent circonflexe'), and the *diaeresis* ('le tréma'). Letters with diacritic marks do not have a special entry in the dictionary. Diacritic marks are usually omitted with capital letters.

The cedilla combines with just one letter, *c* (*ç*). The '*c*-cédille', as it is called in French, is found only before the vowel-letters *a*, *o*, and *u*, as in *ça* 'that', *garçon* 'boy', and *reçu* 'receipt'. It always represents the sound [s] ([sa], [garsõ], [rœsy], to be compared with *car* [kar] 'bus', *flacon* [flakõ] 'flask', *reculer* [rœkyle] 'to pull back').

The acute accent occurs only in combination with the letter *e* (*é*), as in *été* 'summer' and *hétérogénéité* 'heterogeneity'; *é* occurs very frequently in French.

The grave accent may combine with the three letters *a*, *e*, and *u*. *à* appears only in a few words and always at the end (*à* 'at', *là* 'there', *là-haut* 'up there', *çà et là* 'here and there', *déjà* 'already', *au-delà* 'beyond', *voilà* 'there is'). *è* occurs frequently; it is mainly found before a written syllable whose vowel is *e* (as in *problème* 'problem', *trèfle* 'clover', and *achètera* 'will buy') or before the final consonant *s* (as in *après* 'after', *progrès* 'progress', and *succès* 'success'). *ù* appears only in the word *où* 'where'.

The circumflex accent may combine with all vowel-letters, except *y* (see Table B.1).

The presence of an accent may have phonetic consequences or be just an orthographic ornament of a more or less functional nature. The accents on the letter *e* constitute one of the means used by French orthography to distinguish *e*s pronounced [e] or [ɛ] from *e*s pronounced [œ] or not pronounced, as illustrated in Table B.2. In general, *é* represents the sound [e] (*été* [ete] 'summer'), while *è* and *ê* both represent the sound [ɛ] (*chèvre* [ʃɛvr] 'goat', *bête* [bɛt] 'beast').

The grave accent on the letters *a* and *u* never indicates a particular

Table B.1. The circumflex accent

â: âge, âtre, grâce, infâme, pâte	(age, hearth, grace, infamous, dough)
ê: bête, être, forêt, suprême, tête	(beast, to be, forest, supreme, head)
î: boîte, connaître, huître, île, maître	(box, to know, oyster, island, master)
ô: côte, hôpital, hôtel, le nôtre, le vôtre	(coast, hospital, hotel, ours, yours)
û: août, dû, fût, piqûre, sûr	(August, due, vat, sting, sure)

Table B.2. Accents on *e*

acheté	[aʃte]	'bought'	achète	[aʃɛt]	'buy'
réforme	[refɔrm]	'reform'	reformé	[rœfɔrme]	'formed again'
congrès	[kõgrɛ]	'congress'	congres	[kõgr]	'conger eels'
rêvé	[rɛve]	'dreamed'	rêve	[rɛv]	'dream'

pronunciation in opposition to the absence of the accent. It simply contributes to making visual distinctions between words with different meanings, but which are homophones (pronounced the same) and would otherwise be homographs (written the same) as well. Compare, for instance, the verb form *a* 'has' and the preposition *à* 'at', both pronounced [a]; the feminine definite article *la* and the adverb *là* 'there', both pronounced [la]; the coordinating conjunction *ou* 'or' and the question-word/relative pronoun *où* 'where', both pronounced [u].

The circumflex accent often plays a role in indicating specific pronunciations. As already mentioned, *ê* may contrast phonetically with *é* and *e*; in addition, the spelling *â* often corresponds to the sound [ɑ] rather than to the sound [a] (compare, for example, *pâte* [pɑt] 'dough' and *patte* [pat] 'paw'); and the spelling *ô* often corresponds to the sound [o] rather than to the sound [ɔ] (compare, for example, *côte* [kot] 'coast' and *cote* [kɔt] 'rating'). In contrast, a circumflex accent on *i* or *u* changes nothing in the pronunciation of words (for instance, the adjective *sûr* 'secure' and the preposition *sur* 'on' are pronounced [syr]); the circumflex here plays a differentiating role only for the eye. In most cases, the circumflex accent has an etymological value; it replaces a letter which used to be present in the orthography and in the pronunciation (often a subsequent *s* or a preceding *e*). This 'missing' letter is frequently found in related words in French or in other languages such as Spanish or English (see Table B.3).

We close this overview of diacritic marks in French with the diaeresis, which may combine with the vowel-letters *e*, *i*, and *u*, as shown in Table B.4. The role of the diaeresis is essentially to indicate that two contiguous vowel-letters must be treated independently, rather than together, for pronunciation purposes. Thus, the feminine adjective *ambiguë* [ãbigy] does not rhyme with *figue* [fig] 'fig', but is pronounced like the masculine *ambigu* [ãbigy]; *Noël* [nɔɛl] does not rhyme with *moelle* [mwal] 'mar-

Table B.3. The circumflex accent and 'missing' letters

	French	*Spanish*	*English*
château	castel	castillo	castle
hâte			haste
bête	bestial	bestia	beast
honnête		honesto	honest
île		isla	island
maître		maestro	master
côte	accoster	costa	coast
hôpital	hospitaliser	hospital	hospital
coûter		costar	to cost
sûr	sécurité	seguro	secure

Table B.4. The diaeresis

ë: ambiguë, Noël	(ambiguous, Christmas)
ï: héroïque, haïr	(heroic, to hate)
ü: capharnaüm, Saül	(mess, Saul)

row', but with *oh! elle!* [ɔɛl] 'oh! her!'; the sequence *oï* of *héroïque* is pronounced [ɔi], as in *oh hisse!* [ɔis] 'yo heave yo!', and not [wɑ] as in *roi* 'king'; *haïr* [air] does not rhyme with *air* [ɛr] 'air', but with *trahir* [trair] 'to betray'; *capharnaüm* [kafarnaɔm] does not rhyme with *baume* [bom] 'balm', but with *d'homme à homme* [dɔmaɔm] 'from man to man'; lastly, *Saül* [sayl] does not rhyme with *saule* [sol] 'willow', but contains the first two vowels of *ahuri* [ayri] 'stunned'.

Appendix C
Outline of the history
of French orthography

Writing systems in the languages of the world differ in what basic linguistic units are represented by the basic symbols of the systems. For instance, Chinese characters typically represent words and Japanese characters syllables. In alphabetical writing systems, sounds are the basic linguistic units represented by the letters of the various alphabets (e.g. the Latin alphabet in English and French, the Greek alphabet in Greek, the Cyrillic alphabet in Russian), and in each case a specific *code* can be said to determine the correspondences between sounds and letters. In the simplest type of code, sounds and letters would stand in one-to-one correspondences, as they do in the International Phonetic Association's system, where, for instance, the symbol *i* exclusively represents the sound [i] and only the sound [i], and the symbol *y* the sound [y] and only the sound [y]. Languages rarely use such a simple code, but their deviations from it can vary widely. French (with English) is one of the languages where the deviation is most extraordinary, and where in fact knowledge of the code is in itself insufficient to allow one to spell according to the norm. As a simple illustration, consider the sound [i]: in French it may be represented by the letter *i* or by the letter *y* (cf. *lire* [lir] 'to read' and *lyre* [lir] 'lyre'). The French code very generally offers such options for writing sounds, but as every school child and every student of French knows, often from painful personal experience, there is in reality no choice, and it is thus considered a mistake to write *lyre* for 'to read' and *lire* for 'lyre' (extremely rare are the words for which the norm does tolerate different spellings). Knowing French orthography is therefore not just knowing the inventory of possible correspondences between sounds and letters (the *phono-graphic* code), it also involves knowing for a given word how to limit to one the various spellings allowed by the code. This supplement to the code is sometimes termed *ideographic*, because it associates meaning and spelling by giving words a specific written look (so, in our example *lyre*, the idea of a musical instrument and the letter *y* become associated in an idiosyncratic ideographic connection). The question we shall briefly consider in this appendix is how French orthography came to have a complex phono-graphic code and an ideographic supplement.

The fundamental reason for the complexity of the French phono-graphic code and the existence of an ideographic supplement lies in a history replete with layers of traditions. One basic tradition is the etymological tradition, mainly the language's Latin and Greek heritage. Many options in the French phono-graphic code, such as the *i/y* choice in our earlier example, ultimately go back to Latin and Greek spellings, and to the ideas that word etymology must be respected (the *etymological* principle) and that homophones must be distinguished in the written language (the *differentiating* principle, which is the other side of the *morphological* principle, the linking of related words through like spellings).

These principles, which began to play an important role in the thirteenth century (when French started dislodging Latin from official documents), have not been rigorously applied in the course of time. For instance, there are words that have kept or retrieved their Greek letters (e.g. *ph* for [f] in *pharmacie* 'pharmacy', attested as *farmacie* in the fourteenth century), there are words that have lost them (e.g. *fantôme* 'ghost'), and there are even a few that have alternate spellings (e.g. *fantasme ~ phantasme* 'phantasm'). The elimination of Greek letters from French words (*ch* for [k], *ph* for [f], *rh* for [r], *th* for [t], and *y* for [i]) has been a pillar of the innumerable reform projects proposed since the sixteenth century to simplify French orthography.

Occasionally, etymological errors occurred; some were later corrected (e.g. sixteenth-century *sçavoir* 'to know' was changed back to *savoir* at the beginning of the eighteenth century, in recognition of the word's Latin origin *sapere*, not *scire*), but others were not: e.g. *poids* 'weight', which does not come from *pondus*, but from *pensum*, and was actually written *pois* in the twelfth century, has kept its *d*, probably in order to remain distinct from *pois* 'pea'.

Like all languages, French has undergone sound changes in its history, and up to a point its orthography has reacted to these changes. Two factors, however, have strongly contributed to limiting the scope of the responses. First, the Latin alphabet, which French basically took over, offered an insufficient number of symbols to cover the new sound systems which emerged. Second, spelling changes made in reaction to sound changes typically became fixed themselves in a tradition often dating back to Old French pronunciations. (A late, but isolated, important spelling change was officially adopted in 1835: *ai* replaced *oi* pronounced [ɛ], as in *connaître* 'to know' and *français* 'French'.)

The orthography of nasal vowels can serve to illustrate these two points. The Latin alphabet did not provide special symbols for nasal vowels, which started appearing in Old French; although these new sounds were sometimes noted with a tilde (as in today's International

Phonetic Alphabet), the prevailing tradition came to represent them with as few changes as possible in the existing orthography, namely, by means of a written 'vowel + nasal consonant' sequence. Before a consonant or word-finally, there was thus no change in the spelling itself (as in *conte* 'story' and *don* 'gift'); before another vowel, the spelling change was minimal: the written nasal consonant was doubled (as in *honneur* 'honor' and *donner* 'to give'); in this way, a nasal consonant after a vowel served to represent nasality, and all other nasal consonants kept their regular value. Then, in Middle French, the nasal vowels which gave rise to a written doubling of nasal consonants typically denasalized; the original motivation for the double written nasal consonants had thus vanished, but tradition preserved the existing double spelling. To make matters worse, after the nasalization wave was over, words were directly borrowed from Latin, with their Latin spelling, which resulted in pairs like *honneur/honorable* and *donner/donation*, violating the morphological principle since two different spellings are used for the same basic stem. Like Greek letters, the double consonants of French orthography (and not just double nasal consonants) have been a staple of reform-minded authors.

Although French orthography can thus be characterized as conservative with respect to both its Latin and Greek heritage and its own early tradition, two very important innovations must be noted in its history: first, the distinction between *i* and *j* and between *u* and *v*; and second, the introduction of accent marks, in particular on the letter *e*. But as we shall see shortly, even the use of these new devices can be characterized as conservatively restricted.

For several centuries, French spelling followed the Latin system in using the letters *i/j* and *u/v* ambiguously. For example, in the sixteenth century, *i/j* could stand for [i] ~ [j] or [ʒ], and *u/v* could stand for [y] ~ [ɥ] or [v]. Basically, the graphic distinctions *i/j* and *u/v* did not correspond to sound distinctions, but were typographically governed (thus, for the pair *u/v*, *v* was used word-initially and *u* elsewhere). At the end of the seventeenth century, the usage we now know was officially put into effect, reserving for *i* and *u* the vowel and glide values ([i] ~ [j], [y] ~ [ɥ]), and for *j* and *v* the consonant values ([ʒ], [v]). This move helped clarify the orthography considerably by yielding different symbols for different sounds. For example, in sixteenth-century *debuoir* 'to owe', the etymological *b* (cf. Latin *debere*) was not pronounced, but in all likelihood functioned to indicate that the following *u* was to be read with the consonant value [v]; the new graphic distinction resulted in the more straightforward spelling *devoir*. But not all previous indirect disambiguating attempts were eliminated in favor of the new device. For instance, the words *ville* 'town' and *huile* 'oil' used to be spelled the same: *vile*; the letter *h* (by itself a consonant-letter without phonetic value, but always followed by a vowel within a word) was introduced at the beginning of the second word to give the *v* its glide value unambiguously (the *v* was then written *u* because it was no longer in word-initial position). But when the graphic distinction *u/v* was finally correlated with the phonetic distinction, words like *huile* kept their roundabout spelling. Similarly, before the introduction of the phonetic distinction between *i* and *j*, the letter *i* had been changed to the letter *y* in the word for 'eyes' (*ieux* → *yeux*), thereby differentiating it from the word for 'games', also spelled *ieux*. But after the phonetic separation between *i* and *j* (which gave *jeux* for 'games'), the spelling *yeux* for 'eyes' was kept. In one case (the word for the elder-plant), both the spelling device used for *yeux* and the one used for *huile* have been retained: the norm thus tolerates the two spellings *yèble* and *hièble*, but not **ièble* (the asterisk indicates that this form is not accepted).

The official introduction of accent marks also dates back to the end of the seventeenth century, with a number of changes and refinements occurring later and a few still pending today. The most significant of these particular innovations concerns the accents on the letter *e*. A lasting ambiguity in French orthography, due to the inheritance of the Latin writing system and French-specific sound changes, was the phonetic value of the letter *e*, which could represent [ə], [e], or [ɛ]. Various devices were used in the course of history to try to disambiguate the situation, mainly to separate [ə] from [e, ɛ]. For example, the letter *e* was sometimes replaced by the sequence *ai* (after the diphthong represented by *ai* had simplified to [ɛ]); this is how spellings like *clair* 'clear' and *frais* 'fresh' finally replaced earlier *cler* and *fres*; but some other words formerly written with *ai* ended up with an accented *e* (e.g. *alaigre* → *allègre* 'brisk', *graisle* → *grêle* 'slender'). Consonants were also used to help specify the phonetic value of the letter *e*; thus, a preconsonantal *s* (whether or not it was etymological) was often introduced after *e* to eliminate the [ə] interpretation (e.g. *esglise* 'church', *estroit* 'narrow', *teste* 'head'); the introduction of accent marks eventually led to the disappearance of these *s*s (*église, étroit, tête*), except in *est* 'is'. Another device was consonant doubling: the letter *e* before (still written) etymological double consonants typically had the phonetic value [ɛ]; this correlation was generalized to non-etymological cases, yielding spellings like *achette* 'buys' and *jette* 'throws'. As today's established spellings for the same words show (*achète, jette*), the progressive introduction of accent marks was arbitrarily selective.

French orthography today seems to be in a state of arrested development. The most minute seemingly logical changes simply do not get through, and reform project after reform project goes in vain after the very same spelling oddities (such as the already mentioned Greek letters and double consonants). Borrowed words which conform in all respects with the phonetics of French do not get incorporated into its basic phono-graphic code; e.g. the English borrowings *look* [luk] and *football* [futbɔl] remain as spelling anomalies, when they could perfectly well be integrated as *louk* and *foutbol* (cf. *plouk* [pluk] 'peasant' and *bol* [bɔl] 'bowl'). Such lack of orthographic integrating power (which strikingly separates French from languages like Spanish; cf. Spanish *fútbol* [futbɔl]) is, of course, not the result of chance. It correlates with the strong ideographic component of French orthography, whereby it is precisely the 'look' of words which plays an important role in meaning assignment. As we have tried to illustrate, this strong ideographic component itself derives from the fact that the phono-graphic code has been over the centuries affected by multiple layers of often conflicting and usually unsystematically applied traditions, principles, and changes. Not too surprisingly, instead of orthography conforming to pronunciation, it has frequently been pronunciation which has ended up conforming to orthography (e.g. some speakers pronounce *football* [fɔtbal]).

The orthography of a language is very much a socio-historical product. In the preceding paragraphs, we identified important governing tendencies in the course of the history of French orthography, but we stayed away from an equally important social factor, which we now briefly take up, namely: who are the decision makers in matters of French orthography?

The official norm today is ultimately in the hands of the French Academy, but with a complex set of intervening forces, including the French government, certain groups in society (e.g. linguists, teachers, writers, publishers, the press), public opinion, and a number of modern dictionaries (such as *Petit Larousse* and *Petit Robert*). In the twentieth century, the role of the French government can be seen in a number of special commissions named by the Ministry of National Education and charged with presenting projects for the reform of French orthography. Such projects, however, have typically met with strong opposition from one or another sector of society, and they have invariably been tabled (and many other non-officially sponsored proposals have been ignored). Government decrees have also been issued (1901, 1977), legislating in favor of a few very specific spelling 'tolerances' at examinations.

Modern dictionaries, with the frequent publication of revised editions, have in practice filled the void left by the ever-so-slow work of the French Academy on its own dictionary (fifty years have elapsed since its last edition, and the completion of the next edition is nowhere in sight). From one edition to the next, these modern dictionaries duly register new words and new meanings and eliminate obsolete ones, but in the domain of orthography, they usually limit themselves to a few minor changes in the spelling of compounds and borrowed words.

At present, then, everything contributes to the status quo, i.e. a kind of orthographic paralysis contrasting somewhat with what occurred in past centuries. The French Academy goes back to 1635, when it was created by Richelieu to write a dictionary and a grammar of the French language. The first edition of the dictionary appeared in 1694, with subsequent revised editions in 1718, 1740, 1762, 1798, 1835, 1878, and 1935 (the first and only edition of the grammar appeared in 1932). The official status of the French Academy naturally lent to its dictionary a special aura of authority concerning orthographic matters, although the Academy itself repeatedly stated that its goal was to follow 'usage'. The question, of course, is 'which usage?'

From the first written records in the ninth century up to the thirteenth century, the reading public was extremely limited, and the way French was written depended essentially on the writer; variability was thus the rule, often within a given manuscript. With the thirteenth century and the penetration of French into official documents, jurists began to play an important role in controlling spelling. Then, the increasing diffusion of written texts to a growing literate population gave printers a special influence, in particular from the sixteenth to the eighteenth centuries. With this continuous expansion of the written word, the need for a unification of spelling progressively emerged and it was made particularly urgent by the French Revolution of 1789. It is basically this task which in practice the various editions of the French Academy's dictionary achieved, by officializing certain usages over others.

Today's essential paralysis of French orthography lies in the following catch-22 situation: dictionaries claim to rely on usage, but the foundation of usage among influential practitioners (such as writers, printers, and the press) is dictionaries. Usage has thus become norm and norm usage.

Appendix D
Sounds and letters in French: summary

Table D.1. French vowels and glides

		front		back		Examples	
		unrounded	rounded	unrounded	rounded		
glides		j	ɥ		w	miette muette mouette	(crumb, mute, seagull)
oral vowels	closed	i	y		u	lit *lu loup*	(bed, read, wolf)
	half closed	e	ø		o	*dé deux dos*	(thimble, two, back)
	half open	ɛ	œ		ɔ	l'*air leur* l'*or*	(the air, their, the gold)
	open	a		ɑ		*patte pâte*	(paw, dough)
nasal vowels		ɛ̃	œ̃	ɑ̃	ɔ̃	*lin* l'*un lent long*	(flax, the one, slow, long)

Table D.2. French consonants

Manner of articulation			bilabial	labiodental	dental	alveolar	alveopalatal	palatal	velar	uvular	Examples
stops	nasal		m		n			ɲ			mou nous gnon (soft, we, blow)
stops	oral	voiceless	p		t				k		pou tout cou (louse, all, neck)
stops	oral	voiced	b		d				g		bout doux goût (end, mild, taste)
fricatives	voiceless			f		s	ʃ				fou sous chou (mad, under, cabbage)
fricatives	voiced			v		z	ʒ				vous zou joue (you, [interjection], cheek)
approximants	lateral					l					loup (wolf)
approximants	central									ʁ	roue (wheel)

Main orthographic realizations of French sounds

This section presents for each sound of French its main orthographic realizations, together with illustrative examples.

(i) Oral vowels

[i] *i* (lire 'to read'), *y* (lyre 'lyre'), *î* (île 'island'), *ï* (haïr 'to hate')

[e] *é* (été 'summer'), *er* (chanter 'to sing'), *ez* (chantez 'sing')

[ɛ] *e* (sec 'dry'), *è* (père 'father'), *ê* (tête 'head'), *ai* (lait 'milk'), *ei* (seize 'sixteen'), *et* (effet 'effect'), *é* (crémerie 'dairy')

[a] *a* (patte 'paw'), *â* (chantâmes '(we) sang'), *e* (femme 'woman'); *oi* = [wa] (moi 'me')

[y] *u* (lu 'read'), *û* (sûr 'sure'), *eu* (past participle of *avoir*)

[ø] *eu* (feu 'fire'), *œu* (nœud 'knot')

[œ] *e* (le 'the'), *eu* (leur 'their'), *œu* (œuf 'egg'), *œ* (œil 'eye'), *ai* (faisons '(we) do')

[u] *ou* (loup 'wolf'), *oû* (goût 'taste'), *où* (où 'where')

[o] *o* (rose 'rose'), *ô* (côte 'coast'), *au* (chaud 'hot'), *eau* (beau 'beautiful')

[ɔ] *o* (fort 'strong'), *au* (Paul 'Paul'), *ô* (rôti 'roast'), *u* (album 'album')

[ɑ] *a* (gaz 'gas'), *â* (pâte 'dough'); *oi* = [wɑ] (mois 'month')

(ii) Nasal vowels

[ɛ̃] *iN* (fin 'end'), *aiN* (pain 'bread'), *eiN* (plein 'full'), *eN* (chien 'dog'); *uN* (un 'one'), *yN* (syntaxe 'syntax'); *oiN* = [wɛ̃] (loin 'far')

[œ̃] *uN* (un 'one')

[ɑ̃] *eN*, *aN* (enfant 'child')

[ɔ̃] *oN* (bon 'good')

(*N* = *m* or *n*)

(iii) Glides

[j] *i* (pierre 'stone'), *y* (Lyon [town]), *ill* (paille 'straw'), *ll* (billet 'ticket'), *il* (œil 'eye')

[ɥ] *u* (lui 'him')

[w] *ou* (Louis 'Lewis'), *w* (kiwi 'kiwi'); *oi* = [wa]/[wɑ] (loi 'law')

(iv) Consonants

[m] *m* (mot 'word'), *mm* (pomme 'apple')

[n] *n* (nos 'our'), *nn* (donner 'to give')

[ɲ] *gn* (agneau 'lamb')

[p] *p* (peau 'skin'), *pp* (apporter 'to bring')

[t] *t* (taux 'rate'), *tt* (battre 'to beat'), *th* (théâtre 'theater')

[k] *c* (car 'bus'), *cc* (accrocher 'to hang'), *ch* (écho 'echo'), *k* (kilomètre 'kilometer'), *q* (coq 'rooster'), *qu* (quand 'when')

[b] *b* (beau 'beautiful'), *bb* (abbé 'abbot')

[d] *d* (dos 'back'), *dd* (addition 'addition')

[g] *g* (gare 'station'), *gg* (aggraver 'to aggravate'), *c* (second 'second')

[f] *f* (faux 'false'), *ff* (affirmer 'to affirm'), *ph* (phare 'headlight')

[s] *s* (seau 'pail'), *ss* (assez 'enough'), *c* (ce 'this'), *ç* (ça 'that'), *sc* (science) 'science'), *t* (nation 'nation'), *x* (dix 'ten')

[ʃ] *ch* (chaud 'hot')

[v] *v* (veau 'calf'), *w* (wagon 'wagon')

[z] *s* (oiseau 'bird'), *z* (zèbre 'zebra'), *x* (dixième 'tenth')

[ʒ] *j* (jeu 'game'), *g* (Georges 'George')

[l] *l* (l'eau 'the water'), *ll* (aller 'to go')

[ʁ] *r* (rare 'rare'), *rr* (arriver 'to arrive')

Main phonetic values of the letters of the alphabet in French

For each letter of the alphabet (excluding letters with diacritic marks), Table D.3 provides the various phonetic values the letter represents in French orthography. The notions of basic value, positional value, auxiliary value, digraph, and null value are explained in Chapter 1 (Section 1.3.1). Table D.3 is adapted from charts in V. G. Gak's *L'Orthographe du français* (1976, pp. 34–40) and Claire Blanche-Benveniste and André Chervel's *L'Orthographe* (1978, p. 134).

Table D.3. Main phonetic values of the letters of the alphabet in French

Letter	(1) Basic value	(2) Positional value	(3) Auxiliary value	(4) Digraph		(5) Null value
A	[a] art		américain (cf. cinq) gain (cf. Gigi)	ai [ε] fait au [o] haut ay [ei] pays aN [ā] grand		pain (cf. pin)
B	[b] bar					plomb (cf. nom)
C	[k] car	[s] cire	exciter (cf. exil)	ch [ʃ] chat		banc (cf. ban)
D	[d] dur		pied (cf. pie)			bond (cf. bon)
E	[œ] gredin	[e] errer, nez [ε] complet, jette	grise (cf. gris) douceâtre (cf. ducat) Georges (cf. gorge) essaient (cf. saint)	ei [ε] baleine eu [ø] eux [œ] heure œ [œ] œil eN [ā] entendre		bulletin (cf. ultime) sole (cf. sol) eau (cf. au)
F	[f] fer		clef (cf. oncle)			bœufs (cf. peu)
G	[g] gare	[ʒ] gel		gn [ɲ] agneau		vingt (cf. vint) coing (cf. coin)
H	In certain words, an initial h indicates the absence of elision and liaison with the preceding word (la hache, le hibou; les haches, les hiboux)		orchestre (cf. cette) ghetto (cf. geler) trahir (cf. traire)	ch [ʃ] chat ph [f] phonétique		écho (cf. écot) homme (cf. omelette)

Table D.3. cont.

Letter	(1) Basic value	(2) Positional value	(3) Auxiliary value	(4) Digraph		(5) Null value
I	[i] petit, défi	[j] petiot, défier		ai [ɛ] fait ei [ɛ] baleine oi [wa] moi iN [ɛ̃] fin il [j] œil		oignon (cf. grognon)
J	[ʒ] joli					
K	[k] képi					stock (cf. toc)
L	[l] lit			il, ill, ll [j] œil, paille, billet		fils (cf. vis)
M	[m] mère			Vm [Ṽ] ample, temps, simple, sombre, parfum, thym		automne (cf. tonal) damner (cf. âne)
N	[n] nu			Vn [Ṽ] enfant, fin, bon, un, syntaxe gn [ɲ] agneau		indemne (cf. œdème)
O	[ɔ] or [o] trop	[w] poêle	œur (cf. douceur)	œ [œ] œil oi [wa] moi ou [u] mou oN [ɔ̃] bon		faon (cf. fantastique) vœux (cf. veux)

Table D.3. cont.

Letter	(1) Basic value	(2) Positional value	(3) Auxiliary value	(4) Digraph		(5) Null value
				ph	[f] phonétique	
P	[p] père					champ (cf. Adam)
Q	[k] quand					
R	[r] rare		aimer (cf. aime)			gars (cf. gagner) / monsieur (cf. cieux)
S	[s] sage	[z] vase	les (cf. le)			jeunes (cf. jeune)
T	[t] table	[s] action	complet (cf. comble)			port (cf. or)
U	[y] usine, sue	[ɥ] linguiste, suer / [w] aquatique	cueillir (cf. ceux) / guide (cf. Gide)	au [o] haut / eu [ø] eux / [œ] heure / oɪ [u] mou / uN [œ̃] un		fatiguant (cf. fatigant)
V	[v] vase					
W	[w] watt					
X	[ks] taxi	[gz] exemple / [s] six / [z] deuxième				deux (cf. feu)
Y	[i] lys	[j] cobaye		y·N [ɛ̃] syntaxe / ay [ei] pays		
Z	[z] zèbre		nez (cf. ne)			raz (cf. sera)

Appendix E
A selection of h-aspiré words

H-aspiré words can be roughly described as words which phonetically begin with a vowel, but behave as if they began with a consonant. Thus, as Table E.1 illustrates, regular vowel-initial words allow elision and liaison, but h-aspiré words do not (just like consonant-initial words).

Regular vowel-initial words also require the use of special forms for some determiners and adjectives occurring immediately before them. For example, the masculine noun *arbre* must be used with *cet* 'this' (and not *ce*), with *vieil* 'old' and *bel* 'beautiful' (and not *vieux* or *beau*), and the feminine noun *arme* 'weapon' must be used with *son* 'his/her' (and not *sa*): *cet arbre*, *ce vieil arbre*, *ce bel arbre*, *son arme* (compare with consonant-initial nouns like the masculine *tapis* and the feminine *table* 'table': *ce tapis*, *ce vieux tapis*, *ce beau tapis*; *sa table*). Here too, h-aspiré words behave like consonant-initial words, as the masculine *héros* and the feminine *hache* 'axe' show in the following examples: *ce héros*, *ce vieux héros*, *ce beau héros*; *sa hache*.

Table E.2 presents a list of relatively common h-aspiré words divided for convenience into parts of speech.

Note that derivatives of h-aspiré words are generally h-aspiré words themselves: for example, *hautain* and *hauteur* are h-aspiré words, like *haut*; *hacher* and *hachoir* 'grinder' are h-aspiré words, like *hache*. Notable exceptions to this general principle are the derivatives of the word *héros*, which are not h-aspiré words: cf. *l'héroïne* 'the heroine', *l'héroïsme* 'heroism'.

Table E.1. The behavior of h-aspiré words in elision and liaison

Vowel-initial words		Consonant-initial words
Regular	H-aspiré	
(e.g. arbre [arbr] 'tree') l'arbre [larbr] les arbres [lezarbr]	(e.g. héros [ero] 'hero') le héros [lœero] les héros [leero]	(e.g. tapis [tapi] 'carpet') le tapis [lœtapi] les tapis [letapi]
Elision and liaison	No elision – No liaison	

Table E.2. List of selected h-aspiré words

Masculine nouns					
haillons	'tatters'	hareng	'herring'	hic	'snag'
hall	'hall'	haricot	'bean'	hibou	'owl'
hamac	'hammock'	harpon	'harpoon'	hold-up	'hold-up'
hameau	'hamlet'	hasard	'chance'	homard	'lobster'
handicap	'handicap'	hérisson	'hedgehog'	hoquet	'hiccough'
hangar	'hangar'	héron	'heron'	hors-d'œuvre	'hors d'oeuvre'
hanneton	'June bug'	héros	'hero'	hublot	'porthole'
harem	'harem'	hêtre	'beech tree'		

Feminine nouns					
hache	'axe'	hargne	'ill temper'	Hollande	'Holland'
haie	'hurdle'	harpe	'harp'	Hongrie	'Hungary'
haine	'hatred'	hâte	'haste'	honte	'shame'
halte	'stop'	hausse	'increase'	housse	'dust cover'
hanche	'hip'	hauteur	'height'	huées	'boos'
hantise	'fear'	hernie	'hernia'	hutte	'hut'
harangue	'harangue'				

Adjectives		*Verbs*			
hardi	'bold'	hacher	'to chop'	héler	'to hail'
hâtif	'hasty'	haïr	'to hate'	heurter	'to hit'
haut	'high'	haleter	'to pant'	hisser	'to hoist'
hautain	'haughty'	hanter	'to haunt'	hocher (la tête)	'to shake' (one's head)
hideux	'hideous'	harasser	'to wear out'	huer	'to boo'
		harceler	'to badger'	hurler	'to scream'
		hâter	'to hasten'		

Appendix F
Fundamental principles of French pronunciation: summary

The following principles summarize the fundamental practical rules of pronunciation that native speakers of English should strive to follow if they wish to speak French with a minimum of a foreign accent. [The numbers in square brackets refer to the chapters and pages in the text where these questions are discussed.]

1. Pronounce each syllable with approximately equal stress. Maintain for each vowel a full, unreduced quality. [3.33–5]
2. Do not diphthongize vowels; maintain a constant quality during their entire production. [3.39–42]
3. Distinguish between the front rounded vowels and the back rounded vowels, especially between [y] (*tu*) and [u] (*tout*). [3.42–3]
4. In the production of rounded vowels, project the lips forward while rounding them well. [3.43–5]
5. Avoid nasalizing oral vowels before nasal consonants. [5.69–73]
6. Do not aspirate the voiceless stops [p, t, k]. [8.129–30]
7. Be sure to produce a clear *l* in all instances; pay especially close attention to the pronunciation of *l* in syllable-final position. [9.137–9]
8. Be sure to produce a back *r*; pay especially close attention to the pronunciation of *r* after a vowel and before a consonant. [9.142–6]

Bibliography

References mentioned in the text

Blanche-Benveniste, Claire and André Chervel. 1978. *L'Orthographe* (Edition augmentée). Paris: Maspéro.

Delattre, Pierre, 1965. *Comparing the Phonetic Features of English, French, German and Spanish: An Interim Report*. New York: Chilton Books/ Heidelberg: Julius Groos Verlag.

Denes, Peter and Elliot Pinson. 1963. *The Speech Chain: The Physics and Biology of Spoken Language*. Bell Telephone Laboratories.

Gak, V. G. 1976. *L'Orthographe du français: Essai de description théorique et pratique*. Paris: SELAF [Société d'Etudes Linguistiques et Anthropologiques de France, Numéro Spécial N° 6].

Juilland, Alphonse. 1965. *Dictionnaire inverse de la langue française*. The Hague: Mouton.

Léon, Monique. 1976. *Exercices systématiques de prononciation française* (nouvelle édition). Paris: Hachette/Larousse.

Martinon, Philippe. 1913. *Comment on prononce le français*. Paris: Larousse. Larousse.

Straka, Georges. 1967. *Album phonétique*. Quebec: Les Presses de l'Université Laval.

The Principles of the International Phonetic Association. 1949. London: International Phonetic Association, Department of Phonetics, University College.

General phonetics and phonology

Denes, Peter and Elliot Pinson. 1963. *The Speech Chain: The Physics and Biology of Spoken Language*. Bell Telephone Laboratories.

Halle, Morris and G. N. Clements. 1983. *Problem Book in Phonology: A Workbook for Introductory Courses in Linguistics and Modern Phonology*. Cambridge, Ma.: MIT Press.

Hyman, Larry. 1975. *Phonology: Theory and Analysis*. New York: Holt, Rinehart & Winston.

Kenstowicz, Michael and Charles Kisseberth. 1979. *Generative Phonology: Description and Theory*. New York: Academic Press.

Ladefoged, Peter. 1982. *A Course in Phonetics* (Second edition). New York: Harcourt Brace Jovanovich.

Lass, Roger. 1984. *Phonology: An Introduction to Basic Concepts*. Cambridge: Cambridge University Press.

Sommerstein, Alan. 1977. *Modern Phonology*. London: Edward Arnold/ University Park Press.

French orthography

Blanche-Benveniste, Claire and André Chervel. 1978. *L'Orthographe*
(Edition augmentée). Paris: Maspéro.
Catach, Nina. 1982. *L'Orthographe* (Deuxième édition). Paris: Presses
Universitaires de France (Collection 'Que sais-je?', N° 685).
Gak, V. G. 1976. *L'Orthographe du français: Essai de description théorique et
pratique.* Paris: SELAF.
Thimonnier, René. 1976. *Le Système graphique du français: Introduction à
une pédagogie rationnelle de l'orthographe* (nouvelle édition). Paris:
Plon.

French phonetics and phonology

Cornulier, Benoît de. 1981. 'H-aspirée et la syllabation: Expressions
disjonctives'. In *Phonology in the 1980's*, edited by Didier Goyvaerts,
pp. 183–230. Ghent: E. Story-Scientia.
Delattre, Pierre. 1965. *Comparing the Phonetic Features of English, French,
German and Spanish: An Interim Report.* New York: Chilton Books/
Heidelberg: Julius Groos Verlag.
Delattre, Pierre. 1966. *Studies in French and Comparative Phonetics.* The
Hague: Mouton.
Dell, François. 1980. *Generative Phonology and French Phonology.*
Cambridge: Cambridge University Press/Paris: Hermann. [Translation,
with revisions, of *Les Règles et les sons: Introduction à la phonologie
générative*, 1973, Paris: Hermann; a second 'revised and augmented'
French edition appeared in 1985.]
Grammont, Maurice. 1914. *Traité pratique de prononciation française.* Paris:
Delagrave.
Martinet, André. 1969. *Le Français sans fard.* Paris: Presses Universitaires de
France.
Martinet, André and Henriette Walter. 1973. *Dictionnaire de la
prononciation française dans son usage réel.* Paris: France-Expansion.
Morin, Yves. 1978. 'The status of mute "e"'. In *Studies in French
Linguistics* I (2), pp. 79–140.
Tranel, Bernard. 1981. *Concreteness in Generative Phonology: Evidence from
French.* Berkeley: University of California Press.
Walter, Henriette. 1976. *La Dynamique des phonèmes dans le lexique
français contemporain.* Paris: France-Expansion.